Refined Probabilistic Abstraction

Dissertation

Zur Erlangung des Grades des
Doktors der Ingenieurwissenschaften
der Naturwissenschaftlich-Technischen Fakultäten
der Universität des Saarlandes

von
Björn Wachter

Saarbrücken
2010

Bibliografische Information der Deutschen Nationalbibliothek

Die Deutsche Nationalbibliothek verzeichnet diese Publikation in der
Deutschen Nationalbibliografie; detaillierte bibliografische Daten sind
im Internet über http://dnb.d-nb.de abrufbar.

ISBN 978-3-8325-2764-8

Logos Verlag Berlin GmbH
Comeniushof, Gubener Str. 47,
10243 Berlin
Tel.: +49 (0)30 42 85 10 90
Fax: +49 (0)30 42 85 10 92
INTERNET: http://www.logos-verlag.de

Tag des Kolloquiums:	8.12.2010
Dekan:	Prof. Dr. Holger Hermanns
Prüfungsausschuss:	
Vorsizender:	Prof. Dr. Bernd Finkbeiner
Gutachter:	Prof. Dr. Dr. h.c. mult. Reinhard Wilhelm
	Prof. Dr. Holger Hermanns
	Prof. Dr. Martin Fränzle
Akademischer Mitarbeiter:	Dr. Raghavendra Rao

Abstract

Network technology enables smarter and more adaptive computing devices in the context of vehicles, communication and energy networks. Performance and quality-of-service guarantees are vital concerns for such systems. Meaningful guarantees are typically of a probabilistic nature due to the use of randomized algorithms inside network protocols and other phenomena like message loss. Probabilistic verification provides methods and tools to quantify the performance and quality of service of systems. A central problem in probabilistic verification is to determine the probability that a system enters a particular set of goal states, e.g., states in which packages have been transmitted successfully. Despite the remarkable versatility of existing methods, they are inherently limited to systems with very small state spaces.

This dissertation proposes new methods that solve the problem of probabilistic reachability for large or even infinite state spaces. The key is to automatically obtain small abstractions of a system. To this end, we start with a very coarse abstraction and successively refine it. The process is fully automatic and has been implemented in the tool PASS. PASS achieves significant performance improvements compared to previous methods and, further, applies to infinite-state systems which could previously not be handled by any existing automatic method.

Zusammenfassung

Netzwerktechnologie ermöglicht intelligentere und adaptivere Rechnersysteme, z.B. in Fahrzeugen, sowie im Bereich Kommunikation und Energie. Leistungsgarantien sind dabei von entscheidender Bedeutung und meist von probabilistischer Natur, da Netzwerkprotokolle auf randomisierten Algorithmen basieren und Phänomenen ausgesetzt sind, welche dem Zufall unterliegen, wie etwa dem Verlust von Nachrichten. Eine wichtige Grösse, mit der sich die Leistungsfähigkeit und Verfügbarkeit von Systemen quantifizieren lässt, ist die Wahrscheinlichkeit gewisse Zielzustände in einem System zu erreichen, z.B. von Zuständen in denen eine Nachricht erfolgreich versendet wurde. Trotz der bemerkenswerten Vielseitigkeit bestehender Berechnungsverfahren sind diese auf Systeme mit kleinen Zustandsräumen beschränkt.

Diese Dissertation stellt ein neues Verfahren vor, um solche Wahrscheinlichkeiten für Systeme mit großen und sogar unendlichen Zustandsräumen zu berechnen. Dabei werden automatisiert kompakte Abstraktionen eines Systems berechnet und nach Bedarf sukzessive verfeinert. Das Verfahren wurde im Werkzeug PASS implementiert und ist vollständig automatisch. PASS erzielt deutliche Geschwindigkeitszuwächse im Vergleich zu vorherigen Ansätzen und behandelt zustandsunendliche Systeme, welche zuvor nicht automatisiert behandelt werden konnten.

Acknowledgements

I would like to begin by thanking my advisors, Holger Hermanns and Reinhard Wilhelm. They shaped my understanding of research and their stewardship has guided me through this dissertation. I am very grateful to my friend and colleague Lijun Zhang, for a great collaboration that was more fruitful than I had ever imagined.

Furthermore, I would like to thank my colleagues at both the Dependable Systems Group and the Compiler Design Lab for providing a friendly and supportive environment. Especially I would like to thank Claire Maïza and Ernst Moritz Hahn for the time they devoted to reading the thesis and their valuable feedback.

I am very thankful to Martin Fränzle for serving as an examiner on my thesis committee.

I gratefully acknowledge the support of the German Research Foundation (DFG) as part of the transregional research center SFB/TR 14 AVACS. AVACS has been an excellent platform to develop ideas. Discussions within the Quasimodo project have been helpful to improve the presentation of the material. I should also like to thank the Saarbrücken Graduate School of Computer Science for their support.

Meiner Familie und Freunden danke ich für Ihre Unterstützung. Ich widme diese Dissertation meinem Vater.

Contents

III. Conclusion

9. Summary and Future Work

Bibliography

IV. Annexes

A. Additional Proofs

B. Implementation Details

1

Introduction

Computing systems pervade all areas of life, from embedded systems in vehicles and medical devices to phones. Millions of people place reliance on these systems: we expect cars to remain under control in critical situations and that networked devices deliver a certain quality of service under load. Numerous accidents and costly failures in the past, e.g., [Lacan et al., 1998], have shown that we need rigorous verification techniques to make sure that this reliance is justified. Formal verification consists in formalizing the desired behavior in specifications and checking a given system against its specification.

Temporal logics [Pnueli, 1977, Owicki and Lamport, 1982] are popular specification languages for both hardware and software systems, e.g., they admit to express that an airbag fires instantly after a collision has been detected by an acceleration sensor. To check if a system meets a specification in temporal logic, there are model checking algorithms that exhaustively explore all system behaviors. If the property is not met, they even provide a counterexample to diagnose the cause of violation [Clarke and Emerson, 1981, Queille and Sifakis, 1982]. However, these algorithms are impractical for complex systems with large state spaces, a notorious problem called "state-space explosion".

Driven by the need to verify large systems, verification techniques based on abstract interpretation [Cousot and Cousot, 1977] emerged and enabled automatic verification of certain temporal properties of software in operating systems [Ball and Rajamani, 2002] and avionics systems [Blanchet et al., 2003]. These techniques overcome state-space explosion by approximating sets of program states with symbolic assertions, e.g., $x > 0$ for an integer variable x. The computed symbolic assertions yield program invariants that can be used to exclude runtime errors such as division by zero.

Beyond classical temporal logic, quantitative, in particular probabilistic, properties are coming into focus because computing systems increasingly interact with their environment via networks. External phenomena entail a probabilistic aspect, e.g., messages are lost with a certain probability. Further, network protocols themselves rely on randomization. For example, in order to avoid collisions on shared communication channels without synchronization overhead, network devices adapt their transmission rate using a randomized algorithm. This leads to a low, albeit non-zero, probability of collision. One would like to compute or bound the probability that collisions occur and also the probability that packages arrive, as these probabilities are indicators for the performance and reliability of a network protocol.

Algorithms to compute such probabilities and to verify more sophisticated temporal properties [Hansson and Jonsson, 1994, Bianco and de Alfaro, 1995] are studied in the field of probabilistic model checking. These methods enable the analysis of the performance and reliability of networked systems and randomized algorithms, e.g., to determine the probability of collision in presence of randomization.

Markov decision processes (MDP) [Puterman, 1994] are an important semantic model in the context of probabilistic model checking, as MDPs offer both non-deterministic choice to model concurrency and probabilistic choice to express random phenomena. In fact, many interesting properties, including the one just mentioned, can be reduced to computing reachability probabilities: the probability to reach a set of states in an MDP.

Reachability probabilities depend on non-deterministic choices in the MDP, which model aspects of uncertainty such as the execution order in a concurrent system. To obtain a probability measure in an MDP, a resolution of non-determinism, called adversary, is needed. Typically, worst-case or best-case guarantees that hold for all possible adversaries are of interest. These minimal or maximal probabilities can be computed for finite MDPs by linear programming [Bianco and de Alfaro, 1995], and tool support is provided by probabilistic model checkers such as PRISM [Hinton et al., 2006].

Despite their remarkable versatility, probabilistic model checkers are severely limited by the state-space explosion problem. The problem is even aggravated compared to conventional model checkers due to the cost of numerical computations. On the quest for a solution, it seems promising to apply abstract interpretation to probabilistic verification because of its striking success in other areas of verification. Still, before our work, fully automatic probabilistic verification based on abstract interpretation had not been explored and it was not clear whether such techniques would be effective in practice.

1.1 Contributions

Network protocols and randomized algorithms can conveniently be modeled by concurrent probabilistic programs, which map to MDPs with a potentially infinite state space. However, until recently, *infinite-state* probabilistic programs were not amenable to any existing automatic verification technique and reachability probabilities for such systems could not be computed automatically.

We are the first to develop automatic abstraction techniques for infinite-state concurrent probabilistic programs. As a result, we are able to analyze programs which are beyond the scope of previous methods. To develop our automatic approach, we address the following subproblems:

- what is a suitable abstract-interpretation framework for the probabilistic setting,
- how to construct abstraction of programs automatically,
- and how to refine abstractions to tune them to a particular property.

These problems involve both challenges of theoretical and practical nature which we address in this thesis. In the remainder of the section, our contributions are summarized.

Probabilistic Abstraction

In abstract interpretation, the program is given an abstract semantics, an interpretation over an abstract domain which safely approximates the original semantics. In software verification, abstract domains typically consist of symbolic assertions, e.g., assertions like $x > 0$. The symbolic assertion $x > 0$ represents all states for which the expression $x > 0$ evaluates to true. In general, symbolic assertions are indicator functions over the program states, i.e., functions that map states to Boolean values.

We are interested in reachability probabilities of concurrent probabilistic programs. These probabilities can be described by *valuations*, i.e., functions that map program states to probability values, i.e., real numbers between zero and one, rather than Boolean values. Thus valuations can be regarded as *probabilistic* indicator functions.

As discussed, the number of program states can be very large, even infinite, and, in this case, directly computing these valuations becomes very expensive or even intractable. Instead we aim to efficiently obtain lower bounds and upper bounds on the reachability probabilities of given program. To this end, we employ an abstraction that merges states to a finite number of blocks keeping only a single probability value per block. Thus our abstract domain consists of abstract valuations, which map each *block* to a probability value. There is only a finite number of blocks even if there are infinitely many states.

To obtain an effective analysis, an abstract semantics over the abstract domain is needed. To this end, abstract interpretation provides a systematic approach to derive an abstract semantics based on the abstract domain and the original program semantics. Abstract interpretation thus helps disentangle the subtle interplay between abstraction, non-determinism and probabilism, an interplay leading to an abstract semantics which is equivalent to certain stochastic two-player games [Condon, 1992].

We arrive at a probabilistic abstraction framework – the first to support this systematic derivation of abstractions in the context of concurrent probabilistic programs and the first framework based on abstract interpretation that yields both lower and upper bounds on reachability probabilities. The framework provides not only a theoretical foundation, it is also the basis for effective program abstraction in practice.

Program Abstraction

The probabilistic abstraction framework *specifies* the abstract semantics in a declarative manner. To obtain effective analyses that *implement* the abstract semantics, we develop methods to compute program abstractions. In presence of infinite state spaces, the program abstraction must be computed using symbolic methods, i.e., the abstraction is computed at the language level from the program code without unfolding the state space of the program. Before our work, such symbolic infinite-state abstractions had not been explored in the probabilistic setting.

Our approach is inspired by predicate abstraction [Graf and Saïdi, 1997] which has evolved as a symbolic method to construct abstractions, and is the basis of verification tools for C programs [Ball and Rajamani, 2002], Verilog models [Clarke et al., 2003] and hybrid systems [Alur et al., 2006]. Predicate abstraction is based on symbolic assertions involving program variables. These assertions are called predicates and they partition the (potentially infinite) state space into a finite number of blocks. The partition, in turn, induces a finite abstraction of the original system. To obtain such program abstractions, predicate-abstraction tools integrate automatic decision procedures for decidable fragments of first-order logic, known as Satisfiability Modulo Theory (SMT) solvers [Ganzinger et al., 2004].

While previous predicate abstraction techniques were only designed for non-probabilistic models, we need to account for both probabilistic and non-deterministic choice. To this end, we combine our abstract domain with predicate abstraction, so that abstract valuations are represented using predicates. Devising corresponding methods to compute program abstractions is more challenging than in the non-probabilistic case. Here our probabilistic abstraction framework provides guidance to develop suitable abstractions.

Predicate abstraction for concurrent probabilistic programs computes an abstraction in the form of a stochastic game based on standard functionality implemented in off-the-shelf SMT solvers. Thereby we address the aspect of concurrency with an approximation, called menu-based abstraction, that dramatically reduces the cost of abstraction. By solving the game, we obtain a lower bound and an upper bound on the reachability probability in the original program. This gives a symbolic method for program abstraction which is completely automatic, except that a set of predicates must be provided.

Refinement

Automatic abstraction refinement incrementally refines an abstraction of the program beginning with an initial abstraction. Because the cost of constructing abstractions is worst-case exponential in the number of predicates, the initial abstraction involves few predicates, and is, as a result, inexpensive to compute but typically too imprecise. Abstraction refinement identifies the cause for a potential imprecision and generates predicates to refine the abstraction accordingly. Then the program abstraction is recomputed taking the new predicates into account. If sufficient precision has been achieved at that point, the refinement process terminates, if *not*, the refinement process starts over again.

Automatic generation of suitable predicates is thus a key element of abstraction refinement. To this end, predicate abstraction is typically coupled with *counterexample-guided abstraction refinement* (CEGAR) [Clarke et al., 2000]. Software verification tools like SLAM [Ball and Rajamani, 2002] use CEGAR to check safety properties of C programs, i.e., whether the program may reach an error state. If the program abstraction does not contain an abstract path to an error state, the soundness of the abstraction guarantees that the program is safe. If, on the other hand, such a counterexample exists, counterexample analysis checks if there is a corresponding run of the program that enters an error state. If there is no corresponding run, the abstraction is too coarse. The spurious counterexamples then delivers diagnostic information (predicates) to refine the abstraction. The process is repeated with the refined abstraction until safety is proved or refuted, i.e., until either no abstract error paths remain or an actual error is discovered.

Inspired by this idea, we explore the automation of predicate abstraction for concurrent probabilistic programs by counterexample-guided abstraction refinement. We consider maximal probabilistic reachability and aim to determine if the probability of reaching a particular set of goal states remains below a given threshold. Then the program is safe in a probabilistic sense.

The core challenge of developing probabilistic CEGAR lies in the notion and analysis of counterexamples. In the traditional setting, an abstract counterexample is a single finite path (to any of the error states). In turn, counterexample analysis consists in checking if the program exhibits a corresponding error path. In contrast, a counterexample against a probabilistic reachability property can be viewed as a finite Markov chain [Chatterjee et al., 2005] which generally contains cycles. Due to these cycles, probabilistic counterexample analysis is not directly amenable to conventional methods.

We deal with this problem by preprocessing the abstract counterexample using the strongest evidence idea of [Han and Katoen, 2007]. That is, we generate a finite set $\mathcal{C}_{real}$ of abstract finite paths whose abstract probability mass sums up to a value larger than the threshold. Different than Han and Katoen, we are dealing with abstract paths. Therefore the abstract probability mass does not necessarily correspond to the same realizable concrete probability mass. Computing the realizable probability mass of $\mathcal{C}_{real}$ admits to decide whether the paths correspond to a counterexample in the original program. We reduce the problem of computing the realizable probability to a weighted MAX-SMT problem [Papadimitriou and Yannakakis, 1991], an optimization problem where we seek the maximal solution to a set of weighted constraints.

These ingredients result in a theory for probabilistic CEGAR. We have evaluated the approach on various case studies. Indeed, CEGAR entirely mechanizes the verification process: predicates are added mechanically on demand based on counterexample analysis. To this end, our implementation employs interpolation [McMillan, 2006] to generate new predicates from spurious paths. For the first time, our technique admits the automatic verification of concurrent probabilistic programs with infinite state spaces.

Probabilistic CEGAR checks thresholds on reachability probabilities. However, probability thresholds may not always be given and one may want to compute probabilities without giving a threshold a priori. Further, probabilistic CEGAR is limited to maximal reachability probabilities, i.e., it does not treat minimal reachability. Therefore we present an additional refinement technique, called backward refinement, which does not require the specification of a threshold and supports both minimal *and* maximal probabilistic reachability. The technique approximates these probabilities successively and refines the partition until the bounds differ by less than a user-specified precision.

The proposed refinement techniques have different characteristics regarding their capabilities and computational cost. Both techniques employ lower and upper bounds obtained from the abstract games. Additionally, the counterexample analysis of probabilistic CEGAR computes lower bounds that can be more precise than the lower bounds computed directly from the abstract game. In contrast, backward refinement employs a light-weight analysis which only synthesizes predicates and neither yields additional bounds nor counterexamples. We evaluate and compare both techniques in practice.

Abstraction in Practice

We have implemented abstraction refinement for concurrent probabilistic programs in a prototype tool called PASS. PASS is the first automatic abstraction-based verification tool for concurrent probabilistic programs. It checks probabilistic reachability properties and computes lower bounds and upper bounds on reachability probabilities.

The tool PASS combines techniques from software verification with probabilistic model checking – a combination which has not been reported before. The routines for program abstraction resemble software verification tools such as BLAST [Henzinger et al., 2005a] including SMT-based predicate abstraction and interpolation. However, while BLAST abstracts programs to Boolean programs, PASS abstracts to stochastic games and solves these games using similar algorithms as probabilistic model checkers.

We have used PASS to evaluate the presented techniques on several case studies from the area of network protocols. Some of these case studies are beyond the capability of any previous techniques. First of all, PASS is able to verify infinite-state programs. Compared to conventional techniques which do not use abstraction, significant reductions in running time can be achieved on large finite-state programs.

1.2 Related Work

In this thesis, we address the problem of analyzing probabilistic models with very large state spaces, a problem that has received continued research interest in recent years. In this section, we summarize related work and outline the connection to our work.

De Alfaro *et al.* have explored probabilistic model checking with implicit representations [de Alfaro et al., 2000, Parker, 2002] inspired by research on symbolic model checking [Burch et al., 1990]. Other works merge states to shrink the size of the model itself, e.g., using bisimulation reduction as a pre-processing step before model checking to obtain smaller but equivalent models, e.g. [Katoen et al., 2007, Derisavi, 2007].

Other approaches pursue abstraction refinement for finite MDPs [D'Argenio et al., 2002, de Alfaro and Roy, 2007]. Theoretical work in [Chatterjee et al., 2005] presents abstraction refinement for finite stochastic games. Chada and Viswanathan investigate counterexamples and refinement for finite MDPs [Chadha and Viswanathan, 2010].

A common aspect of the aforementioned methods is that they build the full semantics of the model at some point. This can be expensive and is evidently impossible for infinite-state models. Our approach constitutes the first [Wachter et al., 2007] practical application of predicate abstraction to probabilistic models and, at the same time, the first method that obviates the construction of the MDP semantics.

Concepts of probabilistic counterexamples as well as algorithms to deal with counterexamples have been developed in [Aljazzar et al., 2005] and [Han and Katoen, 2007]. However these works do not consider counterexamples in the context of abstraction. Probabilistic CEGAR [Hermanns et al., 2008] is the first work that combines abstraction refinement with predicate abstraction for probabilistic systems.

The use of stochastic games in our work, as well as our interest in lower and upper bounds are inspired by game-based abstraction [Kwiatkowska et al., 2006], which is a construction that abstracts MDPs to stochastic two-player games. The salient point is that the resulting abstract games admit to compute both lower and upper bounds on reachability probabilities in the original MDP.

In [Kattenbelt et al., 2009], game-based abstraction is combined with predicate abstraction for probabilistic C programs and, in [Kwiatkowska et al., 2009], with region abstraction for timed automata [Alur and Dill, 1994]. A significant difference between the probabilistic software model checking approach of [Kattenbelt et al., 2009] and our work is that we target concurrent rather than sequential programs, which poses additional efficiency challenges regarding the construction of program abstractions. Our predicate abstraction technique for concurrent probabilistic program, menu-based abstraction, is an approximation of game-based abstraction. Menu-based abstraction sacrifices precision in certain cases but can be exponentially cheaper to compute than game-based abstraction and is easier to implement.

The related work discussed so far takes an automata-based view on program semantics and the process of abstraction. While these works do not explicitly refer to concepts of abstract interpretation, we show that it is natural to view game-based abstraction as a most precise abstraction in the sense of abstract interpretation [Wachter and Zhang, 2010], which has several practical consequences. On the one hand, optimal precision is a very desirable theoretical property and simplifies the process of refinement. On the other hand, optimal abstractions are typically expensive to compute so that approximations are often used instead (see e.g. [Tonetta and Sharygina, 2006]).

Several works investigate abstract interpretation in the context of probabilistic verification [Pierro and Wiklicky, 2000a, Monniaux, 2005, Smith, 2008, Coletta et al., 2009]. Except for Monniaux, all of these papers address fully probabilistic programs without non-determinism. Monniaux introduces an abstraction framework that aims at upper bounds on reachability probabilities for probabilistic programs that correspond to MDPs. The underlying abstraction techniques require manual design of abstract domains, which can be very challenging in the probabilistic setting. Further, the method has yet to be evaluated in practice. In contrast, we develop abstraction refinement techniques and supplement our work with a running implementation.

Wrapping up the related work section, our abstraction refinement techniques are the first to admit automatic verification of infinite-state concurrent probabilistic programs. The key to this is a novel combination of predicate abstraction, refinement and probabilistic methods with a firm foundation in the theory of abstract interpretation.

1.3 Structure of the Thesis

This thesis consists of two main parts. Part one recalls background material from the area of abstract interpretation and probabilistic verification.

Chapter 2 We give a gentle introduction into abstract interpretation. We start with Galois connections which relate the abstract domain with the original domain of computation. Then we turn to lattices and the abstraction of fixed points.

Chapter 3 We discuss the family of Markov models including MDPs. Our focus is thereby on probabilistic reachability probabilities and their characterization in terms of fixed points.

Chapter 4 Concurrent probabilistic program are introduced. We give their MDP semantics and a symbolic semantics which is useful for their abstraction.

Part two presents the contributions of the thesis: our abstraction framework, methods to compute program abstractions, refinement techniques and experimental results.

Chapter 5 We present a novel probabilistic abstraction framework which lays the foundation for program abstraction. The chapter focuses on the abstract valuation domain and abstract analyses based on this domain.

Chapter 6 We develop symbolic techniques to compute program abstractions. In particular, we present menu-based abstraction, an abstraction suited for *concurrent* probabilistic programs, and give SMT-based techniques to effectively compute menu-based abstractions.

Chapter 7 We introduce novel refinement techniques. The first part of the chapter focuses on probabilistic CEGAR and the second part on backward refinement. The chapter ends with a comprehensive discussion of related work in the area.

Chapter 8 We present PASS, the first automatic verification tool for concurrent probabilistic programs. Experimental results with various network protocols show the effectiveness of the refinement techniques and their respective strengths and limitations. Further, we compare PASS with other probabilistic verification tools.

Finally, Chapter 9 concludes the thesis with a summary of the main contributions and several avenues for future work. Appendix A contains additional proofs and Appendix B gives certain implementation details.

Part I.

Background

2

Abstract Interpretation

Many interesting verification problems are of high theoretical complexity or even undecidable. To solve these problems in practice, program analyses have been developed which approximate the original semantics with abstract values in a conservative way, i.e., preserving correctness. This approach is successful in many different application domains, and, throughout these domains, the theoretical foundation is abstract interpretation. Abstraction interpretation is a semantics-based theory for program analysis. This chapter gives a gentle introduction into the topic, so that we can later on employ abstract interpretation to design analyses for probabilistic programs.

2.1 Introduction

Abstract interpretation has its roots in the compiler domain. From early on, compilers used static program analyses to discover opportunities to carry out optimizing transformations. First theoretical results in the area of static program analysis date back to the 1970s [Kildall, 1973, Kam and Ullman, 1977]. At that time, Patrick Cousot developed the theory of abstract interpretation [Cousot, 1978] with the goal of providing a general theoretical framework for program analyses.

The mathematical foundations of abstract interpretation such as Tarski's fixed point theorem [Tarski, 1955] and Galois connections originate in lattice theory. Galois connections were first studied in the 1940s; for a brief history, refer to [Erne et al., 1992].

Beyond compilers [Wilhelm and Maurer, 1992], abstract interpretation is widely applied in formal verification today. Success stories are, for example:

- the analysis of the reasons for the failure of the Ariane5 rocket [Lacan et al., 1998],
- the proof of the absence of run-time errors in safety-critical avionics code in the ASTREÉ project [Blanchet et al., 2003],
- static timing analysis which is used to analyze the timing behavior of avionics software [Ferdinand et al., 2001, Thesing et al., 2003].
- the verification of device drivers in the SLAM project [Ball and Rajamani, 2002].

This thesis leverages abstract interpretation in the area of probabilistic verification. In this chapter, we discuss basics of abstract interpretation relevant to the thesis.

Outline

We introduce abstract interpretation and illustrate the theory with examples:

Section 2.2 We begin with Galois connections, which relate abstract values of the analysis domain with the domain of the original program semantics.

Section 2.3 Domains with a lattice structure enjoy several properties which are particularly favorable for program analysis. We recall the notion of lattices.

Section 2.4 Probabilistic verification requires specialized domains. We introduce the lattice of valuations, which admits to represent probabilities.

Section 2.5 We discuss properties of monotone functions over a lattice and, in particular, Tarski's fixed point theorem which guarantees the existence of certain fixed points.

Section 2.6 We formalize the relationship between the original program semantics and the information computed by a program analysis.

Section 2.7 We explain how to design analyses that are correct by construction and optimal in terms of precision.

Section 2.8 Finally we conclude the chapter with a summary and give an outlook where concepts of abstract interpretation will be used later on in the thesis.

2.2 Galois Connections

Program analyses interpret a given program over an abstract domain rather than its original domain of computation. Thus the soundness and precision of a program analysis is founded on the relationship between these two domains. This section introduces the underlying theory supplemented with illustrating examples.

Domains in program analysis are typically *partially ordered sets*. Recall that a partially ordered set is a pair $(P, \leq)$ consisting of a set P and a partial order $\leq \subseteq P \times P$, i.e., a reflexive, antisymmetric and transitive binary relation. The partial order expresses the relative information content of domain elements. As a convention, an element $p \in P$ is more precise than another element $p' \in P$ if $p \leq p'$. In other words, p' approximates p. This notion of approximation is crucial for abstract interpretation.

The program analysis is carried out on the abstract domain $(A, \leq)$ and approximates the original semantics over the concrete domain $(C, \leq)$. Both domains $(C, \leq)$ and $(A, \leq)$ are partially ordered sets. To ensure that the analysis obtains meaningful information about the original semantics, there must be a meaningful relationship between the domains.

This relationship is expressed by Galois connections, pairs of functions (α, γ), which transfer information between the two domains. The *abstraction function* $\alpha : C \to A$ maps a concrete element to an abstract element which represents it. Conversely, each element of the abstract domain has a particular meaning in terms of the concrete domain, and the *concretization function* $\gamma : A \to C$ maps an abstract element to that concrete meaning.

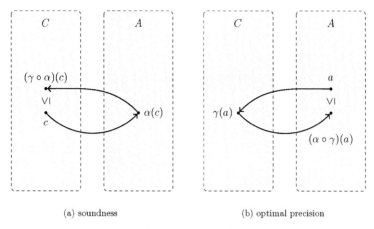

(a) soundness   (b) optimal precision

Figure 2.1.: The defining properties of a Galois connection.

To qualify as a Galois connection, such a pair of functions needs to fulfill certain properties regarding the loss of information incurred by moving between the two domains. Namely, a Galois connection guarantees both soundness and optimal precision in the following sense:

- *soundness* means that a concrete element is always conservatively approximated by its abstraction. Thus loss of information in the abstraction process is always sound. The idea is illustrated in Figure 2.1a: a concrete element c is safely approximated by its abstraction $\alpha(c)$, i.e. $c \leq \gamma(\alpha(c))$.

- the *precision* of the abstraction is optimal: the abstraction function yields the most precise abstraction of a concrete element expressible in the abstract domain. The idea is illustrated in Figure 2.1b: an abstract element a maps to a concrete element $\gamma(a)$ and, in turn, the abstraction $(\alpha \circ \gamma)(a)$ of $\gamma(a)$ is at least as precise as element a itself, i.e. $\alpha(\gamma(a)) \leq a$.

The definition of a Galois connection formalizes these notions of soundness and precision:

Definition 2.1 (Galois connection). *Let $(C, \leq)$ and $(A, \leq)$ be partially ordered sets. Consider functions $\alpha : C \to A$, $\gamma : A \to C$. The pair (α, γ) is a Galois connection if and only if α and γ are monotone, $\gamma \circ \alpha$ is extensive:*

$$\forall c \in C : \ c \leq (\gamma \circ \alpha)(c) \qquad \boxed{2.1}$$

and $\alpha \circ \gamma$ is reductive:

$$\forall a \in A : \ (\alpha \circ \gamma)(a) \leq a \ . \qquad \boxed{2.2}$$

There is also an equivalent characterization which is more concise and sometimes more convenient to use in proofs:

Theorem 2.2. *Let $(C, \leq)$ and $(A, \leq)$ be partially ordered sets. Consider functions $\alpha : C \to A$, $\gamma : A \to C$. The pair (α, γ) is a Galois connection if and only*

$$\forall a \in A \; \forall c \in C : \quad \alpha(c) \leq a \Longleftrightarrow c \leq \gamma(a) . \tag{2.3}$$

Proof. A proof can be found in e.g. [Cousot and Cousot, 1992]. ∎

Galois connections admit the construction of new Galois connections by composition:

Theorem 2.3 (Compositionality). *Let $(A_1, \leq)$, $(A_2, \leq)$ and $(A_3, \leq)$ be partially ordered sets. Let*

$$(A_1, \leq) \xrightleftharpoons[\alpha_1]{\gamma_1} (A_2, \leq) \quad and \quad (A_2, \leq) \xrightleftharpoons[\alpha_2]{\gamma_2} (A_3, \leq)$$

be Galois connections. Then $(A_1, \leq) \xrightleftharpoons[\alpha_2 \circ \alpha_1]{\gamma_1 \circ \gamma_2} (A_3, \leq)$ is also a Galois connection.

For illustration of these properties, we consider examples of Galois connections.

2.2.1. Interval Abstraction

Interval abstraction [Cousot and Cousot, 1977] is a classical example for a Galois connection. Interval abstraction is used, for example, to compute value ranges for variables in embedded software [Thesing et al., 2003] by replacing the value domain $\mathbb{Z}$ for integer variables by the following interval domain:

$$\mathbb{I} = \{[l, u] \mid l \in \mathbb{Z} \cup \{-\infty\}, u \in \mathbb{Z} \cup \{+\infty\}, l \leq u\} .$$

An interval $[l, u] \in \mathbb{I}$ represents the non-empty set of integers between l and u. This notion is formalized by the concretization function:

$$\gamma_{\mathbb{I}}([l, u]) = \{z \in \mathbb{Z} \mid l \leq z \leq u\} .$$

A set $M \subseteq \mathbb{Z}$ of integers maps to an interval with the infimum and supremum of M as end points, as defined by the abstraction function: $\alpha_{\mathbb{I}}(M) = [\inf_{z \in M} z, \sup_{z \in M} z]$. The set of intervals is ordered by "$\leq_{\mathbb{I}}$", the counterpart of set inclusion, which is defined by:

$$[l_1, u_1] \leq_{\mathbb{I}} [l_2, u_2] \qquad \text{iff} \qquad l_2 \leq l_1 \wedge u_1 \leq u_2 .$$

The presented abstraction and concretization function form a Galois connection:

$$(2^{\mathbb{Z}} \setminus \emptyset, \leq) \xrightleftharpoons[\alpha_{\mathbb{I}}]{\gamma_{\mathbb{I}}} (\mathbb{I}, \leq) .$$

Proof. Monotonicity of $\gamma_\mathbb{I}$ and $\alpha_\mathbb{I}$ is easy to see. We show Conditions 2.1 and 2.2. Let be a $M \subseteq \mathbb{Z}$ a non-empty set of integers. Then we have:

$$M \subseteq \{z \in \mathbb{Z} \mid \inf{}_{z' \in M} z' \leq z \leq \sup{}_{z' \in M} z'\}$$
$$= \gamma_\mathbb{I}([\inf{}_{z' \in M} z', \sup{}_{z' \in M} z'])$$
$$= (\gamma_\mathbb{I} \circ \alpha_\mathbb{I})(M) \ .$$

Let $[l, u] \in \mathbb{I}$ be an interval. Then the following equality holds:

$$(\alpha_\mathbb{I} \circ \gamma_\mathbb{I})([l, u]) = \alpha_\mathbb{I}(\{z \in \mathbb{Z} \mid l \leq z \leq u\}) = [l, u] \ .$$

The function $(\alpha_\mathbb{I} \circ \gamma_\mathbb{I})$ is the identity function on $\mathbb{I}$. ∎

Function $\alpha_\mathbb{I}$ enjoys soundness and optimality. For illustration, we consider some *bad* abstraction functions, i.e., functions that do not form a Galois connection with $\gamma_\mathbb{I}$:

- Consider the function $\alpha_1 : 2^\mathbb{Z} \to \mathbb{I}$ with $\alpha_1(M) = [0, 1]$ for all $M \subseteq \mathbb{Z}$ which always returns interval $[0, 1]$. The function is monotone. However, it is an unsound abstraction since it violates Condition 2.1. For example, the condition is violated for the concrete element $\{z \in \mathbb{Z} \mid 0 \leq z \leq 2\}$. The interval $[0, 2]$ (or even $[0, 100]$) is a sound abstraction of this set. However, function α_1 returns $[0, 1]$ and the concretization of $[0, 1]$ does not contain $\{z \in \mathbb{Z} \mid 0 \leq z \leq 2\}$:

$$\{z \in \mathbb{Z} \mid 0 \leq z \leq 2\} \not\subseteq \{z \in \mathbb{Z} \mid 0 \leq z \leq 1\} = (\gamma \circ \alpha_1)(\{z \in \mathbb{Z} \mid 0 \leq z \leq 2\}) \ .$$

- Consider the function $\alpha_2 : 2^\mathbb{Z} \to \mathbb{I}$ with $\alpha_2(M) = [-\infty, +\infty]$ for all $M \subseteq \mathbb{Z}$ which always returns interval $[-\infty, \infty]$. This abstraction function is sound, it fulfills Condition 2.1, since $2^\mathbb{Z} = \gamma \circ \alpha_2(M)$ for all $M \subseteq \mathbb{Z}$. However, it does not yield the most precise abstraction in the interval domain, i.e. it violates Condition 2.2. For example, consider the interval $[0, 2]$. Its concretization is $\{z \in \mathbb{Z} \mid 0 \leq z \leq 2\}$. However, the abstraction of this set under α_2 is $[-\infty, +\infty]$, which is not optimal in terms of precision:

$$(\alpha_2 \circ \gamma)([0, 2]) = [-\infty, +\infty] \not\sqsubseteq_\mathbb{I} [0, 2] \ .$$

2.2.2. Partition Abstraction

The idea behind partition abstraction is to merge the states of a system or program according to a partition of its state space, so that only a finite number of abstract states need to be considered. Partition abstractions are an important class of abstractions. For example, predicate abstraction [Graf and Saïdi, 1997] is a special kind of partition abstraction. In this section, we recall partition abstraction and its characterization in terms of abstract interpretation [Cousot, 1981, page 315].

Partitions.   Partition abstractions are based on a finite partition of the state space. A partition of a set S consists of a set Q of subsets of S, i.e. $Q \subseteq 2^S$. The subsets that make up a partition are called blocks. The blocks of a partition are pairwise disjoint and their union covers the set S. We denote blocks with the upper-case letter B. We consider finite partitions, which means that the number of blocks in a partition is finite. Note that the number of elements in a block is allowed to be infinite.

Formally, we have the following notion of partitions:

Definition 2.4 (Partition). *Let S be a set and $Q = \{B_1, \ldots, B_k\} \subseteq 2^S$ a finite set of subsets of S, i.e. $B_i \subseteq S$ for all $i \in \{1, \ldots, k\}$. The set Q is a partition of S if the following two conditions are fulfilled:*

- *the elements of Q are pairwise disjoint:*

$$\forall i, j \in \{1, \ldots, k\} : i \neq j \Rightarrow B_i \cap B_j = \emptyset \ ,$$

- *the union of the elements of Q covers S:*

$$S = \bigcup_{B \in Q} B \ .$$

The elements of Q are then called blocks of the partition Q.

Approximation.   Under- and overapproximation respectively of a given set of states is a crucial operation in partition abstraction. Let $M \subseteq S$. An underapproximation is a set of blocks which lie completely in M. Conversely, a set of blocks that contain M is an overapproximation of M.

As an example, consider the state-space partition in Figure 2.2a. Thereby the blocks are given by a grid of equal-sized boxes. Note that these equal-sized blocks are just an example and that, in general, partitions need not even have a geometric interpretation. Consider the set depicted by the round shape in Figure 2.2b. Figure 2.2c shows an underapproximation of this set and Figure 2.2d an overapproximation. With this geometric intuition in mind, let us return to the general case and make the notion of approximation more formal.

Trivially, the empty set $\emptyset$ of blocks is an underapproximation and the set of all blocks Q is an overapproximation of M (or any other subset of S). However, for the sake of precision, we aim for approximations that come as close to the original set M as possible. We now give abstraction functions that return such approximations.

The larger underapproximations are, the more precise they are. Therefore, for a given set of states $M \subseteq S$, the set of blocks $B \in Q$ that are completely contained in M, i.e. $B \subseteq M$, form its most precise underapproximation. This notion is expressed by abstraction function $\alpha^\downarrow$:

$$\alpha^\downarrow : \ 2^S \to 2^Q, \quad \alpha^\downarrow(M) = \{B \in Q \mid B \subseteq M\} \ .$$

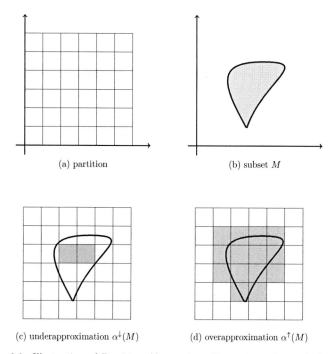

(a) partition

(b) subset M

(c) underapproximation $\alpha^{\downarrow}(M)$

(d) overapproximation $\alpha^{\uparrow}(M)$

Figure 2.2.: Illustration of Partition Abstraction. Figure 2.2a shows the blocks of the partition as boxes. The set to be abstracted is depicted by the region depicted in Figure 2.2b. The under-approximating abstraction is shown in Figure 2.2c and the over-approximating abstraction in Figure 2.2d.

For example, the underapproximation of the set in Figure 2.2b is shown in Figure 2.2c.

Opposite to underapproximations, overapproximations are the more precise, the smaller they are. For a subset $M \subseteq S$, the smallest set of blocks that contains M – and thus the most precise overapproximation of M – consists of the set of blocks whose intersection with M is non-empty. This defines the over-approximating abstraction function $\alpha^\uparrow$:

$$\alpha^\uparrow : \ 2^S \to 2^Q, \quad \alpha^\uparrow(M) = \{B \in Q \mid B \cap M \neq \emptyset\} \ .$$

The overapproximation of the set in Figure 2.2b is shown in Figure 2.2d.

Formalization as a Galois connection. The intuition of most precise approximation in the context of partitions has an elegant formalization by Galois connections. Thereby the concrete domain is the set 2^S and the abstract domain the set 2^Q, both ordered by set inclusion. While we have discussed abstraction functions, namely $\alpha^\downarrow$ and $\alpha^\uparrow$, we now describe concretizations: functions that return the meaning of a set of blocks in terms states. A set of blocks $M^\sharp \subseteq Q$ represents a set of states, i.e., the union of the blocks in $M^\sharp$. The *concretization* function γ formalizes this notion:

$$\gamma : \ 2^Q \to 2^S, \quad M^\sharp \mapsto \bigcup_{B \in M^\sharp} B \ .$$

We obtain the following Galois connection which formalizes (over-approximating) partition abstraction in terms of abstract interpretation:

Proposition 1. *The pair* $(\alpha^\uparrow, \gamma)$ *forms a Galois connection:*

$$(2^S, \leq) \xleftrightarrow[\alpha^\uparrow]{\gamma} (2^Q, \leq) \ .$$

Proof. We check the conditions in Definition 2.1. It is easy to see that both concretization and abstraction function are monotone. It remains to show both the conditions of soundness (Condition 2.1) and precision (Condition 2.2).

- We begin with the soundness condition 2.1. We need to show that $M \subseteq \gamma(\alpha^\uparrow(M))$ for every $M \subseteq S$.

  If M is the empty set the claim is trivially fulfilled. Otherwise let $s \in M$. There exists a unique block $B \in Q$ in the partition containing s, i.e. $s \in B$. This block B is contained in $\alpha^\uparrow(M)$ because B has a non-empty intersection with M. Therefore, s is contained in $\gamma(\alpha^\uparrow(M))$.

- For the optimality of the abstraction, i.e. Condition 2.2, we need to show that $\alpha^\uparrow(\gamma(M^\sharp)) \subseteq M^\sharp$ for every set of blocks $M^\sharp \subseteq Q$. Again we are done if the set of blocks $\alpha^\uparrow(\gamma(M^\sharp))$ is empty. So assume that B is a block in $\alpha^\uparrow(\gamma(M^\sharp))$. We need to show that $B \in M^\sharp$. By definition, the condition $\alpha^\uparrow(\gamma(M^\sharp))$ implies that $\emptyset \neq B \cap (\bigcup_{B' \in M^\sharp} B')$. Since Q is a partition, i.e. a disjoint union of blocks, we get $B \in M^\sharp$. ∎

This Galois connection has already been studied [Cousot, 1981, page 315].

Dually, there exists the Galois connection for underapproximation

$$(2^S, \geq) \xleftrightarrow[\alpha^\downarrow]{\gamma} (2^Q, \geq)$$

where the order is inverted. The concept of dual over- and underapproximation functions appears in a similar form in predicate abstraction where such approximations are used to compute abstract transformers [Ball et al., 2001, Lahiri et al., 2006].

2.2.3. Indicator Functions

We recall the notion of indicator functions and discuss partition abstraction for indicator functions. The material in this section helps to understand the connection between probabilistic abstractions and conventional partition abstraction later on.

Indicator functions provide an equivalent representation of sets. For a given set M, the corresponding indicator function $\mathbf{1}_M$ returns one if and only if an element is contained in M and zero otherwise. For example, we can represent the even numbers by the indicator function $\mathbf{1}_{even} : \mathbb{N} \to \{0, 1\}$ where, for every natural number $n \in \mathbb{N}$, we have:

$$\mathbf{1}_{even}(n) = \begin{cases} 1 & ; \text{ if } n \text{ is even} \\ 0 & ; \text{ if } n \text{ is odd} \end{cases} .$$

The subsets of a set and the indicator functions over that set are isomorphic domains. We use Galois connections to formalize this well-known fact. We have so far considered Galois connections where abstraction is associated with a loss of information. This time we consider an example where a Galois connection relates two isomorphic domains.

Let S be a set. We denote the domain of indicator functions over S by:

$$\{0, 1\}^S := \{c \mid c : S \to \{0, 1\}\} .$$

If we transfer the set-inclusion order $\subseteq$ of the power-set domain $(2^S, \subseteq)$ to indicator functions, we get, for all $c_1, c_2 \in \{0, 1\}^S$:

$$c_1 \leq c_2 \quad \text{iff} \quad \forall s \in S : \ c_1(s) \leq c_2(s) .$$

The indicator function of a subset $M \subseteq S$ is given by $\mathbf{1}_M : S \to \{0, 1\}$ where $\mathbf{1}_M(s) = 1$ if $s \in M$ and $\mathbf{1}_M(s) = 0$ otherwise. This defines a function which maps each subset to its indicator function:

$$\chi : 2^S \to \{0, 1\}^S, M \mapsto \mathbf{1}_M .$$

Conversely, we can also map indicator functions to subsets which defines the inverse χ^{-1} of χ:

$$\chi^{-1} : \{0, 1\}^S \to 2^S, c \mapsto \{s \in S \mid c(s) = 1\} .$$

Functions χ and χ^{-1} are monotone. The larger a set, the more elements the corresponding indicator function maps to one. The more elements a function maps to one, the larger the set it represents. Because $\chi \circ \chi^{-1}$ and $\chi^{-1} \circ \chi$ are both identity functions, it follows immediately that the pair (χ, χ^{-1}) forms a Galois connection:

$$(2^S, \leq) \xleftrightarrow[\chi]{\chi^{-1}} (\{0,1\}^S, \leq) \ .$$

Partition Abstraction

We now aim at a notion of partition abstraction for indicator functions. More specifically, the starting point is a state space S and a partition Q. We want to relate the domain of indicator functions $\{0,1\}^S$ over S with the indicator functions $\{0,1\}^Q$ over Q. This section is concerned with the construction of the associated Galois connections corresponding to underapproximation and overapproximation respectively.

We construct the corresponding Galois connections by composing set-based partition abstraction with the bijective Galois connections of Section 2.2.3 and then give an equivalent definition in closed form. By definition, the resulting abstractions for indicator functions are equivalent to the corresponding abstractions for sets in Section 2.2.2.

As previously discussed, we have the following Galois connection between the power set domains and the indicator function domains:

$$(2^S, \subseteq) \xleftrightarrow[\chi]{\chi^{-1}} (\{0,1\}^S, \leq) \qquad (2^Q, \subseteq) \xleftrightarrow[\chi]{\chi^{-1}} (\{0,1\}^Q, \leq) \ .$$

Further, there is the over-approximating Galois connection:

$$(2^S, \leq) \xleftrightarrow[\alpha^\uparrow]{\gamma} (2^Q, \leq) \ .$$

Thanks to compositionality of Galois connections, there exists a Galois connection between indicator functions over states and indicator functions over blocks:

$$(\{0,1\}^S, \leq) \xleftrightarrow[\alpha_\chi^\uparrow = (\chi \circ \alpha^\uparrow \circ \chi^{-1})]{\gamma_\chi = (\chi \circ \gamma \circ \chi^{-1})} (\{0,1\}^Q, \leq) \ .$$

The abstraction and concretization functions can also be written in closed form. The abstraction[1] of a concrete indicator function c is the abstract indicator function that maps a block B to 1 if and only if c maps at least one state in block B to 1:

$$\alpha_\chi^\uparrow : \{0,1\}^S \to \{0,1\}^Q, \quad \alpha_\chi^\uparrow(c)(B) = \max_{s \in B} c(s) \ . \tag{2.4}$$

The concretization of an abstract indicator function $c^\sharp$ maps a state s to 1 if and only if abstract indicator function $c^\sharp$ maps the block $\overline{s}$ that contains s to 1:

$$\gamma_\chi : \{0,1\}^Q \to \{0,1\}^S, \quad \gamma_\chi(c^\sharp)(s) = c^\sharp(\overline{s}) \ . \tag{2.5}$$

This concludes our treatment of partition abstraction for indicator functions.

In the next section, we discuss lattices, partially-ordered sets with stronger algebraic properties that are favorable for program analysis.

---

[1]The corresponding under-approximating abstraction function can be obtained by replacing the maximum with a minimum. The concretization function is the same for both cases.

2.3 Lattices

Lattices are partially ordered sets in which pairs of elements have a greatest lower bound (also called *infimum* or *meet*) and least upper bound (also called *supremum* or *join*). Lattices play an important role as semantic domains in program analysis.

Definition 2.5. *Let $(P, \leq)$ be a partially ordered set.*

- *For a subset $P' \subseteq P$, a lower bound is an element $a \in P$ that is smaller than all elements of P', i.e., for all $a' \in A'$, $a \leq a'$.*
- *An element $a \in P$ is a greatest lower bound of P' if it is a lower bound of P' and all lower bounds $a^\dagger \in P$ of P' fulfill $a^\dagger \leq a$.*
- *Similarly, an upper bound of P' is an element that is greater than all elements of P', and a least upper bound is a smallest upper bound of P'.*

Partially ordered sets in which every subset possesses both a least upper and greatest lower bound are called lattices:

Definition 2.6 (Lattice). *Let $(L, \leq)$ be a partially ordered set. The pair $(L, \leq)$ is a (complete) lattice if each subset of L has both a greatest lower and a least upper bound.*

If least upper bounds and greatest lower bounds exist, they are unique. This uniqueness holds since partial orders are anti-symmetric.

To denote the least upper and greatest lower bounds of sets of elements in a lattice L, we employ an operator notation. The *meet* operator $\sqcap : 2^L \to L$ returns the greatest lower bound of a subset of L. The *join* operator $\sqcup : 2^L \to L$ returns least upper bounds. The notation alludes to that of set intersection $\cap$ and set union $\cup$ respectively, as meet and join are often intended as abstract counterparts that mimic these set operations. We now give several examples for lattices.

Power Sets. The classical example for lattice structures are power sets. The power set 2^S of a set S together with set inclusion $\subseteq$ is a lattice. For a subset $M \subseteq 2^S$, a set of sets, its greatest lower bound is the intersection of all sets in M:

$$\left(\bigsqcap M\right) = \bigcap \{S' \in S \mid S' \in M\}$$

and the least upper bound is given by the union of all sets in M:

$$\left(\bigsqcup M\right) = \bigcup \{S' \in S \mid S' \in M\}.$$

Indicator Functions. In section 2.2.3, we have considered the domain of indicator functions $\{0, 1\}^S$ over a set S. As already discussed this domain is isomorphic to the power set domain over S. Not surprisingly $\{0, 1\}^S$ also forms a lattice. For a set of indicator functions $M \subseteq \{0,1\}^S$, the greatest lower bound is given by the indicator function

$$\left(\bigsqcap M \right) = \lambda s \in S. \; \min_{c \in M} c(s)$$

and the least upper bound is given by

$$\left(\bigsqcup M \right) = \lambda s \in S. \; \max_{c \in M} c(s) \; .$$

The lambda notation indicates that $(\bigsqcap M)$ and $(\bigsqcup M)$, respectively, are functions from states to values in $\{0,1\}$.

In this section, we have discussed the general notion of lattices and two examples: power-set domains and indicator functions. Indicator functions are a special case of valuations, a more general lattice which admits to represent probabilities. We come to valuations in the next section.

2.4 Valuations

We now introduce the lattice of valuations, the domain of probabilistic reachability analyses. Mathematically, our valuations are functions from states to probability values. They can thus be seen as a generalization of indicator functions where the range of indicator functions, the discrete set $\{0,1\}$ of Booleans, is extended to the interval $[0,1]$ of real values between zero and one.

We formally define valuations, give a partial order and the corresponding meet and join operators.

Definition 2.7 (Valuations). *Let S be a set. A valuation over a set S is a function $w : S \to [0,1]$ that maps elements of S to probabilities $[0,1] \subseteq \mathbb{R}$.*

We denote the set of valuations over S by:

$$[0,1]^S = \{ w \mid w : S \to [0,1] \} \; .$$

The valuations are ordered according to the relation $\leq$:

$$\forall w, w' \in [0,1]^S : \; w \leq w' :\Leftrightarrow \forall s \in S : \; w(s) \leq w'(s) \; .$$

Example. *The figure below shows two valuations w_1 and w_2 over a set S with 16 elements. Each element of the set S is drawn as a circle. The corresponding value is annotated above each circle. Note that the regular geometric arrangement of the circles does not carry a deeper meaning beyond layout.*

$$
\begin{array}{cccc}
0.1 & 0.1 & 1.0 & 1.0 \\
\circ & \circ & \circ & \circ \\
0.1 & 0.1 & 1.0 & 1.0 \\
\circ & \circ & \circ & \circ \\
0.0 & 0.0 & 0.0 & 0.0 \\
\circ & \circ & \circ & \circ \\
0.0 & 0.0 & 0.0 & 0.0 \\
\circ & \circ & \circ & \circ
\end{array}
\quad \leq \quad
\begin{array}{cccc}
1.0 & 0.5 & 1.0 & 1.0 \\
\circ & \circ & \circ & \circ \\
0.2 & 0.1 & 1.0 & 1.0 \\
\circ & \circ & \circ & \circ \\
0.3 & 0.7 & 0.4 & 0.1 \\
\circ & \circ & \circ & \circ \\
0.0 & 0.8 & 0.3 & 0.2 \\
\circ & \circ & \circ & \circ
\end{array}
$$

$$w_1 \qquad\qquad\qquad w_2$$

We have $w_1 \leq w_2$, i.e., w_2 is an upper bound for w_1, and, vice versa, w_1 a lower bound for w_2.

Lemma 2.8. *The valuations $([0,1]^S, \leq)$ form a lattice.*

The join and meet operators of valuations are given by infima and suprema. This is a generalization of the join and meet operators we defined for indicator functions and the power-set domain respectively.

For a set of indicator functions $V \subseteq [0,1]^S$, the greatest lower bound is given by:

$$\left(\bigsqcap V\right) = \lambda s \in S. \inf_{w \in V} w(s)$$

and the least upper bound by:

$$\left(\bigsqcup V\right) = \lambda s \in S. \sup_{w \in V} w(s) .$$

Lower and Upper Bounds. We would like to obtain both under- and overapproximations. We shall use the same set to represent analysis information. Therefore, we have to be careful with the partial order on this set because the notion of precision for lower bounds is inverse to the one for upper bounds.

The smaller the value of an upper bound the more precise it is. In the example, we have $w_1 \leq w_2$ because the probabilities of w_1 are smaller than the one of w_2.

The partial order $\leq$, which we have defined for valuations, is only suitable if we want to compare approximations from above. However, for lower bounds, the notion of precision is inverse to the numerical ordering of values: the larger probabilities the more precise the lower bound. We therefore invert the order when we aim for lower bounds instead of upper bounds. By inverting the order $\leq$, we obtain the lattice $([0,1]^S, \geq)$. Lattice $([0,1]^S, \geq)$ is used to express analyses that aim at lower bounds and lattice $([0,1]^S, \leq)$ for upper bounds. Note that the symbols $\bigsqcap$ and $\bigsqcup$ always refer to the least elements and greatest elements respectively in $([0,1]^S, \leq)$, and *not* the ones in $([0,1]^S, \geq)$.

This concludes our discussion of lattices and the lattice of valuations. In the next section, we consider monotone functions and fixed points over lattices.

2.5 Monotone Functions and Fixed Points

Monotone functions play an important role for abstract interpretation: they are used to represent the program semantics. Both concrete and abstract semantics of a program are typically expressed as a least (or greatest) fixed point of a monotone function. Monotonicity guarantees that these functions preserve the soundness of the approximation. In this section, we recall the notion of monotone functions and the fixed-point theorem of Tarski.

Definition 2.9 (Monotone Functions). *Let* $(A, \leq)$ *and* $(B, \leq)$ *be partially ordered sets. Let* $f : A \rightarrow B$ *be a function. Function* $f : A \rightarrow B$ *is monotone if for all* $a, a' \in A$, $a \leq a' \implies f(a) \leq f(a')$.

For notational convenience, we lift the order over the range B to a partial order on monotone functions. Let $f, g : A \rightarrow B$ be monotone functions. We define $f \leq g$ if and only if $f(a) \leq g(a)$ for all $a \in A$.

Fixed points. Let $f : L \rightarrow L$ be a function. A fixed point is an element $x \in L$ with $f(x) = x$. We denote the set of fixed points of a function f by:

$$Fix(f) = \{x \in L \mid f(x) = x\} \ .$$

In general, fixed points of monotone functions need not exist for general partially ordered sets. However, for lattices, there are well-known theorems that guarantee existence of such fixed points.

Alfred Tarski [Tarski, 1955] published an existence result, which is easy to prove but fundamental: every monotone function over a lattice is guaranteed to have least and greatest fixed points. Further, these fixed points can be characterized by the bounds of the pre- and post-fixed points respectively of a function. The pre-fixed points of f are the elements $\{x \in L \mid f(x) \leq x\}$ and the post fixed points are given by $\{x \in L \mid f(x) \geq x\}$ respectively.

Tarski's Fixed Point Theorem states that the least fixed point $lfp_{\leq}(f)$ is the greatest lower bound of the pre fixed points and, dually, the greatest fixed point $gfp_{\leq}(f)$ the least upper bound of the post fixed points.

Theorem 2.10 (Fixed-Point Theorem [Tarski, 1955]). *Let* $f : L \rightarrow L$ *be a monotone function over a lattice* $(L, \leq)$. *Then the set of fixed points* $Fix(f)$ *is a lattice. The least and the greatest fixed points can be characterized as follows:*

$$lfp_{\leq}(f) = \bigsqcap Fix(f) = \bigsqcap\{x \in L \mid f(x) \leq x\}$$
$$gfp_{\leq}(f) = \bigsqcup Fix(f) = \bigsqcup\{x \in L \mid f(x) \geq x\} \ .$$

This section has recalled Tarski's fixed point theorem which guarantees the existence of fixed points for monotone functions over a lattice. We are now prepared to discuss fixed points in the context of abstraction in the next section.

2.6   Fixed-Point Abstraction

The design process for an analysis involves the creative step of devising an abstract semantics, and ensuring its correctness with respect to the concrete semantics. In this section, we discuss how abstract interpretation helps to address these design tasks and the necessary theoretical foundations based on the theory of fixed points.

Abstract interpretation views both the concrete and the abstract semantics as fixed points of monotone functions, a so-called concrete transformer and an abstract transformer respectively. To establish correctness of an analysis, we need to relate the underlying fixed points. This can be achieved by reasoning about the relationship between the respective concrete and abstract transformers. The proper relationship between the transformers can be formulated using the Galois connection between the domains.

Concrete Semantics. The original program semantics, also called concrete semantics is defined over a lattice $(C, \leq)$, called concrete domain. The concrete semantics is defined in terms of a concrete transformer, a monotone function $f : C \to C$. The program semantics is a (least or greatest) fixed point of the concrete transformer.

Abstract Semantics. The fixed point defined by the concrete semantics is not always computable. Therefore, one considers an abstract semantics over an abstract domain, a lattice $(A, \leq)$, in which an abstract fixed point that approximates the concrete fixed point is effectively computable. Formally, the abstract semantics is defined in terms of a fixed point of an abstract transformer, a monotone function $g^\sharp : A \to A$.

At the level of the domains $(C, \leq)$ and $(A, \leq)$, Galois connections relate the concrete with the abstract world by means of the abstraction function $\alpha : C \to A$ and the concretization function $\gamma : A \to C$. To relate the concrete with the abstract semantics, a relationship has to be established at the level of functions over these domains.

An abstract transformer $g^\sharp$ over-approximates a concrete transformer $f : C \to C$ if applying $g^\sharp$ to an abstract element a yields an approximation of applying f to the concretization of a, as depicted in Figure 2.3. In this case we call $g^\sharp$ a valid abstraction of f (sometimes this condition is also referred to as "local consistency"):

Definition 2.11 (Valid Abstraction). *We call an abstract transformer* $g^\sharp : A \to A$ *a* valid *abstraction of concrete transformer* f *if:*

$$(f \circ \gamma) \leq (\gamma \circ g^\sharp) \ . \tag{2.6}$$

Valid transformers admit fixed-point abstraction as formalized below:

Lemma 2.12 (Fixed-Point Abstraction Using Valid Transformers). *Let A and C be lattices. Assume that we have Galois connection: $(C, \leq) \xleftrightarrow[\alpha]{\gamma} (A, \leq)$. Let $f : C \to C$ and $f^\sharp : A \to A$ be transformers such that $f^\sharp$ is a valid abstraction of f, i.e., $(f \circ \gamma) \leq (\gamma \circ f^\sharp)$. Then the following statements hold regarding the fixed points:*

(a) for the least fixed point, we have:

$$lfp_\leq(f) \leq \gamma \left(lfp_\leq(f^\sharp) \right) \ .$$

(b) and, for the greatest fixed point, we get:

$$gfp_\leq(f) \leq \gamma \left(gfp_\leq(f^\sharp) \right) \ .$$

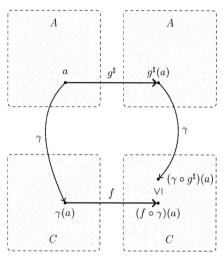

Figure 2.3.: Valid abstraction. The diagram shows an abstract transformer $g^\sharp$ which is a valid abstraction of concrete transformer f.

Proof. The proof exploits existence of the Galois connection and Tarski's fixed-point theorem, which characterizes least and greatest fixed point in terms of pre- and post-fixed points respectively:

(a) Let $a^* = lfp_{\leq}(f^\sharp)$. Value a^* is a fixed point, so it holds that $f^\sharp(a^*) = a^*$. Therefore, we have $(\gamma \circ f^\sharp)(a^*) = \gamma(a^*)$. Because $f^\sharp$ is a valid abstraction, i.e., $f \circ \gamma \leq \gamma \circ f^\sharp$, we have $(f \circ \gamma)(a^*) \leq (\gamma \circ f^\sharp)(a^*) = \gamma(a^*)$. Therefore, $\gamma(a^*)$ is a pre-fixed point of f, i.e. $\gamma(a^*) \in \{x \in [0,1]^S \mid f(x) \leq x\}$. Hence we obtain, as claimed, the inequality for the least fixed point: $lfp_{\leq}(f) = \bigsqcap\{x \in [0,1]^S \mid f(x) \leq x\} \leq \gamma(a^*)$.

(b) Let $b^* = gfp_{\leq}(f)$. We have $b^* = f(b^*) \leq f((\gamma \circ \alpha)(b^*)))$. Since $f^\sharp$ is a valid abstraction of f, we have $(f \circ \gamma)(\alpha(b^*)) \leq (\gamma \circ f^\sharp)(\alpha(b^*))$. Summing up these two steps, we get $b^* \leq \gamma(f^\sharp(\alpha(b^*)))$. This is equivalent to $\alpha(b^*) \leq (f^\sharp(\alpha(b^*))$, which implies that $\alpha(b^*) \in \{a \in A \mid f^\sharp(a) \geq a\}$, i.e. $\alpha(b^*)$ is post-fixed point of $f^\sharp$. As a direct consequence, we get $\alpha(b^*) \leq \bigsqcup\{a \in A \mid f^\sharp(a) \geq a\} = gfp_{\leq}(f^\sharp)$. This in turn implies, thanks to the Galois connection, $b^* \leq \gamma(gfp_{\leq}(f^\sharp))$ as claimed.

The proofs can also be found in [Cousot and Cousot, 1992]. ■

Beside methods to establish correctness, abstract interpretation provides ample support to design abstract analyses. The key is to obtain suitable abstract transformers which form a valid abstraction. The next section describes how valid abstractions with good theoretical properties can be derived.

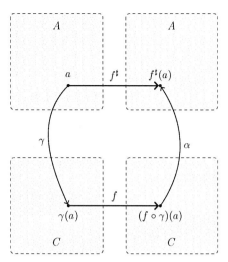

Figure 2.4.: Best transformer. The diagram illustrates the best transformer $f^\sharp$ for a given concrete transformer f.

2.7 Best Transformer

Program analyses are based on valid abstractions (see Lemma 2.12). In this section, we describe how valid abstractions can be obtained. We present the notion of the best transformer, a construction that admits to derive a valid abstraction from the abstraction and the given concrete transformer. Best transformers provide a systematic way to design analyses.

We assume that a Galois connection (α, γ) is established. Then we can derive an abstract transformer by function composition. First, we concretize an abstract element, then apply the concrete transformer f and abstract again, yielding an abstract element. This gives the function:

$$\alpha \circ f \circ \gamma \, .$$

The composition of monotone functions is a monotone function. Function $\gamma \circ \alpha$ is extensive which immediately implies that $\alpha \circ f \circ \gamma$ is a valid abstraction of f:

$$f \circ \gamma \le (\gamma \circ \alpha) \circ (f \circ \gamma) = \gamma \circ (\alpha \circ f \circ \gamma) \, .$$

Furthermore, the abstract transformer $\alpha \circ f \circ \gamma$ is not only valid, it also exhibits the best achievable precision among all valid abstractions. This follows because $\alpha \circ \gamma$ is reductive. Assume that $g^\sharp$ is some valid abstraction, which means by definition that the inequality $f \circ \gamma \le \gamma \circ g^\sharp$ holds. If we apply the abstraction function α to both sides we obtain

$\alpha \circ f \circ \gamma \leq (\alpha \circ \gamma) \circ g^\sharp$, due to the monotonicity of α. Since (α, γ) is a Galois connection, $(\alpha \circ \gamma)$ is a reductive function, we get $(\alpha \circ \gamma) \circ g^\sharp \leq g^\sharp$ and thus:

$$\alpha \circ f \circ \gamma \leq g^\sharp .$$

This means that the function given by the composition $\alpha \circ f \circ \gamma$ is at least as precise as any valid transformer.

The function $\alpha \circ f \circ \gamma$ is called *best transformer*. The best transformer is considered as the ideal transformer. Implementing it by actually computing concretizations of abstract elements is often infeasible. However one can often implement the best transformer with operations that stay at the level of the abstract domain.

Definition 2.13 (Best Transformer [Cousot and Cousot, 1992]). *For a transformer* $f : C \to C$, *the* best transformer *is defined by the following composition of functions:*

$$f^\sharp = \alpha \circ f \circ \gamma . \qquad (2.7)$$

We summarize the properties of the best transformer, which we have just discussed, in the following Theorem 2.14 :

Theorem 2.14 (Validity and Optimality of Best Transformer). *Let f and $f^\sharp$ be as in Definition 2.13. The best transformer $f^\sharp$ is the most precise abstract transformer, i.e. we have that:*

1. *the best transformer is a valid abstraction of f,*
2. *it holds that $f^\sharp \leq g^\sharp$ for any valid abstraction $g^\sharp : A \to A$ of f.*

In this section, we have described how to derive abstract analyses based on a given concrete semantics and a Galois connection. This concludes the agenda for the current chapter.

2.8 Conclusion

In this chapter, we have presented basics of abstract interpretation recalling how to design correct analyses, and how to reason about relative precision and optimality. Thereby we have covered abstract interpretation in its full generality along with several examples that illustrate how abstract interpretation can be used to determine properties of programs. In coming chapters, the focus will be on the analysis of a particular class of properties, namely probabilistic properties. Thus domains are needed which can represent probability values. Here the lattice of valuations comes into play. To obtain abstractions for the probabilistic setting, we will consider variants of partition abstractions which apply to valuations and thus constitute a quantitative generalization of the qualitative partition abstraction studied in this chapter. Valuations then range over blocks, i.e., abstract states, rather than states of the original program. Abstract interpretation formalizes the relationship between domains and induces (optimal) analyses. Based on these concepts, we will construct analyses for probabilistic programs.

3

Markov Models

This chapter discusses Markov models, a family of models which includes Markov chains and extensions of Markov chains. In a nutshell, Markov chains have a set of states and define probabilities to take a transition from one state to another. The transition probability is determined only by the current state and not by the execution history – a characteristic known as the Markov property: for any given state, the probability to go to a successor state is governed by a particular probability distribution over states.

By extending Markov chains with non-determinism, i.e., admitting multiple distributions per state, we arrive at the model of Markov decision processes (MDPs) [Puterman, 1994]. MDPs play a crucial role as a semantic model in the analysis of concurrent systems with random phenomena, e.g., network protocols and randomized algorithms. Stochastic two-player games [Condon, 1992] extend MDPs with an additional level of non-determinism. Abstractions of MDPs can be represented by stochastic games.

Many interesting properties of systems with random phenomena are expressible in terms of probabilistic reachability, the probability to reach a certain set of goal states in a Markov model. The notion of probabilistic reachability depends on the specific type of Markov model under consideration. In a Markov chain, reachability probability is defined by the probability mass of the paths that traverse a goal state. In an MDP, non-deterministic decisions influence the reachability probability and the same goes for stochastic games. In this chapter, we discuss probabilistic reachability along with each of the different Markov models and supplement the formal presentation with examples.

Outline

The structure of the chapter follows the hierarchy of the models:

Section 3.1 We begin with probability distributions, which appear in the transition structure of all Markov models.

Section 3.2 We discuss Markov chains and probabilistic reachability in Markov chains. This forms the foundation of the theory behind MDPs and stochastic games.

Section 3.3 MDPs are introduced which extend Markov chains with non-determinism. We recall probabilistic reachability for MDPs.

Section 3.4 We discuss stochastic games which generalize MDPs by an additional level of non-deterministic choices.

Section 3.4 The last section concludes the chapter with a summary and an outlook on the roles the different Markov models play in the thesis.

3.1   Probability Distributions

Probability distributions define the probability with which Markov models move from one state to the next. They are thus a basic building block of Markov models. In this section, we recall probability distributions and introduce notation.

Definition 3.1 (Probability Distribution). *A simple probability distribution π over a set S is a function $\pi : S \to [0, 1]$ such that $\pi(S) := \sum_{s \in S} \pi(s) = 1$.*

We denote the set of distributions over S by $Distr_S$.

In addition to simple probability distributions, we need the notion of labeled distributions. Labeled distribution are probability distributions over tuples where the first component is a label and the second component is an element of a set S.

Definition 3.2 (Labeled Distribution). *Let U be a finite set. A labeled distribution π over set $U \times S$ is a function $\pi : U \times S \to [0, 1]$ such that $\sum_{(u,s) \in U \times S} \pi(u, s) = 1$ and π is right unique, i.e., for all $u \in U, s, s' \in S$, $\pi(u, s) > 0$ and $\pi(u, s') > 0$ implies $s = s'$. We denote the set of labeled distributions by $Distr_{U \times S}$. A labeled distribution π gives rise to a simple distribution where the weight of $s \in S$ is given by summing over the labels:*

$$\pi(s) := \sum \{\pi(u, s) \mid u \in U\} . \tag{3.1}$$

We abbreviate the sum of the probabilities for a subset $S' \subseteq S$ by $\pi(S') := \sum_{s \in S'} \pi(s)$. We would like to construct distributions based on a given collection of weighted elements. Let $p_1, \ldots, p_n \in \{0, 1\}$ be weights with $1 = \sum_{i=1}^{n} p_i$. Let $u_1, \ldots, u_n \in U$ be pairwise distinct labels and let $s_1, \ldots, s_n \in S$ be elements of S (which are not necessarily distinct). Then we define the labeled distribution, $\bigoplus_{i=1}^{n} p_i : (u, s_i)$, by:

$$\left(\bigoplus_{i=1}^{n} p_i : (u_i, s_i) \right)(u, s) := \begin{cases} p_i & \text{; if there exists } i \in \{1, \ldots, n\} : (u, s) = (u_i, s_i) \\ 0 & \text{; otherwise} \end{cases} .$$

As an alternative notation, we use $p_1 : (u_1, s_1) \oplus \ldots \oplus p_n : (u, s_n)$ if convenient. For illustration, consider a fair die. We denote the corresponding uniform distribution over the numbers $\{0, \ldots, 5\}$ and labels $u := \{u_0, \ldots, u_5\}$ by

$$\frac{1}{6} : (u_0, 0) \oplus \frac{1}{6} : (u_1, 1) \oplus \frac{1}{6} : (u_2, 2) \oplus \frac{1}{6} : (u_3, 3) \oplus \frac{1}{6} : (u_4, 4) \oplus \frac{1}{6} : (u_5, 5) .$$

Alternatively, we can write the same distribution as: $\bigoplus_{i=1}^{n} \{\frac{1}{6} : (u_i, i) \mid 0 \le i \le 5\}$.

Now we are prepared to define the most basic Markov model: Markov chains.

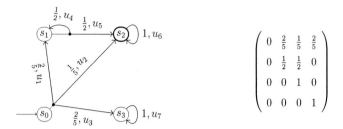

Figure 3.1.: A Markov chain with four states and the corresponding matrix.

3.2 Markov Chains

Markov chains are a modeling formalism for probabilistic behavior. In a Markov chain, a state is either absorbing, i.e., the state has no successors, or it can choose a successor state according to a labeled probability distribution.

Figure 3.1 shows a Markov chain. Its initial state s_0 has three probabilistic choices: it can go to state s_1 with probability $\frac{2}{5}$, to state s_2 with $\frac{1}{5}$ and to state s_3 with $\frac{2}{5}$ respectively.

Each probabilistic choice is decorated with an element from a set U of update labels. For example, the Markov chain in Figure 3.1 has update[1] labels $\{u_1, \ldots, u_7\}$. The labels are depicted next to the respective probabilities. Formally, the transition probabilities are governed by a partial function from states to labeled probability distributions, where the value of the function for absorbing states is undefined.

The definition of a Markov chain is as follows:

Definition 3.3 (Markov Chain). *A Markov chain $\mathcal{M}$ is a triple (S, U, I, R) where*

- *S is a set of states,*
- *$I \subseteq S$ is a set of initial states,*
- *U is an update alphabet,*
- *R is the transition function, a partial function of the form $R : S \to Distr_{U,S}$.*

Markov chains can be viewed as weighted directed graphs. The transition function of a Markov chain defines a weighted adjacency matrix, which gives the transition probability from a state s to another state s' via label u. Such a matrix is depicted on the right of Figure 3.1. Following this intuition, we use the transition function R of a Markov chain in the style of a matrix. We define $R(s, u, s') := 0$ if state s is absorbing, i.e., if s is not in the domain of the partial function R, and $R(s, u, s') := \pi(u, s')$ for $\pi := R(u, s)$.

---

[1]Update labels link the respective probabilistic branch with a probabilistic choice in a program.

We are interested in the paths that are generated by Markov chains because these paths correspond to runs of the system which is modeled by a given Markov chain.

Paths. Let $\mathcal{M} = (S, I, U, R)$ be a Markov chain. A *finite path* β in $\mathcal{M}$ is a non-empty sequence of states and update labels:

$$\beta = s_0 u_0 s_1 u_1 \ldots s_n$$

where $R(s_i, u_i, s_{i+1}) > 0$ for all $i \in \{0, \ldots, n-1\}$. For a finite path β, the last state is written $last(\beta)$. We denote the set of all finite paths over $\mathcal{M}$ starting in state $s \in S$ by $Path_s^{fin}(\mathcal{M})$. If a finite path β is a prefix of β', we write $\beta \leq \beta'$. A finite path β is maximal if $\beta \leq \beta'$ implies that $\beta = \beta'$ for all finite paths. Similarly, an *infinite path* in $\mathcal{M}$ is a sequence $\beta = s_0 u_0 s_1 u_1 \ldots$ where $R(s_i, u_i, s_{i+1}) > 0$ for all $i \in \mathbb{N}$. Let $Path_s(\mathcal{M})$ denote the set of infinite paths or maximal paths over $\mathcal{M}$ starting in state $s \in S$. The i-th state of a (finite or infinite) path β is denoted by $\beta[i]$.

For illustration, consider the Markov chain in Figure 3.1. The sequence $s_0 u_2 (s_2 u_6)^\infty$ is an infinite path. The path $\beta := s_0 u_2 s_2 u_6 s_2$ is a finite prefix of this infinite path. Further, we have $\beta[0] = s_0$ and $\beta[1] = s_2$.

Probability Measure. In order to reason about the behavior of a Markov chain, we need to quantify the probability that certain paths are taken. To this end, we define a probability measure on paths. The probability measure P_s is defined with respect to a particular start state s, i.e., the measure $P_s : 2^{Path_s(\mathcal{M})} \to [0, 1]$ is defined over the paths $Path_s(\mathcal{M})$ that begin with s.

In general, the set $Path_s(\mathcal{M})$ is an uncountably infinite domain, even for a Markov chain with just two states. To avoid problems with unmeasurable sets, we employ the well-known cylinder construction [Kemeny et al., 1966], which uses finite paths to represent sets of infinite paths. Thereby a finite path β represents a cylinder, a set of infinite paths sharing prefix β. The idea is that a probability measure P_s on finite paths is easily defined, and that this measure can, in turn, be lifted to infinite paths by considering cylinders. Let us now briefly go through the construction in more detail.

A finite path is the outcome of a series of probabilistic choices. The probability $P(\beta)$ of a finite path β is thus the product of the probabilities of the taken probabilistic choices, or 1 if the path has length zero and no choice had to be made:

$$P(\beta) := \begin{cases} \prod_{i=0}^{n-1} R(s_i, u_i, s_{i+1}) & ; \text{ if } \beta = s_0 u_0 s_1 u_1 \ldots s_n \text{ and } n > 0 \\ 1 & ; \text{ if } \beta = s_0 \end{cases}.$$

The cylinder set $Cyl(\beta)$ of a finite path β is the set of all paths with (finite) prefix β, i.e., $Cyl(\beta) = \{\beta' \in Path_s(\mathcal{M}) \mid \beta \leq \beta'\}$. Let Σ_s be the smallest σ-algebra on $Path_s(\mathcal{M})$ which contains the cylinders $Cyl(\beta)$ with $\beta \in Path_s^{fin}(\mathcal{M})$. Intuitively, we want a probability measure that assigns to a cylinder set the probability of its underlying finite path, i.e., $P_s(Cyl(\beta)) = P(\beta)$. Results from probability and measure theory guarantee that such a probability measure P_s on Σ_s exists and is uniquely defined.

Now we can determine the probability that a Markov chain behaves in a certain way by identifying the set of paths satisfying our specification, and taking the measure of this set under P_s.

Probabilistic Reachability. We consider reachability probabilities in Markov chains. That is, for each state s, we are interested in the probability to reach a specified set of *goal states* $F \subseteq S$. This reachability probability $p_s(F)$ is defined as the probability of the paths starting in state s that reach a goal state:

$$p_s(F) := P_s(\{\beta \in Paths_s(\mathcal{M}) \mid \exists i \in \mathbb{N} : \beta[i] \in F\}) \quad \text{for each } s \in S .$$

For each state, we can thus quantify the probability to reach F, which defines a function that maps states to probabilities:

$$p(F) \in [0,1]^S, s \mapsto p_s(F) .$$

As an example, consider the Markov chain in Figure 3.1. We are interested in $p_{s_0}(\{s_2\})$, the probability to reach the goal state s_2 from the initial state s_0. The set of paths that begin in s_0 and reach state s_2 is $\{s_0 u_2 (s_2 u_6)^\infty\} \cup \{s_0 u_1 (s_1 u_4)^k s_1 u_5 (s_2 u_6)^\infty \mid k \in \mathbb{N}\}$. The probability measure of this set of paths is given by the geometric series

$$\underbrace{\frac{1}{5}}_{s_0 u_2 (s_2 u_6)^\infty} + \underbrace{\frac{2}{5} \cdot \left(\sum_{k=0}^{\infty} \left(\frac{1}{2} \right)^k \right) \cdot \frac{1}{2}}_{s_0 u_1 (s_1 u_4)^k s_1 u_5 (s_2 u_6)^\infty} = \frac{1}{5} + \frac{2}{5} \cdot \left(\frac{1}{1 - \frac{1}{2}} \right) \cdot \frac{1}{2} = \frac{3}{5} .$$

Thus the probability to reach s_2 from s_0 is $p_{s_0}(\{s_2\}) = \frac{3}{5}$.

Fixed-Point Characterization of Probabilistic Reachability. Reachability probabilities are expressible in terms of least fixed points. The intuition is that the probability to reach a state can be formulated by recursive equations.

For example, in the Markov chain from Figure 3.1, the probability to reach s_2 from state s_0 is given by the sum of the probabilities to reach s_2 from any of its successors and likewise for s_1. State s_2 is the goal state and s_3 cannot reach a goal state. This yields the equation system:

$$p_{s_0}(\{s_2\}) = \frac{2}{5} \cdot p_{s_1}(\{s_2\}) + \frac{1}{5} \cdot p_{s_2}(\{s_2\}) \tag{3.2}$$

$$p_{s_1}(\{s_2\}) = \frac{1}{2} \cdot p_{s_1}(\{s_2\}) + \frac{1}{2} \cdot p_{s_2}(\{s_2\}) \tag{3.3}$$

$$p_{s_2}(\{s_2\}) = 1 \tag{3.4}$$

$$p_{s_3}(\{s_2\}) = 0 \tag{3.5}$$

The smallest solution of this system of equations are the reachability probabilities:

$$p_{s_0}(\{s_2\}) = \frac{3}{5} \quad , \quad p_{s_1}(\{s_2\}) = 1 \quad , \quad p_{s_2}(\{s_2\}) = 1 \quad , \quad p_{s_3}(\{s_2\}) = 0 \ .$$

Remember that we call functions from states to probabilities valuations (see Section 2.4 for a formal definition). For example, the reachability probabilities for the states form a valuation. The recursive equations that define these reachability probabilities can be viewed as a monotone function, a so called valuation transformer (valuation transformers are monotone functions over the domain of valuations). Reachability probabilities can then be expressed as a least fixed point of a *valuation transformer*:

Definition 3.4 (Valuation Transformer). *A valuation transformer is a monotone function* $f : [0,1]^S \to [0,1]^S$. *We refer to the least fixed point of* f *over* $([0,1]^S, \leq)$ *by* $lfp_\leq f$, *to the greatest fixed point over* $([0,1]^S, \geq)$ *by* $gfp_\geq f$ *and analogously for the other cases.*

The valuation transformer $pre_F : [0,1]^S \to [0,1]^S$ for probabilistic reachability is determined by the Markov chain and the goal states F:

$$pre_F(w)(s) := \begin{cases} 1 & ; \text{ if } s \in F \\ 0 & ; \text{ if } s \in F_0 \\ \sum_{u \in U, s' \in S} R(s, u, s') \cdot w(s') & ; \text{ otherwise} \end{cases} \quad . \tag{3.6}$$

The goal states have reachability probability 1, which determines Equation 3.4 in our example. The states that cannot reach any state in F, denoted by $F_0 \subseteq S$, have reachability probability 0, the state s_3 is such a state – this explains Equation 3.5. In the other cases, the reachability probability is given by the weighted sum of the probabilities of the successors of the state, which corresponds to Equation 3.2 and 3.3. Lastly, the reachability probabilities $p(F)$ are given by the least fixed point:

$$p(F) = lfp_\leq pre_F \ .$$

This concludes our discussion of Markov chains. In the next section, we recall Markov decision processes, which combine probabilistic with non-deterministic behavior. Non-determinism is important since it admits to model concurrency. Markov decision processes are thus significantly more expressive than Markov chains. However, Markov chains and the concept of probabilistic reachability play an important role as a foundation for the coming material.

3.3 Markov Decision Processes

From Markov chains, we come to Markov decision processes (MDPs) [Puterman, 1994]. Recall that a state in a Markov chain has at most one distribution associated with it. Markov decision processes generalize Markov chains – a state in an MDP can choose

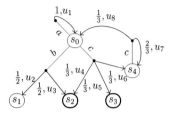

Figure 3.2.: Markov decision process with five states.

non-deterministically from *several* possible distributions. The different distributions are labeled with actions. Figure 3.2 shows an MDP with five states and actions $\{a, b, c\}$.

Because MDPs allow for multiple distributions at a state, MDPs admit to model concurrency including systems composed of several probabilistic systems.

MDPs are formally defined as follows:

Definition 3.5 (Markov Decision Process). *A Markov decision process $\mathcal{M}$ is a tuple $\mathcal{M} = (S, I, A, U, En, R)$ where*

- *S is a set of states,*
- *$I \subseteq S$ is a set of initial states,*
- *A is a finite action alphabet,*
- *U is a finite update alphabet,*
- *function $En : S \to 2^A$ associates with each state $s \in S$ a set $En(s) \subseteq A$ of* enabled *actions,*
- *transition function $R : S \times A \to Distr_{U,S}$ associates with each state s and enabled action $a \in En(s)$ an update-labeled probability distribution $R(s, a) \in Distr_{U,S}$. The value $R(s, a)(u, s') \in [0, 1]$ is the probability of a transition from state s to state s' with action a and update u.*

We denote the set of distributions $Steps(s) \subseteq Distr_{U \times S}$ available at a state s by:

$$Steps(s) := \{\pi \in Distr_{U \times S} \mid a \in En(s) : \ \pi = R(s, a)\} \ .$$

Each state s is associated with a set of enabled actions $En(s)$. The transition function is only defined for those pairs (s, a) of states and transitions where a is enabled at state s, i.e., $a \in En(s)$. Just like for Markov chains, a state s may also be absorbing, i.e., in this case, no action is enabled at that state, i.e., $En(s) = \emptyset$.

For illustration, consider the Markov decision process depicted in Figure 3.2. The probability, for example, of going from state s_0 to s_4 with action c is $\frac{1}{3}$. The set of enabled actions at state s_0 is $En(s_0) = \{a, b, c\}$, while, for state s_4, we have $En(s_4) = \{c\}$.

Paths. A finite path in $\mathcal{M}$ is a sequence $s_0 a_0 u_0 s_1 a_1 u_1 \ldots a_{n-1} u_{n-1} s_n$ which respects the transitions function, i.e. $R(s_i, a_i)(u_i, s_{i+1}) > 0$ for all $i \in \{0, \ldots, n-1\}$. The action labels a_i reflect non-deterministic choice and the update labels u_i probabilistic choice. Let $Path^{fin}(\mathcal{M})$ denote the set of all finite paths over $\mathcal{M}$ and let $Path_s^{fin}(\mathcal{M})$ denote finite paths over $\mathcal{M}$ starting in state s. Like for Markov chains, we write $\beta \leq \beta'$, if the finite path β is a prefix of β'. A finite path β is maximal if $\beta \leq \beta'$ implies that $\beta = \beta'$. Similarly, the last state of a finite path is denoted by $last(\beta)$ and the i-th state of a path is denoted by $\beta[i]$. An infinite path in $\mathcal{M}$ is a sequence such that $s_0 a_0 u_0 s_1 a_1 u_1 \ldots$ where $R(s_i, a_i)(u_i, s_{i+1}) > 0$ for all $i \in \mathbb{N}$. Let $Path_s(\mathcal{M})$ denote the set of all infinite paths or maximal paths over $\mathcal{M}$ starting in state s.

Adversaries. Tracing a path in a Markov decision process requires resolution of both nondeterministic and probabilistic choice. To be able to talk about probability, we need to specify how nondeterminism should be resolved. To this end, we consider the concept of an adversary (also called 'scheduler' or 'policy'), which selects an action based on the choices made so far during execution history. Mathematically, an adversary is a function $\eta : Path^{fin}(\mathcal{M}) \rightarrow A_{\mathcal{D}_\delta}$ mapping every finite path β of the MDP onto either an action $\eta(\beta) \in En(last(\beta))$ or the "undefined" value $\mathcal{D}_\delta$. For a state s, let $Path_s^\eta(\mathcal{M}) \subseteq Path_s(\mathcal{M})$ denote the paths of $\mathcal{M}$ that correspond to η.

As an example, consider the MDP in Figure 3.2. The following adversary chooses action b, if the last state in the path is state s_0, and action c, if the last state in the path is state s_4. The adversary returns the undefined value $\mathcal{D}_\delta$ whenever no action is available, e.g., $En(s_2) = \emptyset$ and $\eta(s_2) = \mathcal{D}_\delta$. Formally, the adversary η is defined by:

$$\eta(\beta) = \begin{cases} b & ; \text{ if } last(\beta) = s_0 \\ c & ; \text{ if } last(\beta) = s_4 \\ \mathcal{D}_\delta & ; \text{ otherwise} \end{cases}.$$

Note that the example adversary only looks at the last state in a path. In general, an adversary can base its decision on the entire path.

The behavior of an MDP under a fixed adversary is fully probabilistic. It can be described by the (generally infinite) Markov chain induced by the adversary. The induced Markov chain is defined as follows: the states are the finite paths in the original MDP and the transition probability between two such states is given by the probability distribution selected by the adversary η. Thus there is a one-to-one correspondence between the paths $Path_s^\eta(\mathcal{M})$ induced by η within the MDP and paths in the induced Markov chain. Namely, the paths in $Path_s^\eta(\mathcal{M})$ correspond exactly to the paths in the induced Markov chain that start with the zero-length path s as a prefix. We can therefore use the probability measure over Markov chains to define the probability measure P_s^η over $Path_s^\eta(\mathcal{M})$. For details of the construction, please refer to [Baier, 1998].

A Markov decision process thus represents a generally infinite family of Markov chains induced by different adversaries. When we compute probabilities, we are generally not interested in one specific adversary, but rather in guarantees that hold for all possible adversaries. One therefore computes *minimal* and *maximal* probabilities over all possible adversaries to capture the 'best-case' and 'worst-case' scenario.

Probabilistic Reachability.   We consider probabilistic reachability properties of MDPs. That is, for each state s, we are interested in the probability to reach a specified set of *goal states* $F \subseteq S$. Under a given adversary η, this reachability probability $p_s^\eta(F)$ is defined as the probability of the paths starting in s that reach a goal state:

$$p_s^\eta(F) := P_s^\eta(\{\beta \in Path_s^\eta(\mathcal{M}) \mid \exists i \in \mathbb{N} : \beta[i] \in F\}) \quad \text{for each } s \in S \ .$$

Thus we can associate with each state its probability to reach F under adversary η, which gives us a valuation $p^\eta(F) \in [0,1]^S, s \mapsto p_s^\eta(F)$.

To obtain guarantees for *all possible adversaries*, the standard approach is to consider both minimal and maximal reachability probabilities. Formally, minimal reachability probabilities $p^-(F) \in [0,1]^S$ are defined by the infimum of the reachability probabilities $p^\eta(F)$ where η ranges over all adversaries, i.e., $p^-(F) = \bigsqcap\{p^\eta(F) \mid \eta \in Adv_\mathcal{M}\}$. Likewise, maximal reachability probabilities $p^+(F) \in [0,1]^S$ are defined by the supremum $p^+(F) = \bigsqcup\{p^\eta(F) \mid \eta \in Adv_\mathcal{M}\}$.

The characterization of reachability probabilities in terms of infima and suprema over an infinite set of adversaries does not lend itself to compute these probabilities in practice. However, probabilistic reachability is expressible in terms of a system of recursive equations [Baier, 1998] where the unknowns correspond to the probability of an individual state. For finite MDPs, these equations can be solved by linear programming [Bianco and de Alfaro, 1995] or by value iteration. Like for Markov chains, the equation system corresponds to a valuation transformer. The solution, the reachability probabilities, are given by the least fixed point of the valuation transformer.

Now we give the valuation transformers. We begin with minimal probabilistic reachability and define the corresponding valuation transformer $pre_F^- : [0,1]^S \to [0,1]^S$. The goal states have reachability probability 1. The states that cannot reach any state in F, denoted by $F_0 \subseteq S$, have reachability probability 0. In the other cases, the reachability probability is given by taking the minimal probability among all enabled actions[2]:

$$pre_F^-(w)(s) := \begin{cases} 1 & ; \text{ if } s \in F \\ 0 & ; \text{ if } s \in F_0 \\ \min_{a \in En(s)} \sum_{s' \in S} R(s,a)(s') \cdot w(s') & ; \text{ otherwise} \end{cases} \ .$$

Figure 3.3 gives an example MDP with the corresponding valuation transformer pre_F^-. The minimal reachability probabilities $p^-(F) \in [0,1]^S$ are given by the least fixed point $p^-(F) = lfp_\leq \ pre_F^-$ (as shown in [Baier, 1998]).

---

[2] For notational convenience, we treat labeled distributions as simple distributions writing $R(s,a)(s')$, as explained in Section 3.1, rather than explicitly summing over updates, i.e., $\sum_{u \in U} R(s,a)(u,s')$.

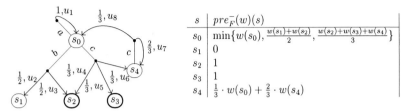

s	$pre_F^-(w)(s)$
s_0	$\min\{w(s_0), \frac{w(s_1)+w(s_2)}{2}, \frac{w(s_2)+w(s_3)+w(s_4)}{3}\}$
s_1	0
s_2	1
s_3	1
s_4	$\frac{1}{3} \cdot w(s_0) + \frac{2}{3} \cdot w(s_4)$

Figure 3.3.: Illustration of valuation transformer pre_F^-. Consider the MDP with states $\{s_0, \dots, s_4\}$ shown on the left. Assume that the goal states are given by the set $F = \{s_2, s_3\}$ and that valuation w assigns probability 1 to s_0, s_2 and s_3 respectively and probability 0 to all other states. Inserting the values and solving for state s_0, we get $pre_F^-(w)(s_0) = \min\{1, \frac{1}{2}, \frac{2}{3}\} = \frac{1}{2}$.

The valuation transformer for maximal probabilistic reachability $pre_F^+ : [0,1]^S \to [0,1]^S$ is defined analogously:

$$pre_F^+(w)(s) := \begin{cases} 1 & ; \text{ if } s \in F \\ 0 & ; \text{ if } s \in F_0 \\ \max\limits_{a \in En(s)} \sum\limits_{s' \in S} R(s,a)(s') \cdot w(s') & ; \text{ otherwise} \end{cases} .$$

We have $p^+(F) = lfp_{\leq} \ pre_F^+$.

Summing up, non-determinism makes the notion of reachability probabilities more involved because it induces a range of possible behaviors. Thereby each possible behavior corresponds to a particular induced Markov chain. The extremal cases lead to minimal and maximal reachability probabilities. In the next section, we discuss stochastic games where the problem of reachability can be reduced to the setting of Markov chains in a similar fashion.

3.4 Stochastic Games

We consider stochastic games [Condon, 1992] which feature two players and probabilistic choice. Therefore stochastic games are also called $2\frac{1}{2}$-player games (where the fraction $\frac{1}{2}$ refers to the probabilistic choice). The players are adversarial, so that one player tries to minimize the probability of a certain outcome while the other player seeks to maximize the probability. MDPs, on the other hand, can be seen as $1\frac{1}{2}$-player games, a special subclass of stochastic games where the decisions of one player are already fixed.

Definition 3.6 (Stochastic game [Condon, 1992]). *A stochastic game $\mathcal{G}$ is a tuple $((V, E), V_{init}, (V_1, V_2, V_p), \delta)$ where*

- $V_{init} \subseteq V_1$ *is the set of initial vertices,*

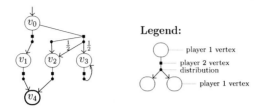

Figure 3.4.: Stochastic game (on the left) and legend.

- (V_1, V_2, V_p) is a partition of the set V, where
  - the vertex set V_1 is called player 1 vertices,
  - the vertex set V_2 is called player 2 vertices,
  - the vertex set V_p is called the probabilistic vertices,
- (V, E) is a directed graph with edges $E \subseteq (V_1 \times V_2) \cup (V_2 \times V_p) \cup (V_p \times V_1)$,
- $\delta : V_p \to Distr_{U,V}$ where $\delta(v)(u, v') > 0$ implies that $(v, v') \in E$.

We denote by $E(v) = \{v' \in V \mid (v, v') \in E\}$ the set of successors of a game vertex v.

Figure 3.4 shows an example for a stochastic game. On the left of the figure, a stochastic game with five player 1 vertices $V_1 = \{v_1, v_2, v_3, v_4\}$ and initial vertex $V_{init} = \{v_0\}$ is depicted. Player 1 vertex v_0 can non-deterministically choose between two player 2 vertices shown as small solid squares. The player 2 vertex on the left can only chose a single distribution, while the right player 2 vertex can choose between two distributions. The legend on the right explains our graphical notation for the different kinds of vertices of a stochastic game.

Plays. Plays are sequences of vertices that result from resolving player 1 and player 2 decisions and probabilistic choice. They are the counterpart of paths in Markov chains or MDPs. A finite *play* in $\mathcal{G}$ is a sequence of game vertices and update labels with:

$$\omega = (v_{1,0}, v_{2,0}, v_{p,0}, u_0)(v_{1,1}, v_{2,1}, v_{p,1}, u_1) \ldots v_{1,n}$$

such that $(v_{1,i}, v_{2,i}), (v_{2,i}, v_{p,i}) \in E$ and $\delta(v_{p,i})(u_i, v_{1,i+1}) > 0$. We denote the set of finite plays starting in a vertex v by $Play_v^{fin}(\mathcal{G})$ and set of all finite plays by $Play^{fin}(\mathcal{G})$. The last vertex of a finite play is denoted by $last(\omega)$ and the i-th vertex of a play is denoted by $\omega[i]$. Similarly, we write $\omega \leq \omega'$, if the finite play ω is a prefix of ω'. A finite play ω is maximal if $\omega \leq \omega'$ implies that $\omega = \omega'$. An infinite play in $\mathcal{G}$ is a sequence $\omega = v_{1,0} v_{2,0} v_{p,0}, u_0 \ldots$ such that $(v_{1,i}, v_{2,i}), (v_{2,i}, v_{p,i}) \in E$ and $\delta(v_{p,i})(u_i, v_{1,i+1}) > 0$ for all $i \in \mathbb{N}$. Let $Play(\mathcal{G})$ denote the set of all infinite plays or maximal plays over $\mathcal{G}$ and $Play_v(\mathcal{G})$ the plays that start in vertex v.

Strategies. To define a probability measure on plays, two strategies are needed to resolve player 1 and player 2 decisions respectively. Formally, a player 1 strategy is a function $\sigma_1 : Play^{fin}(\mathcal{G})V_1 \to V$ such that for any finite play $\omega \in Play^{fin}(\mathcal{G})V_1$, $\sigma_1(\omega) = v$ implies that $(last(\omega), v) \in E$. Player 2 strategies are defined analogously.

The behavior of a game under a pair of strategies is fully probabilistic. Analogous to adversaries in MDPs, a pair of strategies σ_1 and σ_2 induces a Markov chain, denoted by $\mathcal{G}_v^{\sigma_1,\sigma_2}$, and a probability measure $P_v^{\sigma_1,\sigma_2}$ [Condon, 1992] over plays $Play_v^{\sigma_1,\sigma_2}(\mathcal{G})$.

A strategy σ_i for player i is called *memoryless* if it is a function $\sigma_i : V_i \to V$. Memoryless strategies are very desirable in practice, since they can be represented compactly in memory, as only one decision per vertex has to be stored. Further, the induced Markov chains are finite and can easily be obtained from the game.

Probabilistic Reachability. For a fixed pair of strategies σ_1, σ_2, we denote the probability to reach a set F of vertices starting from vertex v by $p_v^{\sigma_1,\sigma_2}(F)$. This probability is given by the measure of the plays that reach F:

$$p_v^{\sigma_1,\sigma_2}(F) := P_v^{\sigma_1,\sigma_2}(\{\omega \in Play_v(\mathcal{G}) \mid \exists i \in \mathbb{N} : \omega[i] \in F\}) \ .$$

We denote the resulting valuation that assigns probabilities to game vertices by $p^{\sigma_1,\sigma_2}(F)$.

Let us assume that player 1 tries to maximize and player 2 tries to minimize the probability to reach F from a player 1 vertex $v \in V_1$. For a given player 1 strategy, player 2 cannot push the probability value lower than $\inf_{\sigma_2} p_v^{\sigma_1,\sigma_2}(F)$ with any of its strategies. Hence the optimal probability player 1 can achieve is given by:

$$\sup_{\sigma_1} \inf_{\sigma_2} p_v^{\sigma_1,\sigma_2}(F) \ .$$

We write $\sup_{\sigma_1} \inf_{\sigma_2} p^{\sigma_1,\sigma_2}(F)$ to denote the resulting valuation that assigns optimal probabilities to player 1 vertices. Similarly, we can consider the dual case where player 1 tries to maximize and player 2 tries to minimize the probability to reach F. In this case, we obtain optimal valuation $\inf_{\sigma_1} \sup_{\sigma_2} p^{\sigma_1,\sigma_2}(F)$. We also consider the cases where the players cooperate: $\inf_{\sigma_1,\sigma_2} p^{\sigma_1,\sigma_2}(F)$ and $\sup_{\sigma_1,\sigma_2} p^{\sigma_1,\sigma_2}(F)$. In these latter cases, probabilistic reachability can be computed by using methods for MDPs.

Optimal strategies are effectively computable and representable since the subclass of memoryless strategies is sufficient, i.e. there always exist memoryless strategies that achieve the optimal valuations [Chatterjee et al., 2004].

Valuation Transformers. Optimal reachability probabilities can be computed as least fixed points of valuation transformers. The optimal probabilities $\sup_{\sigma_1} \inf_{\sigma_2} p^{\sigma_1,\sigma_2}(F)$ are the least fixed point of the transformer $pre_F^{+-} : [0,1]^{V_1} \to [0,1]^{V_1}$:

$$\sup_{\sigma_1} \inf_{\sigma_2} p^{\sigma_1,\sigma_2}(F) = lfp_{\leq} \ pre_F^{+-} \ .$$

The transformer $pre_F^{+-} : [0,1]^{V_1} \to [0,1]^{V_1}$ is defined as follows, for all valuations w:

$$pre_F^{+-}(w)(v) := \begin{cases} 1 & ; \text{ if } s \in F \\ 0 & ; \text{ if } s \in F_0 \\ \max\limits_{v_2 \in E(v)} \min\limits_{v_p \in E(v_2)} \sum\limits_{v' \in E(v_p)} w(v') \cdot \delta(v_p)(v') & ; \text{ otherwise} \end{cases} \qquad (3.7)$$

where F_0 denotes the vertices that cannot reach F.

An analogous characterization can be given for optimal probabilities where the roles of the players are changed in terms of minimization and maximization. Overall, we get:

$$\sup\nolimits_{\sigma_1} \inf\nolimits_{\sigma_2} p^{\sigma_1,\sigma_2}(F) = lfp_\leq pre_F^{+-} \qquad (3.8)$$

$$\inf\nolimits_{\sigma_1} \sup\nolimits_{\sigma_2} p^{\sigma_1,\sigma_2}(F) = lfp_\leq pre_F^{-+} \qquad (3.9)$$

$$\inf\nolimits_{\sigma_1} \inf\nolimits_{\sigma_2} p^{\sigma_1,\sigma_2}(F) = lfp_\leq pre_F^{--} \qquad (3.10)$$

$$\sup\nolimits_{\sigma_1} \sup\nolimits_{\sigma_2} p^{\sigma_1,\sigma_2}(F) = lfp_\leq pre_F^{++} \qquad (3.11)$$

The corresponding valuation transformers $pre_F^{--}, pre_F^{-+}, pre_F^{++}$ are defined along the lines of the transformer pre_F^{+-}. The difference is that the extrema are adapted in the non-trivial case of the case distinction of Equation 3.7, i.e. for the case where $s \in V_1 \setminus (F \cup F_0)$. Here the transformer pre_F^{-+} minimizes over player 2 vertices and maximizes over probabilistic vertices. In contrast pre_F^{--} minimizes over both player 2 vertices and probabilistic vertices, and, lastly, pre_F^{++} maximizes over both.

These optimal valuations can be approximated by iterating valuation transformers, i.e. performing value iteration [Condon, 1992].

We have now covered stochastic games, the most complex member of the family of Markov models. This completes the treatment of Markov models. We conclude the chapter with several remarks and an outlook.

3.5 Conclusion

In this chapter we have introduced variants of Markov models relevant to this thesis. Markov chains are the fundamental model with probabilistic choice. Markov decision processes additionally offer non-deterministic choice and thus lend themselves to describe concurrent and distributed systems. Stochastic games introduce an additional level of non-determinism which will later on play a role to express uncertainty introduced by the abstraction. Across all models, we have studied reachability probabilities.

In the next chapter, we will introduce concurrent probabilistic programs. The semantics of a concurrent probabilistic program is a Markov decision process.

Remark. Typically, Markov models are defined in terms of simple rather than labeled distributions. We consider labeled distributions in order to develop abstraction refinement succinctly (actions and update labels identify points in the program that are responsible for the respective non-deterministic and probabilistic choice). Labeled distributions induce simple distributions, as described by Equation 3.1, and, in turn, Markov models over labeled distributions can be transformed into Markov models over simple distributions in a very straightforward way. Namely, the probability of a state with respect to different update labels is simply summed up, e.g., $\pi(u_1, s) = \frac{1}{2}$ and $\pi(u_2, s) = \frac{1}{2}$ becomes $\pi(s) = \pi(u_1, s) + \pi(u_2, s) = 1$. For the sake of notational convenience, we can thus identify labeled distributions with the simple distributions they induce, except in the context of refinement where the distinction is important.

4

Concurrent Probabilistic Programs

We would like to analyze network protocols, randomized algorithms and other systems involving concurrency and probabilistic behavior. Concurrent probabilistic programs provide a suitable modeling language to express these systems. In this chapter, we discuss the syntax and semantics of concurrent probabilistic programs.

Concurrent probabilistic programs admit both variables with bounded range and unbounded integers. Bounded integers can be used to model control locations, Boolean flags or other data from finite domains. Unbounded integers, on the other hand, can be used to model counters, e.g., how many chunks of a file have been transmitted, or package identifiers, network addresses and so on. Due to unbounded integer variables, the semantics of a program may be an MDP with infinitely many states.

Programs consist of guarded commands, which manipulate the programs variables and induce probabilistic choices. As an example, consider the following command

    [aF] (k=0) -> 0.98 : (k'=1) + 0.02 : (k'=2);

which describes a lossy communication channel. Program variable k models the state of the channel where $k = 0$ means that the channel is free, $k = 1$ means that a message has been sent successfully and $k = 2$ means that a message has been lost. The guard $k = 0$ specifies that the command is only enabled if the channel is free, i.e., $k = 0$. Executing the commands corresponds to a message transmission. Thereby a message is either transmitted successfully ($k = 1$) with a probability of 98%, or it gets lost ($k = 2$) with a probability of 2%. These different probabilistic outcomes are expressed in the command by two different probabilistic alternatives weighted with the respective probabilities.

Beside probabilistic choice, there is also non-deterministic choice. Namely, whenever guards of commands are not exclusive, the program non-deterministically chooses from a menu of enabled commands. In this way, concurrency can be expressed.

The language of concurrent probabilistic programs is inspired by the language of the probabilistic model checker PRISM [Hinton et al., 2006]. PRISM is currently the most popular modeling and verification environment in the domain with a large repository of case studies [Kwiatkowska et al., 2010]. Compared to the PRISM language, concurrent probabilistic programs additionally support unbounded integers, while the original PRISM language restricts to bounded integer variables, since the analysis engines implemented in the PRISM tool support finite-state programs only.

The PRISM language, in turn, is a probabilistic extension of the language of reactive modules [Alur and Henzinger, 1999]. Reactive modules is a guarded-command language that admits to model concurrent systems in a modular fashion, e.g., in case of a network protocol, sender, receiver and transmission medium can be modeled by separate modules that interact with each other. Each module has its own commands and variables. The PRISM language extends reactive modules with composition operators as in Communicating Sequential Processes (CSP) [Hoare, 1978, Roscoe et al., 1997] and probabilistic choice. CSP-style parallel composition admits synchronization between commands of different modules on the same action. For example, our example command is part of a channel and synchronizes with a command in the sender module via action aF.

Concurrent probabilistic programs do not feature modules as a construct. However, a given set of modules can be flattened to a single module by merging synchronizing commands. Katoen *et al.* describe such transformations for a probabilistic process algebra that includes the PRISM language [Katoen et al., 2010]. Thus PRISM models can be translated into concurrent probabilistic programs. The transformation flattens the module structure to obtain a program consisting only of commands. Users of our tool PASS can conveniently use both the modules in the style of PRISM and the extensions enabled by abstraction such as unbounded integers. Internally, programs with modules are transformed into concurrent probabilistic programs. In this thesis, we focus on concurrent probabilistic programs without modules.

Outline. This chapter gives an overview of concurrent probabilistic programs:

Section 4.1 We give a detailed description of the syntax of concurrent probabilistic programs and introduce our running example for this chapter.

Section 4.2 We describe the program semantics. The semantics of a concurrent probabilistic program is an MDP with a potentially infinite state space.

Section 4.3 We give a symbolic semantics in terms of transition constraints, which will later serve for abstraction refinement.

Section 4.4 Finally we conclude.

4.1 Syntax

In this section, we introduce the syntax of concurrent probabilistic programs. A program consists of a set of variables, commands and a Boolean expression that defines the initial states. These expressions and commands are defined over a set of variables.

Variables. We fix a finite set of typed program variables X. We assume that expressions over program variables are part of some fragment of first-order logic that encompasses Boolean combinations of arithmetic expressions. We denote the expressions over the variables X by $Expr_X$ and Boolean expressions by $BExpr_X$.

```
module example_program
m : [0..3];        // control flow
x : int;           // counter variable

[a] m=0 -> 1.0: (x'=4) & (m'=1);
[b] m=0 -> 1.0: (x'=2) & (m'=1);
[c] m=1 & x>0 -> 0.3: (x'=x-1) + 0.7: (m'=3);
[d] m=1 & x<=0 -> 1.0: (m'=2);
endmodule

init
  m = 0 & x = 0
endinit
```

Figure 4.1.: Example program.

The example program in Figure 4.1 has variables $X = \{m, x\}$ and contains the Boolean expression m = 0 & x = 0.

The next step to is define the syntax of commands in concurrent probabilistic programs.

Commands. A command consists of an action, a guard and a finite number of probabilistic alternatives. The action is used to *uniquely* identify the command, i.e., commands have unique, pairwise distinct[1] actions. The guard is a Boolean expression that determines when the command is enabled. If the command is enabled, it may either be the only enabled command or it competes with other enabled commands for the nondeterministic choice. When a particular command is selected for execution, its probabilistic alternatives make a probalistic choice. Each probabilistic alternative consists of a probability and an *assignment*. For each alternative, the corresponding assignment determines how the program variables should be updated. Mathematically, an assignment E is a function that maps each program variable to an expression, i.e., $E : X \to Expr_X$.

For an illustration of a command in a probabilistic program, consider the program in Figure 4.1 and the command:

[c] m=1 & x>0 -> 0.3: (x'=x-1) + 0.7: (m'=3); .

The label of the command is c. Its guard is the expression m=1 & x>0. There are two probabilistic alternatives. The first alternative is weighted with probability 0.3 and the second one with 0.7. We focus on the first alternative with probability 0.3, which decreases variable x by one. The decrement operation is expressed by the assignment E belonging to the alternative by setting $E(x) = x-1$. Variable m is not explicitly mentioned in the concrete syntax. The convention is that, if a variable is not mentioned, its value remains unchanged, i.e., we have $E(m) = m$.

---

[1] This is in contrast to CSP-style parallel compositions where actions are used for synchronization and, typically, different commands are labeled with the same action.

We are now ready to formalize the abstract syntax of commands:

Definition 4.1 (Command). *A command* c *consists of*

- *a unique action a,*
- *a guard $g \in BExpr_{\boldsymbol{I}}$*
- *assignments $E_1, ..., E_k$ weighted with probabilities $p_1, ..., p_k \in [0,1]$ which sum up to one, i.e., $\sum_{i=1}^{k} p_i = 1$.*

We denote a command as follows ("+" separates the different alternatives):

$$[a] \; g \rightarrow p_1 : \boldsymbol{X'} = E_1 \; + \; ... \; + \; p_k : \boldsymbol{X'} = E_k \; .$$

where $\boldsymbol{X'} = E$ denotes the simultaneous update of variables X.

We denote by $deg(c) := k$ the number of probabilistic alternatives $k \in \mathbb{N}$ of a command.

For c, write a_c for its action, g_c for its guard. We omit subscripts if the command is clear from context.

A program consists of a set of variables, an initial condition and commands. Our example program 4.1 has two variables, initial condition m = 0 & x = 0 and four commands.

Definition 4.2 (Program). *A program $P = (\boldsymbol{X}, I, \mathcal{C})$ consists of*

- *a finite set of variables $\boldsymbol{X}$*
- *an initial condition I where $I \in BExpr_{\boldsymbol{I}}$*
- *a finite set of commands $\mathcal{C}$.*

Having discussed the syntax of programs, we now come to semantics in the next section.

4.2 Semantics

The semantics of a program is an MDP. For illustration, Figure 4.2 shows the semantics of the example program from Figure 4.1.

States. Let X be the set of program variables. A *state* (over variables X) is a type-consistent total function from variables in X to their semantic domains. We denote the set of states by $S(\boldsymbol{X})$, or S for short, and a single state by s.

For example, the MDP in Figure 4.2 contains the state $\{m \mapsto 1, x \mapsto 4\}$ where variable m has value 1 and variable x value 4.

Semantics of Expressions. We can evaluate an expression in a given state and get a semantic value. For an expression $e \in Expr_{\boldsymbol{X}}$, we denote by $[\![e]\!]_s$ its valuation in state s. In particular, evaluating a Boolean expression $e \in BExpr_{\boldsymbol{X}}$, yields $[\![e]\!]_s \in \{0,1\}$. We say that a state s fulfills a Boolean expression e if e evaluates to 1. Then we write $s \vDash e$. We denote by $[\![e]\!] = \{s \in S \mid [\![e]\!]_s = 1\}$ the set of states that fulfill e.

For example, state $s := \{m \mapsto 1, x \mapsto 4\}$ fulfills the Boolean expression x>0, formally written $s \vDash$ x>0.

Semantics of Commands. The semantics $[\![c]\!]$ of a command c is a set of probabilistic transitions, i.e. $[\![c]\!] \subseteq S \times Distr_{U,S}$. A transition induced by c is a pair (s, π) where s is a state that fulfills the guard of the command and the distribution π is determined by the probabilistic alternatives. In addition to the state, we store the probabilistic alternative responsible for the probabilistic branch. To this end, we use an update label of the form $u_i = (a_c, i)$ where a_c is the action of the command and i is the index of the probabilistic alternative, i.e., $i \in \{1, \ldots, deg(c)\}$. The update labels U are thus determined by the program and consist of pairs of actions and indices.

To construct distributions, we employ the distribution operator $\bigoplus$ which is defined in Section 3.1. The distribution π of the transition is defined by $\pi = \bigoplus_{i=1}^{k} p_i : (u_i, s_i)$ where p_i is the probability of alternative i. The successor state s_i is determined by the assignment E_i of the probabilistic alternative which updates the state variables based on their values at the present state s. Technically, state s_i is obtained by evaluating the assignment E_i in state s, i.e. $s_i = \lambda x \in X. \; [\![E_i(x)]\!]_s$. The lambda expression indicates that s_i is a mapping from variables to semantic values.

Before giving a concrete example, we define the semantics of commands formally:

Definition 4.3 (Semantics of Commands). *Let c be a command:*

$$[a] \; g \to p_1 : x'{=}E_1 + \ldots + p_k : x'{=}E_k .$$

The semantics of command c is a set of transitions

$$[\![.]\!] : c \to 2^{S \times Distr_{U,S}}$$

where $[\![c]\!]$ is given by:

$$\left\{ \left(s_0, \bigoplus_{i=1}^{k} p_i : ((a,i), s_i) \right) \;\middle|\; \begin{array}{ll} s_0, \ldots s_k \in S : & \\ s_0 \vDash g & \text{"guard"} \\ \forall i \in \{1, \ldots, k\} : \; s_i = \lambda x \in X. \; [\![E_i(x)]\!]_{s_0} & \text{"updates"} \end{array} \right\} .$$

For illustration of this definition, consider again the following command from the example program in Figure 4.2 (note that "[c]" refers to the action of that command):

```
[c] m=1 & x>0 -> 0.3:  (x'=x-1) + 0.7:  (m'=3); .
```

Its semantics is the following set:

$$\left\{ \left(s_0, \bigoplus_{i=1}^{k} p_i : ((c,i), s_i) \right) \;\middle|\; \begin{array}{ll} s_0, \ldots s_2 \in S : & \\ s_0 \vDash \text{m=1 \& x>0} & \text{"guard"} \\ s_1(\text{m}) = s_0(\text{m}), s_1(\text{x}) = s_0(\text{x}) - 1, & \text{"probability 0.3"} \\ s_2(\text{m}) = 3, s_2(\text{x}) = s_0(\text{x}) & \text{"probability 0.7"} \end{array} \right\}$$

where $p_0 = 0.3$ and $p_1 = 0.7$.

For example, the MDP from Figure 4.2 contains the transition

$$(s_0, \; 0.3 : ((c,0), s_1) \; \oplus \; 0.7 : ((c,1), s_2)) \in [\![c]\!]$$

with states $s_0 := \{\text{m} \mapsto 1, \text{x} \mapsto 4\}$, $s_1 := \{\text{m} \mapsto 1, \text{x} \mapsto 3\}$ and $s_2 := \{\text{m} \mapsto 3, \text{x} \mapsto 4\}$.

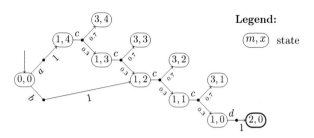

Figure 4.2.: Semantics of the example program in Figure 4.1.

Semantics of Programs. The semantics of a program is an MDP whose states are determined by the program variables. The initial states are defined by the initial expression and the MDP transitions are generated by the commands. Each transitions is labeled by the action a_c of the command that generated it, and every probabilistic choice within the transition has an update label, represented by a pair (a_c, i) consisting of the action label of the command and the index number of the corresponding probabilistic alternative. The transitions are expressed by the transition function of the MDP, which is a partial function because certain actions are only enabled in states where the guard of the corresponding command is true.

Overall we get the following semantics:

Definition 4.4 (Program Semantics). *The semantics of a program* $P = (X, I, C)$ *is the MDP* $\mathcal{M} = (S, I, A, U, En, R)$ *with*

- *states* $S := S(X)$,
- *initial states* $I := [\![I]\!]$,
- *actions* $A := \{a_c \mid c \in C\}$,
- *updates* $U := \{(a_c, i) \mid c \in C, i \in \{1, \ldots, deg(c)\}\}$
- *enabled actions defined by*

$$En(s) := \{a_c \mid (s, \pi) \in [\![c]\!]\}$$

for every state s.

- *transition function* R *where :*

$$R(s, a_c) := \begin{cases} \pi & ; \; if \; (s, \pi) \in [\![c]\!] \\ undefined & ; \; otherwise \end{cases}$$

for every state s *and action* a_c.

This concludes our discussion of the semantics of programs in terms of MDPs. In the following section, we characterize the semantics of programs in terms of logic, which, later on, opens the way to obtain semantic properties without explicitly constructing the MDP semantics of a program.

4.3 Symbolic Semantics

Both for the construction of abstractions and for abstraction refinement, it is useful to have a symbolic semantics, i.e., a description of the semantics in terms of logic. Clearly, expressions already give a symbolic description of sets of states. To describe the behavior of a program, we need to express its transitions. To this end, we use transition constraints and weakest preconditions.

We represent transition constraints using present-state and next-state instances of the program variables. In a non-probabilistic setting, this is often written by using primed and unprimed variable instances. For example, to express a command that increments variable x if x is larger than 0, the transition constraint $x > 0 \land x' = x + 1$ is used. In our setting, one primed instance of the program variables is in general not enough. A command c may feature not only one but $k = deg(c)$ probabilistic alternatives where $k \geq 1$. Each alternative gives rise to one instance X_i of the program variables where $i \in \{1, \ldots, k\}$. The present-state instance is denoted by X_0.

Consider the following command (from the example program in Figure 4.1):

```
[c] m=1 & x>0 -> 0.3: (x'=x-1) + 0.7: (m'=3);
```

The program variables are $X = \{m, x\}$ and we consider instances $X_0 = \{m_0, x_0\}$ for the present state, and the instances $X_1 = \{m_1, x_1\}$ and $X_2 = \{m_2, x_2\}$ for the two probabilistic alternatives.

The transition constraint of the command is determined by the guard and the assignments of the command. The guard of the command is $m = 1 \land x > 0$. In terms of the present-state variables, we get the constraint:

$$g[X/X_0] = (m_0 = 1) \land (x_0 > 0) .$$

There are two probabilistic alternatives with assignments E_1 and E_2 respectively where

$$E_1(m) = m \quad , \quad E_1(x) = x - 1 \quad \text{and} \quad E_2(m) = 3 \quad , \quad E_2(x) = x .$$

The effect of the assignment E_1 is described in terms of a conjunction of equalities $X_1 = E_1[X/X_0]$ involving variables from X_0 and X_1. Specifically we obtain the constraint $m_1 = m_0 \land x_1 = x_0 - 1$. The transition constraint for the command is given by:

$$\mathcal{R}_c = \underbrace{(m_0 = 1 \land x_0 > 0)}_{g[X/X_0]} \land \underbrace{(m_1 = m_0 \land x_1 = x_0 - 1)}_{X_1 = E_1[X/X_0]} \land \underbrace{(m_2 = 3 \land x_2 = x_0)}_{X_2 = E_2[X/X_0]}$$

After this illustrating example, we define transition constraints for the general case:

Definition 4.5 (Transition Constraint). *The concrete transitions of command c given by*

$$[a] \ g \rightarrow p_1 : X' = E_1 + \ldots + p_k : X' = E_k .$$

are expressed by the constraint

$$\mathcal{R}_c := g[X/X_0] \wedge \bigwedge_{i=1}^{deg(c)} (X_i = E_i[X/X_0]) \tag{4.1}$$

A transition constraint defines a set of $(k+1)$-tuples of states

$$\{(s_0, s_1, \ldots, s_k) \in S^{k+1} \mid (s_0, s_1, \ldots, s_k) \vDash \mathcal{R}_c\}$$

These tuples yield probabilistic transitions. Given a tuple $(s_0, s_1, \ldots, s_k)$, the states $s_1, \ldots, s_k$ determine a distribution $\bigoplus_{i=1}^{deg(c)} p_i : (u_i, s_i)$ together with the probabilities p_i from the command. A transition constraint is thus a symbolic description of the semantics of a command:

Proposition 2 (Semantics of Commands). *Let* c *be a command. The semantics of* c *is captured by the transition constraint* $\mathcal{R}_c$. *We have:*

$$[\![c]\!] = \{(s_0, \bigoplus_{i=1}^{k} p_i : (u_i, s_i) \mid (s_0, \ldots, s_k) \vDash \mathcal{R}_c\}$$

where $k = deg(c)$.

In addition to transition constraints, we use weakest preconditions [Dijkstra, 1976]. The weakest precondition of an expression e with respect to an update E describes a condition on the program variables which guarantees that e holds after executing the update u. Formally, the weakest precondition is defined by $WP_u(e) := e[X/E_u(X)]$ where all occurrences of variables are replaced according to u. For example, the weakest precondition $WP_{x'=x-1}(m=1 \ \& \ x>0)$ of the expression m=1 & x>0 with respect to update x'=x-1 is $(m=1 \ \& \ x>0)[X/\{m \mapsto m, x \mapsto x-1\}] = $ m=1 & x > 1. This concludes the description of concurrent probabilistic programs.

4.4 Conclusion

In this chapter we have discussed concurrent probabilistic programs including their syntax and semantics.

Subsequently, we will present suitable abstraction and refinement techniques. These techniques operate at the language level rather than explicitly constructing the original program semantics. To this end, we will employ the symbolic semantics just discussed and, transition constraints in particular.

Part II.

Analysis of Concurrent Probabilistic Programs

5

The Abstract Valuation Domain

Automatic verification of concurrent probabilistic programs requires the use of abstraction to deal with large or even infinite state spaces. In this chapter, we present a framework which lays the theoretical foundation to build abstraction-based analyses for concurrent probabilistic programs which compute lower bounds and upper bounds on reachability probabilities. These lower and upper bounds are represented in the domain of abstract valuations, the abstract domain of our framework. To obtain abstract analyses based on this domain, we need to deal with the complex interplay between the non-determinism and probabilistic choice of the program and uncertainty from abstraction. Here the theory of abstract interpretation provides guidance, so that the specification of the analysis can be derived from the abstract domain and the original semantics by the systematic steps outlined in Chapter 2. This way of building analyses is prevalent in static program analysis. We are the first to pursue it in the context of concurrent probabilistic programs.

The material in this chapter has appeared in condensed form as part of a conference paper [Wachter and Zhang, 2010].

5.1 Introduction

We would like to design analyses to obtain lower and upper bounds on reachability probabilities. The idea behind these analyses is to merge sets of states according to a finite partition and to summarize the probability values of states in the same block, so that only one value need to be represented per block. We formalize this notion of summarization by the domain of abstract valuations and suitable Galois connections. Based on the recipes provided by abstract interpretation and these ingredients, we develop the theoretical foundations which admit to design effective analyses.

To guarantee correct answers, analyses are valid abstractions of the concrete program semantics. There may be myriads of valid abstractions, which vary significantly in terms of their precision. However, there exists a *most precise* analysis among these valid abstractions: its mathematical characterization is given by the composition $f^\sharp = \alpha \circ f \circ \gamma$ of the concretization function γ, the functional f characterizing the program semantics and the abstraction function α. Functional $f^\sharp$ forms the limit on the best achievable precision of *any* valid abstraction [Cousot and Cousot, 2002] for a given Galois connection and is therefore called *best transformer*. The best transformer is a point of reference when designing analyses. Even in cases where an analysis does not achieve the full precision of the best transformer, it is helpful to know in which way it loses precision compared to the best transformer, in particular when devising refinement techniques.

Based on the concepts of abstract interpretation, we develop an abstraction framework for analyses that provide both effective lower and upper bounds on reachability probabilities. The analyses obtained in this way have a clear mathematical justification and are guaranteed to be optimal in terms of precision. Regarding optimal analyses, we show that best transformers can be represented by certain stochastic games studied in [Kwiatkowska et al., 2006], which shows a way to compute and represent best transformers.

Outline

We begin with the abstract domain. Then we turn to valid abstractions and best transformers. The chapter is thus structured as follows:

Section 5.2 We present the domain of abstract valuations and express the relationship between concrete and abstract valuations as a Galois connection.

Section 5.3 We consider abstraction at the level of monotone functions over valuations, i.e., valuation transformers. Using function composition and Galois connections, we derive abstract valuation transformers.

Section 5.4 Properties of interest are defined in terms of fixed points of valuation transformers. In this section, we discuss how to obtain abstractions of such fixed points by computing fixed points of abstract valuation transformers.

Section 5.5 We develop best transformers in the context of valuations. Probabilistic reachability is defined in terms of special valuation transformers of an MDP. We consider best transformers under the aspect of probabilistic reachability and discuss how best transformers can be obtained for a given MDP.

Section 5.6 Throughout the chapter, we assume that state partitions are given a priori. In practice abstract refinement techniques are needed that determine state partitions that are tailored to the property of interest. We formalize partition refinement in our abstraction framework.

Section 5.7 We discuss related work in detail, and outline the novelty and impact of our framework in this context.

Section 5.8 Finally, we conclude the chapter.

5.2 Concrete and Abstract Domain

The cornerstones of a program analysis are concrete and abstract domains that express analysis information. To lay the foundation for the chapter, we develop such domains and formalize the connection between them.

Abstract Valuations

Let us assume that there is some set of states S, which is possibly infinite. Our concrete domain of computation are valuations, i.e., functions $w : S \to [0,1]$ that map states to probabilities.

We would like to abstract these concrete valuations to abstract valuations. To this end, we consider state partitions, i.e., we merge states to blocks. A block B is a subset $B \subseteq S$. Formally, a partition Q of S is a set of pairwise disjoint, non-empty blocks such that

$$S = \bigcup_{B \in Q} B \; .$$

The unique block B containing a state s is denoted by $\bar{s}$, i.e., $s \in B$. We also lift this notion to distributions. Let $\pi \in Distr_{U,S}$ be a labeled distribution. Then we define an abstract labeled distribution $\bar{\pi} \in Distr_{U,Q}$ by $\bar{\pi}(u, B) = \pi(u, s)$ where $B = \bar{s}$.

Moving to the abstract world, blocks take the place of states. We then have abstract valuations, i.e., functions $w^\sharp : Q \to [0,1]$ from blocks to probabilities. The set of abstract valuations is given by the lattice $[0,1]^Q$ of valuations over blocks.

What is the abstraction of a concrete valuation w and what is the concrete meaning of an abstract valuation? This is the topic of the next section.

Abstraction and Concretization Functions

To connect the world of concrete and abstract valuations, we now define abstraction and concretization functions that transfer information between the two domains.

Suppose we want to go from a concrete valuation $w \in [0,1]^S$ to an abstract valuation. Then we need to assign a probability value to each block that summarizes the set of values $\{w(s) \mid s \in B\}$ assumed by the contained states. Obviously, the way values are summarized depends on the kind of information we are interested in. For example, we can take the lower bound (or infimum) of the probabilities within a block:

Definition 5.1 (Lower-bound Abstraction). *The lower-bound abstraction function α^l w.r.t. the partition Q is defined by:*

$$\alpha^l : \; [0,1]^S \to [0,1]^Q, \quad \alpha^l(w)(B) = \inf_{s \in B} w(s) \; \text{for all } B \in Q \; .$$

Likewise, we can take the upper bound of all values (or supremum):

Definition 5.2 (Upper-bound Abstraction). *The upper-bound abstraction function α^u w.r.t. the partition Q is defined by:*

$$\alpha^u : \; [0,1]^S \to [0,1]^Q, \quad \alpha^u(w)(B) = \sup_{s \in B} w(s) \; \text{for all } B \in Q \; .$$

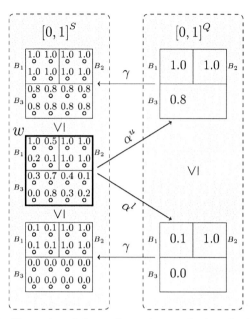

Figure 5.1.: Illustration of abstraction and concretization of valuations.

Having defined abstractions of concrete valuations, we now define the concrete meaning of abstract elements. The concretization of an abstract valuation $w^\sharp \in [0,1]^Q$ is the valuation over states $\gamma(w^\sharp)$ that assigns each state s the value $w^\sharp(\overline{s})$ of its block.

Definition 5.3 (Concretization). *The concretization function γ w.r.t. the partition Q is defined by:*

$$\gamma : \ [0,1]^Q \to [0,1]^S, \quad \gamma(w^\sharp)(s) = w^\sharp(\overline{s}) \text{ for all } s \in S \ .$$

The concretization and abstraction functions are illustrated in Figure 5.1. The large dashed box on the left represents valuations over states $[0,1]^S$ (concrete domain), the one on the right represents valuations over blocks $[0,1]^Q$ (abstract domain). The partition into blocks B_1, B_2, B_3 is depicted by rectangles surrounding states. Consider the valuation w with the thick border. Abstraction $\alpha^l(w)$ provides a lower bound, i.e., $\gamma(\alpha^l(w)) \le w$. Taking the α^u-abstraction yields an upper bound $\alpha^u(w)$, i.e., we get $w \le \gamma(\alpha^u(w))$. A lower bound is the more precise the larger it is, while the converse is true for an upper bound. This notion of precision is reflected by the lattice order: the order is $\ge$ if we compare lower bounds, and $\le$ for upper bounds.

The example in Figure 5.1 illustrates that the lower-bound abstraction function yields the largest and thus most precise lower bound expressible in the abstract domain: abstract valuation $\alpha^l(w)$ is the largest abstract valuation that forms a lower bound for valuation w. Similarly, the upper-bound abstraction yields the smallest upper bound.

Thus abstraction and concretization enjoy soundness and optimality properties. Soundness means that, for a given concrete valuation, the abstractions indeed yield lower and upper bounds. Optimality means that the computed abstract valuations are the most precise abstractions expressible in the abstract domain. We express these properties by Galois connections:

Proposition 3 (Galois Connections). *For a given partition Q, let α^l, α^u, γ be the functions defined above. Then we have the following two Galois connections:*

(a) lower-bound abstraction:

$$([0,1]^S, \geq) \xleftrightarrow[\alpha^l]{\gamma} ([0,1]^Q, \geq)$$

(b) upper-bound abstraction:

$$([0,1]^S, \leq) \xleftrightarrow[\alpha^u]{\gamma} ([0,1]^Q, \leq)$$

Proof. We show that the pairs (α^l, γ) and (α^u, γ) respectively meet the requirements of a Galois connection. To this end, we show the criterion in Theorem 2.2:

(a) We begin with the lower-bound abstraction. We need to show that, for all concrete valuations $w \in [0,1]^S$ and abstract valuations $w^\sharp \in [0,1]^Q$, we have the equivalence $w \geq \gamma(w^\sharp) \Leftrightarrow \alpha^l(w) \geq w^\sharp$.

   $\Rightarrow$: Assume that $w \geq \gamma(w^\sharp)$ holds. Then, for all $B \in Q$, we have the inequality $\left(\alpha^l(w)\right)(B) = \inf_{s \in B} w(s) \geq \inf_{s \in B} \gamma(w^\sharp)(s) = w^\sharp(B)$.

   $\Leftarrow$: Assume that $\alpha^l(w) \geq w^\sharp$ holds. Then, for all $s \in S$, we have the inequality $w(s) \geq \left(\alpha^l(w)\right)(\bar{s}) \geq w^\sharp(\bar{s}) = \gamma(w^\sharp)(s)$.

(b) We proceed with upper-bound abstraction. We show that for all $w \in [0,1]^S$ and $w^\sharp \in [0,1]^Q$, we have $\alpha^u(w) \leq w^\sharp \Leftrightarrow w \leq \gamma(w^\sharp)$.

   $\Rightarrow$: Assume that $w \leq \gamma(w^\sharp)$ holds. Then, for all $B \in Q$, we have the inequality $(\alpha^u(w))(B) = \sup_{s \in B} w(s) \leq \sup_{s \in B} \gamma(w^\sharp)(s) = w^\sharp(B)$.

   $\Leftarrow$: Assume that $\alpha^u(w) \leq w^\sharp$ holds. Then, for all $s \in S$, we have the inequality $w(s) \leq (\alpha^u(w))(\bar{s}) \leq w^\sharp(\bar{s}) = \left(\gamma(w^\sharp)\right)(s)$.

   ∎

Many abstract-interpretation-based analyses feature a Galois connection where the concretization of an abstract element is a set of concrete elements and the concrete domain a power set, e.g., in partition abstraction (Section 2.2.2), the concretization of a block is a set of states. In contrast, the concretization of an abstract valuation is a concrete valuation, rather than a *set* of concrete valuations. Yet our Galois connections are *the* natural way to generalize partition abstraction to the probabilistic setting. More precisely, if we restrict the functions of the Galois connections of Proposition 3 to indicator functions –

which are equivalent to elements of power-set domains (Section 2.2.3), we exactly obtain the Galois connection of partition abstraction (as defined in Section 2.2.2).

For instance, by restricting the lower-bound abstraction function α^l to indicator functions, where the restriction is denoted by $\alpha^l|_{\{0,1\}^S}$, we get the under-approximating abstraction function $\alpha_\chi^\downarrow$ for indicator functions (as given in Section 2.2.3). To see this, recall that the function $\alpha_\chi^\downarrow$ minimizes over blocks. On the other hand, the abstraction function α^l takes the infimum over blocks. Since indicator functions have a discrete range, minima exist and coincide with infima. Thus we immediately get that:

$$\alpha_\chi^\downarrow = \alpha^l|_{\{0,1\}^S} \; .$$

An analogous argument applies for the over-approximating abstraction and upper-bound abstraction function:

$$\alpha_\chi^\uparrow = \alpha^u|_{\{0,1\}^S} \; .$$

Similarly the concretization function for valuation restricted to indicator functions yields the concretization of partition abstraction:

$$\gamma_\chi = \gamma|_{\{0,1\}^Q} \; .$$

Wrapping up, the theory we present here is the natural way to define the quantitative extension of partition abstraction.

Preservation of Operators

In applications of our abstract domain, we need to combine (concrete and abstract) valuations by means of operators, e.g., when considering maximal probabilistic reachability, the program semantics picks the maximum from a menu of available commands. When we apply abstraction, it is therefore important to understand in which way the abstraction functions preserve these operators.

We now briefly discuss this point. In a nutshell, the studied abstraction functions preserve joins of their respective domains. For example, for the upper-bound abstraction, the join operator takes the point-wise supremum of its argument valuations. The abstraction function itself is also supremum operator. Therefore the abstraction of the join of a pair of concrete valuations equals the join of their abstractions:

$$\alpha^u(w_1 \sqcup w_2) = \alpha^u(w_1) \sqcup \alpha^u(w_2) \; .$$

We summarize the preservation of different operators in the following lemma:

Lemma 5.4 (Preservation of Operators). *Abstraction and concretization functions preserve the combination operators, join and merge, in the following way:*

- *For all $M \subseteq [0,1]^S$, we have*

$$\alpha^l(\sqcap M) = \sqcap\{\alpha^l(m) \mid m \in M\}$$
$$\alpha^l(\sqcup M) \geq \sqcup\{\alpha^l(m) \mid m \in M\} \; .$$

- *For all $M \subseteq [0,1]^S$, we have*

$$\alpha^u(\bigsqcap M) \leq \bigsqcap \{\alpha^u(m) \mid m \in M\}$$
$$\alpha^u(\bigsqcup M) = \bigsqcup \{\alpha^u(m) \mid m \in M\} \ .$$

- *For all $M^\sharp \subseteq [0,1]^Q$, we have*

$$\gamma(\bigsqcap M^\sharp) = \bigsqcap \{\gamma(m^\sharp) \mid m^\sharp \in M^\sharp\}$$
$$\gamma(\bigsqcup M^\sharp) = \bigsqcup \{\gamma(m^\sharp) \mid m^\sharp \in M^\sharp\} \ .$$

Proof. This holds because $([0,1]^S, \geq) \xleftrightarrow[\alpha^l]{\gamma} ([0,1]^Q, \geq)$ and $([0,1]^S, \leq) \xleftrightarrow[\alpha^u]{\gamma} ([0,1]^Q, \leq)$ are Galois connections [Cousot and Cousot, 1992, Proposition 6]. ∎

Up till now, we have discussed how Galois connections for lower-bound and upper-bound abstractions relate concrete and abstract valuations. The next step is to move to the level of functions over valuations: we relate concrete transformers with abstract transformers.

5.3 Valid Abstraction

Assume we are given a concrete transformer $f : [0,1]^S \rightarrow [0,1]^S$. Analogous to valuations, we would like to approximate the transformer from below and above. To this end, we consider abstract transformers that form a lower-bound abstraction and an upper-bound abstraction, respectively.

Lower-bound abstraction. An abstract transformer $f_l^\sharp : [0,1]^Q \rightarrow [0,1]^Q$ approximates f from below if it yields a lower bound on the effect of f whenever applied to an abstract valuation. Formally expressed, this means that:

$$\gamma \circ f_l^\sharp \leq f \circ \gamma \ .$$

In the terminology of abstract interpretation, the abstract transformer $f_l^\sharp$ is a valid abstraction with respect to the Galois connection (α^l, γ).

Upper-bound abstraction. Conversely, an abstract transformer $f_u^\sharp : [0,1]^Q \rightarrow [0,1]^Q$ approximates f from above if it yields an upper bound on the effect of f whenever applied to an abstract valuation:

$$f \circ \gamma \leq \gamma \circ f_u^\sharp \ .$$

We also say that abstract transformer $f_u^\sharp$ is a valid abstraction of f with respect to Galois connection (α^u, γ).

abstract valuation

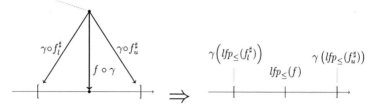

Figure 5.2.: Valid abstraction as a local criterion for fixed point abstraction.

Summing up, we consider abstract transformers that are valid abstractions and approximate a given concrete transformer from above and below, as depicted on the left side of Figure 5.2:

$$\gamma \circ f_l^\sharp \leq f \circ \gamma \leq \gamma \circ f_u^\sharp \qquad (5.1)$$

where $f_l^\sharp$ is the valid lower-bound abstraction of f and $f_u^\sharp$ the valid upper-bound abstraction of f.

This notion of valid abstraction translates to fixed points as well. Namely, valid abstractions provide a local criterion that ensures sound approximation of fixed points.

As discussed in Section 3.3, reachability probabilities are given by the fixed points of suitable concrete transformers. An abstraction of probabilistic reachability can be obtained from valid abstractions of the concrete transformers $f = pre_F^-$ and $f = pre_F^+$ respectively. In this way, lower and upper bounds can then be computed using valid lower- and upper-bound abstractions in the style of Inequality 5.1. The next section gives the necessary theory for fixed point abstraction.

5.4   Fixed-Point Abstraction

In this section, we describe the abstraction of concrete fixed points. In the following, we fix Q as the given partition, and let α^l, α^u, γ be the functions defined previously in Section 5.2.

Suppose a valuation transformer is bounded from below and above by two abstract transformers, i.e., valid abstractions w.r.t. lower-bound and upper-bound abstraction respectively. Then the fixed points of these two abstract transformers bound the fixed point of the valuation transformer. This result is formalized in Lemma 5.5.

Lemma 5.5 (Abstraction of Least Fixed Points). *Let* $f : [0,1]^S \to [0,1]^S$. *Consider valuation transformers* $f_l^\sharp, f_u^\sharp : [0,1]^Q \to [0,1]^Q$ *such that* $f_l^\sharp$ *is a valid lower-bound abstraction of* f *and* $f_u^\sharp$ *a valid upper-bound abstraction of* f, *i.e.,* $\gamma \circ f_l^\sharp \leq f \circ \gamma \leq \gamma \circ f_u^\sharp$.

Then the following inequality holds regarding the fixed points of these functions:

$$\gamma\left(gfp_{\geq}(f_l^\sharp)\right) \quad \leq \quad lfp_{\leq}(f) \quad \leq \quad \gamma\left(lfp_{\leq}(f_u^\sharp)\right) .$$

Proof. The claims follows as a corollary of the fixed point theorem in Lemma 2.12 for general Galois connections, together with Proposition 3:

- We begin with the lower bound. Consider lattices $([0,1]^S, \geq)$ and $([0,1]^Q, \geq)$ and Galois connection $([0,1]^S, \geq) \xleftrightarrow[\alpha^l]{\gamma} ([0,1]^Q, \geq)$. Let $f : [0,1]^S \to [0,1]^S$ be a concrete transformer and $f_l^\sharp : [0,1]^Q \to [0,1]^Q$ a valid lower-bound abstraction of f, i.e. we have $f \circ \gamma \geq \gamma \circ f_l^\sharp$. Further, part (b) of Lemma 2.12 guarantees that $\gamma\left(gfp_{\geq}(f_l^\sharp)\right) \leq gfp_{\geq}(f)$. This proves the claim because $gfp_{\geq}(f) = lfp_{\leq}(f)$.

- The proof for the upper bound works similarly. Consider lattices $([0,1]^S, \leq)$ and $([0,1]^Q, \leq)$ and Galois connection $([0,1]^S, \leq) \xleftrightarrow[\alpha^u]{\gamma} ([0,1]^Q, \leq)$. Consider a concrete transformer $f : [0,1]^S \to [0,1]^S$ and a valid upper-bound abstraction $f_u^\sharp : [0,1]^Q \to [0,1]^Q$ of f, i.e. $f \circ \gamma \leq \gamma \circ f_u^\sharp$. The claim is then $lfp_{\leq}(f) \leq \gamma\left(lfp_{\leq}(f_u^\sharp)\right)$, which is guaranteed by Part (a) of Lemma 2.12.

∎

Next we study a particular kind of valid abstractions, best transformers.

5.5 Best Transformers

The concept of a valid abstraction gives conditions under which an abstract transformer is an abstraction of a concrete transformer. Now we explain how to actually obtain abstract transformers. We aim for best transformers since they are optimal in terms of precision with respect to the given abstract domain.

The ingredients to obtain a best transformer consist in an abstraction and a concrete transformer. We shall first consider general concrete transformers in connection with lower-bound and upper-bound abstraction and then specifically focus on transformers for minimal and maximal probabilistic reachability. Finally, we show how best transformers can be computed for a given Markov decision process.

Fixed-Point Abstraction with Best Transformers

Best transformers can be used to approximate the least fixed point of a concrete transformer. For any concrete valuation transformer f, the fixed points of the best transformers w.r.t. lower- and upper-bound abstraction enclose the least fixed point of f:

Lemma 5.6 (Fix Points of Best Transformers). *Let $f : [0,1]^S \to [0,1]^S$ be a given valuation transformer. Then the following inequalities hold:*

$$\gamma\left(gfp_{\geq}(\alpha^l \circ f \circ \gamma)\right) \quad \leq \quad lfp_{\leq}(f) \quad \leq \quad \gamma\left(lfp_{\leq}(\alpha^u \circ f \circ \gamma)\right) .$$

Proof. The claim follows immediately by applying Lemma 5.5 to the best transformers $f_l^\sharp = (\alpha^l \circ f \circ \gamma)$ and $f_u^\sharp = (\alpha^u \circ f \circ \gamma)$. ∎

We now turn specifically to best transformers for probabilistic reachability.

Best Transformers for Probabilistic Reachability

From now, we consider best transformers for probabilistic reachability. To design best transformers, two things are needed: a concrete transformer and a Galois connection. We begin with the concrete transformer. Here we consider either the transformer for minimal or maximal probabilistic reachability, i.e., we pick either pre_F^- or pre_F^+. Further, we choose the proper Galois connection depending on whether we would like to obtain lower or upper bounds. Altogether this gives four different best transformers for respective cases, as indicated by the diagram below:

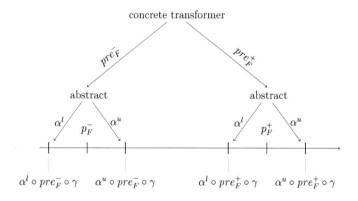

Summing up, the abstraction function controls whether we get lower or upper bounds, and the valuation transformer controls whether maximal or minimal reachability probability is considered.

Exploiting the fact that $p^-(F) = lfp_{\leq} \; pre_F^-$ and $p^+(F) = lfp_{\leq} \; pre_F^+$, we have the connection to probabilistic reachability:

Theorem 5.7 (Bounds for Probabilistic Reachability). *Let $\mathcal{M} = (S, I, A, R)$ be an MDP and let $F \subseteq S$ be a set of goal states. Then we have:*

$$\gamma(gfp_{\geq}(\alpha^l \circ pre_F^- \circ \gamma)) \leq p^-(F) \leq \gamma(lfp_{\leq}(\alpha^u \circ pre_F^- \circ \gamma))$$
$$\gamma(gfp_{\geq}(\alpha^l \circ pre_F^+ \circ \gamma)) \leq p^+(F) \leq \gamma(lfp_{\leq}(\alpha^u \circ pre_F^+ \circ \gamma))$$

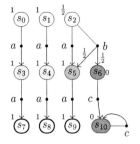 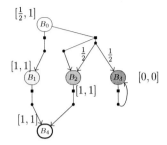

Figure 5.3.: Illustration of an MDP (left) and its abstraction as a game (right).

Best Transformers as Games

The definition of a best transformer in terms of function composition is declarative. It does not directly tell us how to compute the best transformer.

Therefore this subsection answers the question how a best transformer for probabilistic reachability can be obtained given a Markov decision process and an abstraction.

The idea is best illustrated with a concrete example. Consider the MDP on the left half of Figure 5.3. We now focus on a particular partition Q and explain step by step how we arrive at the corresponding best transformer shown on the right side of Figure 5.3.

The partition consists of five blocks $Q = \{B_0, B_1, B_2, B_3, B_4\}$ where the blocks are given by $B_0 = \{s_0, s_1, s_2\}$, $B_1 = \{s_3, s_4\}$, $B_2 = \{s_5\}$, $B_3 = \{s_6, s_{10}\}$ and $B_4 = \{s_7, s_8, s_9\}$. We are interested in the minimal probability to reach states $F = \{s_7, s_8, s_9\}$. These probabilities are already annotated at the states.

Let us take a look at the best transformer for the upper bound of minimal reachability for block B_0 in our example. We need to apply the formal definition of the best transformer. Recall that the general definition is as follows:

$$(\alpha^u \circ pre_F^- \circ \gamma(w^\sharp))(B) = \sup_{s \in B} pre_F^-(\gamma(w^\sharp))(s) \qquad \boxed{5.2}$$

$$= \sup_{s \in B} \min_{a \in En(s)} \sum_{s' \in S} R(s, a)(s') \cdot (\gamma(w^\sharp))(s') \qquad \boxed{5.3}$$

for an abstract valuation $w \in [0, 1]^Q$ and a block $B \in Q$.

Now we compute Equality 5.3 for block B_0. At the top level, the formula maximizes over the different states in block B_0. For each state, the formula minimizes over the available actions, i.e. it applies the concrete transformer. At states s_0 and s_1, only action a is enabled. The states s_0 and s_1 contribute $w^\sharp(B_1)$. In a way, they fall together under abstraction. State s_2 shows a different behavior. The actions a and b are enabled. Therefore the contribution of s_2 to the supremum is the minimum over these actions, i.e., $\min\{w^\sharp(B_2), \frac{1}{2} \cdot w^\sharp(B_2) + \frac{1}{2} \cdot w^\sharp(B_3)\}$. Overall, $(\alpha^u \circ pre_F^- \circ \gamma(w))(B_0)$ equals:

$$\sup\{\underbrace{\min\{1 \cdot w^\sharp(B_1)\}}_{s_1, s_2}, \underbrace{\min\{w^\sharp(B_2), \frac{1}{2} \cdot w^\sharp(B_2) + \frac{1}{2} \cdot w^\sharp(B_3)\}}_{s_3}\} \; . \qquad \boxed{5.4}$$

We can write down the formula in Equality 5.4 as an expression tree. The tree looks exactly like a stochastic game. First, player 1, the abstraction player, maximizes over all states in a block. Then, player 2, the original non-determinism in the MDP, gets to choose an action. Below, the tree and the game are shown side by side:

expression tree of Expression 5.4   corresponding stochastic game

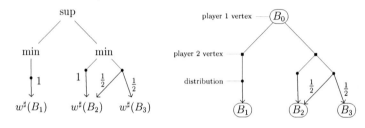

We can carry out this expression-tree construction for all blocks. Thereby the blocks of the partition give rise to the player 1 vertices in the game. The player 2 vertices correspond to the original non-determinism in the MDP. The right side of Figure 5.3 shows the complete stochastic game for our example MDP.

The best transformer is captured precisely by the valuation transformer of the game that maximizes over player 1 vertices and minimizes over player 2 vertices. The stochastic game represents the best transformer of upper-bound abstraction for minimal reachability. In fact, all best transformers, i.e., lower and upper bounds for minimal and maximal reachability, can be obtained: player 1 controls whether lower or upper bounds are obtained and player 2 whether minimal or maximal reachability is considered.

Game-Based Abstraction. The example is a special case of a more general construction. For the studied best transformers, the update of the value of a block depends on the values of its successor blocks. Therefore an abstract transformer can be described by arithmetic expressions that involve addition, multiplication, minima and maxima. These arithmetic expressions induce expression trees that correspond to stochastic games. Player 1 decisions correspond to a concretization step. Minimization yields lower bounds and maximization yields upper bounds respectively. Player 2 decisions reflect the behavior of the concrete transformer.

For a given MDP, goal states and a partition of the state space, we can give a stochastic game that represents the best transformer.

Definition 5.8 (Game-based Abstraction [Kwiatkowska et al., 2006]). *Let $\mathcal{M}$ be an MDP where $\mathcal{M} = (S, I, A, U, En, R)$. Let Q be a partition of the states S of $\mathcal{M}$. Then the game-based abstraction of $\mathcal{M}$ with respect to partition Q is defined as the stochastic game $\mathcal{G}_{\mathcal{M},Q} = ((V, E), V_{init}, (V_1, V_2, V_p), \delta)$ where*

- *the player 1 vertices $V_1 = Q$ are given by the blocks,*
- *the player 2 vertices $V_2 = \{\overline{Steps(s)} \mid s \in S\}$ are sets of distributions where $\overline{D} = \{\overline{\pi} \mid \pi \in D\}$ for $D \subseteq Distr_{U \times S}$.*
- *and the vertices $V_p = \{\overline{\pi} \mid \exists s \in S : \pi \in Steps(s)\}$ are distributions.*

The function $\delta : V_p \to Distr_V$ is defined as the identity function. The initial vertices are the player 1 vertices $V_{init} = \{v_1 \in V_1 \mid v_1 \cap I \neq \emptyset\}$ and the edges E are given by:

$$E = \{(v_1, v_2) \mid v_1 \in V_1, \exists s \in v_1 : v_2 = \overline{Steps(s)}\}$$
$$\cup \{(v_2, v_p) \mid v_2 \in V_2, v_p \in v_2\}$$
$$\cup \{(v_p, v_1) \mid v_p \in V_p, v_p(v_1) > 0\} .$$

Regarding the definition above, a few remarks are in order. There are three types of vertices: player 1 vertices are given by the blocks of the partition, player 2 vertices are sets of probability distributions over blocks and probabilistic vertices are such distributions. The directed edges E connect the game vertices. Thereby a player 1 vertex, a block, is connected to player 2 vertices that correspond to behaviors of states in the block. Player 2 vertices are connected to probabilistic vertices, that is distributions, contained in them. Probabilistic vertices v_p are connected to player 1 vertices v_1 for which they return a non-zero probability when interpreted as a distribution, i.e., $v_p(v_1) > 0$.

Finite Abstraction. In general, the game abstraction of an MDP can be infinite. Let us look at an example MDP and partition.

Example. *Consider an MDP $\mathcal{M} = (S, I, A, U, En, R)$ with a countably infinite number of states $S = \{s_k \mid k \in \mathbb{N}\}$, a single action a and initial state s_0. For each state s_k, the transition function R is defined as follows $R(s_k, a) = \frac{1}{k} : s_k + \frac{k-1}{k} : s_{k+1}$, i.e., it returns the distribution that goes to state s_k with probability $\frac{1}{k}$ and to state s_{k+1} with probability $\frac{k-1}{k}$. The set of transition probabilities in the MDP $\{\frac{1}{k}, \frac{k-1}{k} \mid k \in \mathbb{N}\}$ is infinite. The game-based abstraction for partition $Q = \{\{s_k \mid k \text{ is even}\}, \{s_k \mid k \text{ is odd}\}\}$ is an infinite game. Its number of player 1 vertices is two, however the number of abstract distributions and player 2 vertices is infinite.*

This MDP could only be represented by an infinite program in our modeling language.

When restricting to MDPs expressible in our model language, game-based abstractions are always finite. The reason is that programs can only induce finitely many transition probabilities in the MDP semantics, as probability must be constants. From now on, we assume that game abstractions are finite for simplicity. Finiteness of the games implies that the abstraction functions α^u and α^l are applied to valuations for which not only infima and suprema but even minima and maxima exist.

The central result of this section is that game-based abstraction provides an implementation of best transformers.

Theorem 5.9 (Game-based Abstraction and Best Transformer). *Let $\mathcal{M}$ be an MDP and $F \subseteq S$ a set of goal states. Further, consider the partition Q of S such that the game-based abstraction $\mathcal{G}_{\mathcal{M},Q}$ is finite and the goal states F in $\mathcal{M}$ are exactly representable, i.e., $F = \bigcup_{B \in F^\sharp} B$ for a suitable $F^\sharp \subseteq Q$. Let $pre^{\pm\pm}_{F^\sharp}$ be the valuation transformers in the game $\mathcal{G}_{\mathcal{M},Q}$ as defined in Def. 5.8. Then it holds that:*

$$pre^{--}_{F^\sharp} = \alpha^l \circ pre^{-}_F \circ \gamma \quad , \quad pre^{+-}_{F^\sharp} = \alpha^u \circ pre^{-}_F \circ \gamma$$
$$pre^{-+}_{F^\sharp} = \alpha^l \circ pre^{+}_F \circ \gamma \quad , \quad pre^{++}_{F^\sharp} = \alpha^u \circ pre^{+}_F \circ \gamma$$

Before we come to the formal proof, we give a small remark on the meaning of the result.

Meaning of the Theorem.   Theorem 5.9 implies, on the one hand, that best transformers are computable using the methods of, e.g. [Kattenbelt et al., 2009]. On the other hand, the result puts game-based abstraction into the broader perspective of abstract interpretation showing that game-based abstraction corresponds to the notion of the best transformer. This characterization has several consequences that concern both practice and theory, which are discussed in Section 5.7 in more detail.

Proof of Theorem 5.9. To carry out the proof, we first introduce the notion of behavioral equivalence. We call two states $s, s' \in S$ behaviorally equivalent under abstraction, denoted by $s \equiv^{\rightsquigarrow}_Q s'$, if and only if:

$$s \equiv^{\rightsquigarrow}_Q s' :\Leftrightarrow \overline{Steps(s)} = \overline{Steps(s')} \ . \tag{5.5}$$

In the example of Figure 5.3, e.g., state s_0 and state s_1 are behaviorally equivalent.

We denote the equivalence class of a state s with respect to this equivalence by $[s]^{\rightsquigarrow}_Q$ and denote the quotient by $S/\equiv^{\rightsquigarrow}_Q$. We shall drop the superscript and the subscript if the equivalence is clear from context and write $[s]$ instead. This equivalence also induces an equivalence on the set of states in a block. For a block $B \in Q$, we denote the set of equivalence classes by $B/\equiv^{\rightsquigarrow}_Q$.

From the definition, we have that, for a player 1 vertex[1] $v_1 \in V_1$:

$$E(v_1) = \{\overline{Steps(s)} \mid [s] \in v_1/\equiv^{\rightsquigarrow}_Q\} \tag{5.6}$$

As already described, the *proof idea* is that the best transformer corresponds to an expression. We need to show that this expression is equivalent to transformers of the stochastic game defined by game-based abstraction.

In the game, we first pick a player 2 vertex, corresponding to concretization, and then a probabilistic vertex, corresponding to the concrete transformer. Each player 2 vertex represents a set of states. As just discussed, these sets of states form equivalence

---

[1]Note that player 1 vertices are also blocks, i.e., sets of states

classes with respect to $\equiv_Q^{\leadsto}$. The equivalence classes are in one-to-one correspondence to the player-two vertices of the game, as the player-two vertices are defined by exactly these sets of abstract distributions (see Definition 5.8). Applying the transformer of game-based abstraction is equivalent to taking the optimal probability over all equivalence classes. Equivalence means that the expression induced by the best transformer is equivalent to a certain transformer in the stochastic game.

We prove only $pre_{F^\sharp}^{l+} = \alpha^l \circ pre_F^+ \circ \gamma$, as the other cases follow analogously. Thus we need to show that, for every valuation $w^\sharp \in [0,1]^Q$ and every block $v \in V_1$, the equality $pre_{F^\sharp}^{l+}(w^\sharp)(v) = \alpha^l \circ pre_F^+ \circ \gamma(w^\sharp)(v)$ holds. Let $w^\sharp \in [0,1]^Q$ and $B \in Q$. If $B \in F^\sharp$, the claim is trivially fulfilled by definition. Let us assume that $B \in Q \setminus F^\sharp$.

We show the equality between the valuation transformer $pre_{F^\sharp}^{-+}$ of the game and the best transformer by applying the quotient construction:

$$pre_{F^\sharp}^{-+}(w^\sharp)(v) \stackrel{\text{def.}}{=} \min_{v_2 \in E(v)} \max_{v_p \in v_2} \sum_{v' \in V_1} \delta(v_p)(v') \cdot w^\sharp(v')$$

$$\stackrel{(5.6)}{=} \inf_{[s] \in v/\equiv_Q^{\leadsto}} \max_{\pi^\sharp \in Steps(s)} \sum_{B' \in Q} \pi^\sharp(v') \cdot w^\sharp(B')$$

$$\stackrel{(5.5)}{=} \inf_{s \in v} \max_{\pi^\sharp \in Steps(s)} \sum_{B' \in Q} \pi^\sharp(v') \cdot w^\sharp(B')$$

$$\stackrel{(5.7)}{=} \inf_{s \in v} \max_{\pi \in Steps(s)} \sum_{s' \in S} \pi(s') \cdot w^\sharp(\overline{s'})$$

which is by definition $\left((\alpha^l \circ pre_F^+ \circ \gamma)(w^\sharp)\right)(v)$. This proves the claim.

In the last step, we exploit that, for a distribution π and its abstraction $\pi^\sharp$ where $\pi^\sharp = \overline{\pi}$, the weight of a block is the sum of the weights of the states in the block. This follows from the following equality:

$$\sum_{s' \in S} \pi(s') \cdot w^\sharp(\overline{s'}) = \sum_{B' \in Q} \pi^\sharp(B') \cdot w^\sharp(B') \qquad \boxed{5.7}$$

∎

This concludes our discussion of best transformers and game-based abstraction. Next we explain how partition refinement can be formalized in our framework.

5.6 Partition Refinement

In this section, we show how abstraction refinement fits into our framework (actual algorithms follow later in Chapter 7). In general, refinement means that the underlying partition is refined. We describe the relationship between original abstraction and refined abstraction using a Galois connection. A consequence of this formalization is that *any* refinement of a partition, no matter how it is chosen, leads to an abstraction that is either more precise than the previous one or, at least, as precise as the previous one. This guarantees a monotone evolution of the bounds during abstraction refinement. First we formally define partition refinement.

Definition 5.10 (Partition Refinement). *Let Q and Q' be partitions of state space S. Partition Q' is a refinement of partition Q if and only if every block $B \in Q$ is the union of a set of blocks $B_1', \ldots, B_m' \in Q'$, i.e.,*

$$B = \bigcup_{1 \leq i \leq m} B_i' \, .$$

For a partition Q and a refinement Q', every block in the refined partition Q' is the subset of a unique block of the coarser partition Q. Hence the set Q corresponds to a partition of Q'.

Relationship between Original and Refined Abstraction. The best transformers on the coarser partition Q are valid abstractions of their counterparts over the finer partition Q'. We will now formalize this notion in Lemma 5.11 in terms Galois connections relating abstract valuations over the coarser partition Q to abstract valuations over the finer partition Q'. In the lemma, we denote the corresponding concretization function by $\gamma_{Q':Q}$ and the abstraction functions as $\alpha_{Q':Q}^l$ and $\alpha_{Q':Q}^u$ respectively.

To distinguish instances of abstraction functions and concretization functions that relate *concrete* valuations with abstract valuations, we annotate the respective partition as a subscript. The lower-bound abstraction function with respect to partition Q is denoted by α_Q^l. The concretization function for partition Q' is denoted by $\gamma_{Q'}$, and so on.

Using this notation, the relationship between an abstraction and a refinement of that abstraction can be described as follows:

Lemma 5.11 (Refinement Monotonicity). *Let Q be a partition of S and Q' a partition of S and a refinement of Q. Let $f^\sharp : [0,1]^S \to [0,1]^S$ be a concrete transformer.*

(i) There are Galois connections between the coarser and the finer domain:

$$([0,1]^{Q'}, \geq) \xrightarrow[\alpha_{Q':Q}^l]{\gamma_{Q':Q}} ([0,1]^Q, \geq) \quad and \quad ([0,1]^{Q'}, \leq) \xrightarrow[\alpha_{Q':Q}^u]{\gamma_{Q':Q}} ([0,1]^Q, \leq)$$

where

- *$\alpha_{Q':Q}^u : [0,1]^{Q'} \to [0,1]^Q, \quad \alpha^u(w)(B) = \sup_{B' \subseteq B} w(B')$ for all $B \in Q$*
- *$\alpha_{Q':Q}^l : [0,1]^{Q'} \to [0,1]^Q, \quad \alpha^l(w)(B) = \inf_{B' \subseteq B} w(B')$ for all $B \in Q$*
- *$\gamma_{Q':Q} : [0,1]^Q \to [0,1]^{Q'}, \quad \gamma(w^\sharp)(B') = w^\sharp(B)$ where $B \in Q$ with $B' \subseteq B$*

(ii) The finer partition Q' yields best transformers and bounds that are at least as precise as for the coarser partition Q:

(a) The abstract transformer $(\alpha_Q^l \circ f \circ \gamma_Q)$ is a valid abstraction of $(\alpha_{Q'}^l \circ f \circ \gamma_{Q'})$ with respect to the Galois connection $(\alpha_{Q':Q}^l, \gamma_{Q':Q})$.

(b) *The finer partition yields a lower bound that is at least as precise as the one for the coarser partition:*

$$gfp_{\geq}(\alpha_Q^l \circ f \circ \gamma_Q) \leq gfp_{\geq}(\alpha_{Q'}^l \circ f \circ \gamma_{Q'}) \; .$$

(c) *The abstract transformer* $(\alpha_Q^u \circ f \circ \gamma_Q)$ *is a valid abstraction of* $(\alpha_{Q'}^u \circ f \circ \gamma_{Q'})$ *with respect to the Galois connection* $(\alpha_{Q':Q}^u, \gamma_{Q':Q})$.

(d) *The finer partition yields an upper bound that is at least as precise as the one for the coarser partition:*

$$lfp_{\leq}(\alpha_{Q'}^u \circ f \circ \gamma_{Q'}) \leq lfp_{\leq}(\alpha_Q^u \circ f \circ \gamma_Q) \; .$$

Proof. The proof of part (i) is analogous to the one for Proposition 3. Therefore we skip it. Note that the compositions of the abstraction and concretization functions fulfill the following equalities:

$$\gamma_Q = \gamma_{Q'} \circ \gamma_{Q':Q} \quad \alpha_Q^u = \alpha_{Q':Q}^u \circ \alpha_{Q'}^u \quad \alpha_Q^l = \alpha_{Q':Q}^l \circ \alpha_{Q'}^l \; . \tag{5.8}$$

This implies that the abstract transformers in (ii) over Q are best transformers with respect to the considered Galois connection. Thus claims $(ii)(a)$ and $(ii)(c)$ follow immediately. The claims of $(ii)(b)$ and $(ii)(d)$ follow from $(ii)(a)$ and $(ii)(c)$ respectively by applying Lemma 5.5. ∎

This completes the technical part of the chapter.

5.7 Related Work

We now discuss related work in the area of probabilistic verification. We begin with work that takes an automata-based view on abstraction where MDPs (probabilistic automata) are mapped to abstract MDPs or games. Our work combines an automata-based view with abstract interpretation, and is therefore also related to applications of abstract interpretation in probabilistic verification, which are discussed subsequently.

Partition Abstraction for Probabilistic Reachability. State partitions have been used frequently in previous work on abstraction for probabilistic reachability (for an overview see Section 7.4). In particular, the abstract valuation domain implicitly appears in different previous works [Kwiatkowska et al., 2006, de Alfaro and Roy, 2007, Hermanns et al., 2008, Kattenbelt et al., 2009] without being formalized as an abstract domain in the style of abstract interpretation.

The design approach for these previous analyses is different from ours. While in abstract interpretation an analysis is derived from the abstract domain which is correct by design, previous works start with an abstract analysis [D'Argenio et al., 2002, Kwiatkowska et al., 2006] and then prove it correct, mostly using probabilistic simulation relations.

Our framework gives a deeper understanding where precision is lost (which helps when designing refinement techniques) and generalizes previous work on partition abstraction by allowing fine-grained control of precision. This leads to a systematic way of deriving analyses including [Hermanns et al., 2008, Kattenbelt et al., 2009] and the novel analysis of Chapter 6. The theory from [D'Argenio et al., 2002, Kwiatkowska et al., 2006] does not cover our new analysis, as it only admits to adapt precision via the state partition and implicitly considers best transformers only.

MDP-based Abstraction. In earlier work, we have employed MDPs as abstract models [Wachter et al., 2007, Hermanns et al., 2008]. However, abstract MDPs only yield upper bounds on maximal reachability probability and lower bounds on minimal reachability probabilities. Thus abstract MDPs are limited compared to the approach presented in this chapter, as the remaining bounds, the lower bound on maximal and the upper bound on minimal reachability, cannot readily be derived using Markov decision processes as an abstract model. Kwiatkowska *et. al* have proposed game-based abstraction to overcome this limitation of MDP-based abstraction [Kwiatkowska et al., 2006].

Game-based Abstraction. For a given state partition, game-based abstraction maps an MDP to a stochastic game. The salient point of the game construction is that both lower and upper bounds on minimal and maximal reachability probabilities can be obtained [Kwiatkowska et al., 2006]. In this chapter, we have shown (Theorem 5.9) that the best transformers for probabilistic reachability are exactly the valuation transformers of game-based abstraction. This shows that best transformers are computable for probabilistic programs [Kattenbelt et al., 2009], and, further, gives a systematic mathematical justification for game-based abstraction based on abstract interpretation: we have derived the construction of game-based abstraction as an inevitable consequence of the more general notion of the best transformer (Theorem 5.9).

Hence game-based abstraction is ideal in terms of precision, i.e., for a given partition, game-based abstraction gives the most precise abstract transformer, and all loss of information associated with game-based abstraction can be attributed to the abstraction of states, i.e., to the Galois connection. There is no loss of information in the transition structure, i.e., the best transformer is computed and not only some valid abstraction. This has practical consequences:

- In software model checking, computationally cheaper approximations of the best transformer are sufficient to achieve the necessary precision [Ball et al., 2001]. To establish the correctness of such weaker abstractions we have developed the necessary machinery in the form of valid abstraction. We will put this machinery to work in the next section, where we design abstract transformers which approximate best transformers to gain efficiency.

- For abstraction refinement, it is important to understand where precision is lost. For example, we may use a valid abstraction which is not as precise as the best transformer. If this abstraction is not precise enough, there are two choices: either we refine the abstract domain or the abstract transformer. Our framework enables the distinction between imprecision of the abstract transformer and the abstract domain, which helps to design abstraction-refinement algorithms.

This concludes our discussion of game-based abstraction and of automata-based approaches. We now continue with applications and extensions of abstract interpretation in the probabilistic setting.

Abstract Interpretation of Probabilistic Programs. Monniaux pioneered abstract interpretation for probabilistic programs [Monniaux, 2005] with the aim of adapting concepts and abstract domains from static program analysis to probabilistic programs. Properties are formulated in a special μ-calculus [Monniaux, 2003a, Monniaux, 2005] which can express least and greatest fixed points and Boolean operators. In the interpretation of formulas, Monniaux focuses on maximal reachability probabilities.

Monniaux has proposed two types of probabilistic abstract domains: domains based on step functions [Monniaux, 2001] and on Gaussian distributions [Monniaux, 2003b]. Most closely related to our work are the step-function domains[2]. Based on these domains, the analysis in [Monniaux, 2001] admits to compute upper bounds on the probabilities of properties given as μ-calculus formulas.

The step-function domain is constructed on top of a lattice, typically a numerical domain, e.g., an interval analysis [Cousot and Cousot, 1977]. In contrast, our abstract valuations are constructed on top of a state partition, where the step functions are blocks. Both constructions are based on the concept of linear combination over base domains, where the base domain determines the indicator functions, i.e., the step functions. However, while blocks of a partition are disjoint by definition, Monniaux's base domain contains overlapping indicator functions, since base domains are closed under join operators (joins are the abstract counterpart of set union).

An effect of overlap is that Monniaux's domain contains distinct step functions with the same concretization, i.e., there is no uniqueness of representation [Monniaux, 2001]. Consequently, the ordering in the abstract domain is not anti-symmetric. On these domains, one can define an abstraction relation, rather than an abstraction function. However, there is no partial ordering and no Galois connection.

Monniaux employs sets of valuations as a concrete domain: an abstract valuation, or step function, concretizes to those concrete valuations for which it forms an upper bound. Thus the concrete domain is ordered by set inclusion. So that concrete and abstract domain have a different structure, an abstract element is a valuation and a concrete element is a set of valuations. In our setting, both domains consist of valuations.

To wrap up, both our framework and Monniaux's extend notions from non-probabilistic analyses based on abstract interpretation to the world of probabilities. Monniaux's starting point are base domains known as classical abstract domains (such as the interval domain), which are lifted to probabilistic domains using linear combinations. While the

---

[2] Recall that a function on the real numbers is called a step function if it can be written as a finite linear combination of indicator functions.

base domains are partially ordered sets themselves, the resulting probabilistic domains are not, due to overlapping concretizations of abstract elements. As a consequence, these domains do not lend themselves to develop Galois connections and best transformers. Further, Monniaux considers only abstractions yielding upper bounds on probabilities, while we consider both lower bounds and upper bounds.

Orthogonal to these differences, the ideas on the evaluation of μ-calculus formulas could be fruitfully combined with our framework.

Probabilistic Abstract Interpretation. Di Pierro and Wiklicky have introduced the framework of *probabilistic abstract interpretation* where the abstract domain and the concrete domain are vector spaces with distance metrics [Pierro and Wiklicky, 2000a,Pierro and Wiklicky, 2000b]. Abstraction, concretization and transformers are linear functions between vector spaces. Linearity of the abstraction function precludes the computation of lower and upper bounds. In our framework, both the abstraction functions and the transformers involve non-linear operations because they take minima, maxima, infima or suprema of a set of values. Linearity of the concrete transformer implies a restriction to Markov chains. In Markov decision processes, minimal and maximal reachability involves transformers that minimize or maximize respectively over the enabled actions.

In [Pierro and Wiklicky, 2000a] probabilistic abstract interpretation is discussed for a probabilistic variant of concurrent constraint programming. Classical concurrent constraint systems are non-deterministic, as they offer an interleaving operator and a choice operator. However, probabilistic abstract interpretation does not support non-determinism and thus all interleaving and choice operators are weighted with probabilities. There are cases where, for certain states, some choices are not available and the probabilities of the available choices are normalized to one, skewing the original weights.

Summing up, probabilistic abstract interpretation pursues a different notion of abstraction that aims for expected values and weighted averages rather than lower and upper bounds. Further, it is restricted to a deterministic setting.

Other Applications of Abstract Interpretation. Smith considered deterministic programs whose inputs follow a multivariate normal distribution. The analysis obtains upper bounds for reaching certain program states [Smith, 2008].

Coletta *et al.* describe an abstraction of Markov chains, not MDPs, arising from a process calculus from system biology [Coletta et al., 2009]. Thereby abstract interpretation is only used to relate concrete and abstract states, while the relationship between concrete and abstract model is established by simulation relations. As proposed in [Fecher et al., 2006], they abstract Markov chains to Interval Markov chains, i.e., Markov chains where transition probabilities are intervals of probabilities rather than a single probability.

5.8 Summary and Conclusion

Abstraction is the key to probabilistic model checking of realistic models. In this chapter we have presented the first abstract-interpretation framework for MDPs which admits to compute both lower and upper bounds on reachability probabilities. Previous abstract-interpretation frameworks only gave upper bounds. The lower and upper bounds are beneficial to quantify the loss of precision induced by abstraction and to locate where to refine the abstraction in case of imprecision, as we shall see in subsequent chapters.

In next chapter, we develop effective program abstractions based on the theory of this chapter.

6

Program Abstraction

Effectively computable abstractions are key to the automatic verification of concurrent probabilistic programs. Leveraging the theory of the previous chapter, we design abstract transformers that are computable from the program and present techniques to compute these transformers based on predicate abstraction. Our approach constitutes the first application of predicate abstraction to probabilistic models and allows to construct abstract transformers using SMT solvers. When combined with abstraction-refinement techniques of Section 7, we achieve a fully automatic verification approach.

The material in this chapter is taken from different publications. The abstract transformers appeared in [Wachter and Zhang, 2010]. An early version of the presented predicate-abstraction techniques is contained in [Wachter et al., 2007].

6.1 Introduction

One of the most popular methods for software verification is predicate abstraction [Graf and Saïdi, 1997] which is implemented in software verification tools like SLAM [Ball and Rajamani, 2002] and BLAST [Henzinger et al., 2005a]. Predicate abstraction merges concrete states to abstract states according to their valuation under a finite set of predicates ("Boolean expressions"). This induces a partition of the state space and a finite abstraction/abstract transformer of the original program on which program properties of interest can be checked.

In [Wachter et al., 2007], we developed predicate abstraction for concurrent probabilistic programs yielding the first automatic language-level abstraction for probabilistic models. This admitted to analyze models beyond the reach of preceding abstraction methods that construct the MDP semantics of the original model to extract the abstraction. The approach employs automatic decision procedures for quantifier-free fragments of first-order logic, also known as SMT solvers [Ganzinger et al., 2004].

The predicate abstraction approach in [Wachter et al., 2007] maps to MDPs as abstract models. Hence it is limited in the kinds of bounds that can be computed, i.e. only upper bounds on maximal reachability rather than lower and upper bounds. To get an abstraction that yields both lower and upper bounds, we adapted the machinery using ideas from game-based abstraction [Kwiatkowska et al., 2006].

Our novel predicate-abstraction approach is based on the idea of combining abstract transformers of the individual commands of the program to an abstract transformer for the whole program. Combining abstract transformers is different to a direct application of game-based abstraction. Namely, game-based abstraction can generally not be obtained by combining abstract transformers, as it tracks complex correlations between commands. It therefore has to be computed by abstracting *sets* of commands, as described in [Kattenbelt et al., 2008], which can be *exponentially* more expensive.

Abstract transformers are represented as special stochastic games, which are different from the stochastic games induced by game-based abstraction. By solving probabilistic reachability problems for stochastic games, we can compute lower and upper bounds which may be coarser than the ones obtained from the best transformer, and thus potentially less precise than game-based abstraction.

Outline

The chapter is structured as follows:

Section 6.2 We first define abstract transformers based on a given MDP and a partition of its state space. These transformers are valid abstractions that do not necessarily coincide with the best transformer but are more efficiently computable.

Section 6.3 We introduce methods to effectively compute the abstraction of a given concurrent probabilistic program using predicate abstraction and automatic decision procedures.

Section 6.4 We discuss related work. We compare different abstraction techniques for probabilistic programs analytically and give examples for illustration.

Section 6.5 We conclude the chapter.

6.2 Menu-based Abstraction

We first focus on abstract transformers and introduce the abstraction we will use. We shall call this abstraction *menu-based abstraction*, because the abstract transformer for the whole program non-deterministically picks from a menu of abstract transformers pertaining to the different commands – just like a concurrent probabilistic program where there is a non-deterministic choice from a menu of possible next commands or actions. The aim is thus a command-wise, local abstraction of the program.

We now define the abstract transformers for maximal and minimal probabilistic reachability.

Maximal Probabilistic Reachability

We first focus on abstraction for maximal probabilistic reachability. To make the concept of menu-based abstraction easier to grasp, we begin at the semantic level, i.e., we describe menu-based abstraction in terms of transformers induced by MDPs.

The concrete transformer induced by an MDP picks a transformer $pre_F^+[a]$ from a menu of possible actions $a \in A$ where each action corresponds to a command.

We first give the transformer $pre_F^+[a]$ for an action $a \in A$. In the subsequent step, we then define the complete transformer for maximal reachability in terms of the maximum over the transformers for the individual actions.

Let $w \in [0,1]^S$ be a valuation and $s \in S$ a state. Then $pre[a]_F^+(w)(s)$ equals 1 if s is a goal state, 0 if s cannot reach a goal state. If the action is enabled at state s, i.e., $a \in En(s)$, we have: $pre[a]_F^+(w)(s) = \sum_{s' \in S} \pi_{(s,a)}(s') \cdot w(s')$. For disabled actions, the transformer should not have an effect when composed with transformers for the other actions. Therefore we have $pre[a]_F^+(w)(s) = 0$ if a is disabled at state s, i.e., $a \notin En(s)$. The transformer pre_F^+ for maximal reachability of goal states F is thus given by:

$$pre_F^+(w)(s) \quad = \quad \max_{a \in En(s)} pre[a]_F^+(w)(s) \ . \tag{6.1}$$

We make two assumptions that do not impose any significant limitations but help avoid tedious corner cases. First, we assume that the partition Q is chosen such that the goal states can be represented precisely, i.e. there exists a set of blocks $F^\sharp \subseteq Q$ with $F = \bigcup_{B \in F^\sharp} B$. Second, we assume that, without loss of generality, a block in a partition contains either only absorbing[1] or no absorbing states.

We get the abstract transformer for the whole program by composing abstract transformers for the different actions. The abstract transformer for an action can be obtained by taking the best transformer. The composition operator in this context takes the maximum over all enabled actions. The enabled actions at a block $B \in Q$, denoted by $En(B)$, are given by the set $\{a \in A \mid \exists s \in B : a \in En(s)\}$. Overall we define the abstract transformer by:

Definition 6.1 (Maximal Menu-based Abstraction). *We define the respective abstract transformers for the lower and upper bounds of maximal reachability. For any abstract valuation $w^\sharp \in [0,1]^Q$ and every block $B \in Q$, we let:*

$$\widetilde{pre}_{F^\sharp}^{l+}(w^\sharp)(B) := \max_{a \in En(B)} (\alpha^l \circ (pre[a]_F^+) \circ \gamma)(w^\sharp)(B) \ ,$$
$$\widetilde{pre}_{F^\sharp}^{u+}(w^\sharp)(B) := \max_{a \in En(B)} (\alpha^u \circ (pre[a]_F^+) \circ \gamma)(w^\sharp)(B) \ .$$

Note that the difference to the corresponding best transformers is that the maximum over the actions has moved to the outside.

Before proving the validity of these new abstract transformers, we discuss menu-based abstraction for minimal reachability.

---

[1]Absorbing states are states without out-going transitions.

Minimal Probabilistic Reachability

Similar to maximal reachability, the transformer for minimal reachability is the composition of transformers $pre[a]_F^- : [0,1]^S \to [0,1]^S$ for individual actions a. The transformer $pre[a]_F^-$ differs from its counterpart $pre[a]_F^+$ for maximal reachability in that it returns 1 and not 0 if the corresponding action a is not enabled. Again, this is done to ensure that disabled actions remain without effect when composing these transformers.

In detail, the transformer $pre[a]_F^-$ is defined as follows. For a valuation $w \in [0,1]^S$ and state s, $pre[a]_F^-(w)(s)$ equals 1 if state s is a goal state or the action is not enabled, 0 if the goal states are not reachable from s, and $\sum_{s' \in S} \pi_{(s,a)}(s') \cdot w(s')$ otherwise. Analogous to maximal reachability, the transformer pre_F^- is given by:

$$pre_F^-(w)(s) = \min_{a \in En(s)} pre[a]_F^-(w)(s) . \tag{6.2}$$

Now we define the abstract transformers for the two bounds in terms of the best transformers of individual commands.

Definition 6.2 (Minimal Menu-based Abstraction). *We define the respective abstract transformers for the lower and upper bounds of minimal reachability:*

$$\widetilde{pre}_{F\sharp}^{l-}(w^\sharp)(B) := \min_{a \in En(B)} (\alpha^l \circ (pre[a]_F^-) \circ \gamma)(w^\sharp)(B) ,$$

$$\widetilde{pre}_{F\sharp}^{u-}(w^\sharp)(B) := \min_{a \in En(B)} (\alpha^u \circ (pre[a]_F^-) \circ \gamma)(w^\sharp)(B) .$$

Correctness

For the sake of obtaining correct bounds on reachability probabilities, it is crucial to ensure that menu-based abstraction is indeed a valid abstraction. Further, in the context of refinement, it is very desirable that partition refinement can only improve the precision of menu-based abstraction. We now establish these two important properties of menu-based abstraction, beginning with validity.

Validity. Our goal is to show that maximal and minimal abstract transformers are indeed valid abstractions. For $\widetilde{pre}_{F\sharp}^{u+}$ and $\widetilde{pre}_{F\sharp}^{l-}$ these transformers are exactly the best transformers $\alpha^u \circ pre_F^+ \circ \gamma$ and $\alpha^l \circ pre_F^- \circ \gamma$ respectively. In general, this does not hold for the other two transformers as we will see in Section 6.4.

The following theorem establishes validity of menu-based abstraction:

Theorem 6.3 (Validity of Menu-based Abstraction). *Menu-based abstraction yields valid abstractions for the respective bounds for both minimal and maximal reachability. More specifically, we have that:*

1. *$\widetilde{pre}_{F\sharp}^{u+}$ equals the best transformer $\alpha^u \circ pre_F^+ \circ \gamma$,*

2. *$\widetilde{pre}_{F\sharp}^{l+}$ is a valid abstraction of pre_F^+ w.r.t. the Galois connection (α^l, γ), i.e.,*

$$\gamma \circ \widetilde{pre}_{F\sharp}^{l+} \leq pre_F^+ \circ \gamma \tag{6.3}$$

3. $\widetilde{pre}_{F^{\sharp}}^{l-}$ equals the best transformer $\alpha^{l} \circ pre_{F}^{-} \circ \gamma$.

4. $\widetilde{pre}_{F^{\sharp}}^{u-}$ is a valid abstraction of pre_{F}^{-} w.r.t. the Galois connection (α^{u}, γ), i.e.,

$$\widetilde{pre}_{F^{\sharp}}^{u-} \geq pre_{F}^{-} \circ \gamma\gamma\circ \qquad \boxed{6.4}$$

Proof. The proof is based on properties of the respective Galois connections and applying Definitions 6.1 and 6.2. The full proof can be found in Appendix A. ∎

Note that Theorem 6.3 also implies that, for any given partition, menu-based abstraction is *at most* as precise as game-based abstraction, since the latter implements best transformers.

Menu-based Abstraction and Partition Refinement. We show that menu-based abstraction is well-behaved under refinement. Menu-based abstraction for the finer partition Q' yields *abstract transformers* and bounds that are at least as precise as for the coarser partition Q. We use the notation of Lemma 5.11, where we have shown this for the best transformer.

Lemma 6.4 (Menu-based Abstraction under Refinement). *Let $\mathcal{M}$ be an MDP and F a set of goal states. Let Q be a partition of S and Q' a refinement of Q. Consider the menu-based abstractions for maximal reachability (Definition 6.1) and minimal reachability (Definition 6.2) with respect to partition Q and partition Q' respectively.*

(i) The abstract transformers for the lower bounds of minimal and maximal reachability, respectively, with respect to Q are valid abstractions of the ones for Q' with respect to the Galois connection $(\alpha_{Q':Q}^{l}, \gamma_{Q':Q})$.

(ii) The finer partition yields a lower bound on minimal and maximal reachability that is at least as precise as the one for the coarser partition.

(iii) The abstract transformers for the upper bounds of minimal and maximal reachability, respectively, with respect to Q are valid abstractions of the ones for Q' with respect to the Galois connection $(\alpha_{Q':Q}^{u}, \gamma_{Q':Q})$.

(iv) The finer partition yields an upper bound on minimal and maximal reachability that is at least as precise as the one for the coarser partition.

Proof. It is sufficient to show (i) and (ii). Menu-based abstraction for the lower bound of minimal reachability and the upper bound of maximal reachability amounts to the best transformer. Hence these cases are already covered by Lemma 5.11.

We sketch the proof for the remainder of (i). Consider the menu-based abstraction for the lower-bound on maximal reachability. Thanks to the morphism properties of the concretization $\gamma_{Q':Q}$ (see Lemma 5.4), we can draw the concretization across the maximum over the actions. Equality 5.8 together with extensiveness property of Galois connections implies the claim. The other case works analogously. ∎

Menu Games

The abstract transformers take an abstract valuation as an argument and return an updated valuation. The update of the value of a block depends on the values of its successor blocks. Therefore an abstract transformer of menu-based abstraction can be described by arithmetic expressions that involve addition, multiplication, minima and maxima. The resulting expression trees correspond to stochastic games, which we call menu-based abstraction games or menu games for short. The idea is analogous to the construction we studied for best transformers (see Section 5.5). Menu games are different than these games since the underlying transformers are not the same.

Having already defined the abstract transformers, what is the benefit of considering menu games? There are several good reasons:

- Games provide an efficient and well-understood representation for abstract transformers, which can be stored in cache-friendly sparse-matrix data structures. Furthermore, solution algorithms for stochastic games are well-understood.

- Games admit visualization of analysis results. Annotated with lower and upper bounds, a user of the verification tool can conveniently inspect the results.

- We can illustrate the idea behind menu-based abstraction (see Figure 6.1) and the differences to game-based abstraction (Section 6.4).

Menu games are defined as follows:

Definition 6.5 (Menu game). *Let* $\mathcal{M} = (S, I, A, U, En, R)$ *be an MDP and* Q *a partition of* S. *The menu game is* $\widehat{\mathcal{G}}_{\mathcal{M},Q} = ((V, E), V_{init}, (V_1, V_2, V_p), \delta)$ *with*

- *player 1 vertices* $V_1 = Q \cup \{\star\}$,
- *player 2 vertices* $V_2 = \{(v_1, a) \mid v_1 \in V_1, a \in En(v_1)\}$,
- *probabilistic vertices* $V_p = \{\overline{\pi_{(s,a)}} \mid s \in S, a \in En(s)\} \cup \{v_p^\star\}$,
- *and initial vertices* $V_{init} = \{B \in Q \mid B \cap I \neq \emptyset\}$.

The distribution function δ, *which maps probabilistic vertices to distributions, is the identity. Let* $v_p^\star(\star) = 1$. *The edges* E *are defined by:*

$$
\begin{aligned}
E = & \{(v_1, v_2) \mid v_1 \in V_1, v_2 = (v_1, a) \in V_2, a \in En(v_1)\} \\
& \cup \{(v_2, v_p) \mid v_2 = (v_1, a) \in V_2, \exists s \in v_1 : \ v_p = \overline{\pi_{(s,a)}}\} \\
& \cup \{(v_2, v_p^\star), (v_p^\star, \star) \mid v_2 = (v_1, a) \in V_2, \exists s \in v_1 : \ a \notin En(s)\} \\
& \cup \{(v_p, v') \mid v_p \in V_p, v' \in V_1, v_p(v') > 0\} \ .
\end{aligned}
$$

Note that in the third line of the definition of E the notation $(v_2, v_p^\star), (v_p^\star, \star)$ introduces *two* edges, namely edge $(v_2, v_p^\star)$ and edge $(v_p^\star, \star)$, rather than a single one.

A player 1 vertex v_1 has a player 2 successor for each $a \in En(v_1)$. A player 2 vertex (v_1, a) represents the abstraction of the a-transitions. Further, the partition may contain both states on which a particular action a is enabled and states on which it is not, and, as a result, the abstraction may lose information about which actions are enabled and which ones are not. In this case, player 2 vertex (v_1, a) has distribution $v_p^\star$ as a successor.

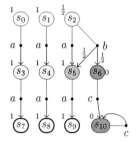 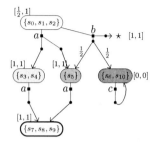

Figure 6.1.: Illustration of an MDP (left) and its abstraction as a menu game (right).

Example. *Figure 6.1 shows an MDP, a state partition, and the corresponding menu game. The MDP has states: $S = \{s_0, \ldots, s_{10}\}$. The different shadings of the states depict the state-space partition $Q = \{\{s_0, s_1, s_2\}, \{s_3, s_4\}, \{s_5\}, \{s_7, s_8, s_9\}, \{s_6, s_{10}\}\}$.*

The enabled actions $En(B_0)$ in block $B_0 = \{s_0, s_1, s_2\}$ are given by $En(B_0) = \{a, b\}$. In the corresponding abstract game, blocks are player 1 vertices. For each enabled action, there is one player 2 vertex. For example, for block B_0, there are two player 2 vertices for action a and b respectively.

The successors of the player 2 vertex for action a reflect that, from B_0, a-transitions into $\{s_3, s_4\}$ and $\{s_5\}$ exist. One successor of the player 2 vertex for b represents the b-distribution out of s_2. Vertex $\star$ reflects that b is not enabled at s_0 and s_1. ∎

The following theorem establishes the formal relationship between menu-based abstraction and menu games:

Theorem 6.6 (Menu Game and Menu-based Abstraction). *Let $\mathcal{M}$, Q and $\widehat{\mathcal{G}}_{\mathcal{M},Q}$ as defined in Definition 6.5. Moreover, let $pre_{V'}^{\pm\pm}$ be the valuation transformers in $\mathcal{G}_{\mathcal{M},Q}$ w.r.t. objective V'. Then we have:*
$$\widetilde{pre}_{F^\sharp}^{l-} = pre_{F^\sharp \cup \{\star\}}^{--}, \quad \widetilde{pre}_{F^\sharp}^{u-} = pre_{F^\sharp \cup \{\star\}}^{-+}, \quad \widetilde{pre}_{F^\sharp}^{l+} = pre_{F^\sharp}^{+-} \quad and \quad \widetilde{pre}_{F^\sharp}^{u+} = pre_{F^\sharp}^{++}.$$

Proof. The proof is based on an argument about expression trees. It proceeds in a similar fashion as the proof for Theorem 5.9. ∎

Note that there is an asymmetry between minimal and maximal probabilistic reachability regarding the goal vertices. Namely, only for minimal reachability, the star vertex is a goal vertex. The asymmetry is a direct consequence of the way concrete transformers are defined: the concrete transformer for an action assigns probability 1 to actions that are not enabled. Of course, absorbing states that are not goal states cannot have reachability probability 1. Why is the construction correct in presence of absorbing states? We have assumed that absorbing states are not in the same block with non-absorbing states. Therefore, blocks containing absorbing states do not have a transition to a star vertex. This assumption is made to ensure correctness of the construction.

We now give an example for illustration of the transformers and games just discussed.

Example. *Figure 6.1 illustrates an MDP and its menu-based abstraction.*

In the MDP the minimal reachability probabilities with respect to goal states $\{s_7, s_8, s_9\}$ are written next to each state. In the game the probability bounds obtained by $\widetilde{pre}_{F\sharp}^{l-}$ and $\widetilde{pre}_{F\sharp}^{u-}$, respectively, are annotated at each block as an interval, e.g., $[\frac{1}{2}, 1]$ for block $\{s_0, s_1, s_2\}$.

Action b is enabled at state s_2. However, at the other two states s_0 and s_1 in the same block, action b is disabled. The $\star$-vertex accounts for the behavior of these two states with respect to action b. Action c is also not enabled at s_0 and s_1 or any other state in the block, and thus the block has no transition to a $\star$-vertex for action c.

Regarding maximal reachability, the lower and upper bound obtained from the game yields the interval $[1, 1]$ for block $\{s_0, s_1, s_2\}$. For action a, we get the interval $[1, 1]$ and, for action b, we get the interval $[0, \frac{1}{2}]$. Taking the maximum over these intervals yields $[1, 1]$.

The next section explains how to compute the menu-based abstraction from a program directly without a detour over the MDP semantics.

6.3 Computing Menu-based Abstraction

In this section we explain how to compute menu-based abstractions. Mathematically, we have defined menu-based abstraction in terms of the MDP semantics of a program. However, for infinite-state programs, this semantics cannot be computed explicitly and, for finite-state programs with large state spaces, the semantics is very expensive to compute.

Therefore we derive the abstraction symbolically from the program, i.e., operating entirely at the language level without constructing its MDP semantics. Menu games are thus obtained by computing abstractions of commands and expressions, which is described in Section 6.3.1. The abstraction of commands and expressions is, in turn, based on predicate abstraction.

We briefly discuss the notion of predicate abstraction in Section 6.3.2. Predicates admit a symbolic representation of the state partition in terms of Boolean expressions over program variables. The abstraction of the program is computed by applying predicate abstraction to expressions (Section 6.3.3) and to commands (Section 6.3.4) using a reduction to certain satisfiability problems. These problems can be solved using the standard functionality of SMT solvers such as YICES [Dutertre and de Moura, 2006].

6.3.1. Symbolic Approach to Abstraction

We assume that a program $P = (X, I, C)$ is given and that Q is a partition of its state space. The goal is to obtain the corresponding menu game by symbolic reasoning.

We give an overview of the components we need to obtain program abstractions and explain how to combine these components to obtain a menu-based abstraction of the program P (Lemma 6.7). Symbolic reasoning and encoding in terms of predicates and SMT are for now treated as a black box and will be explained in detail later on.

Abstraction of Expressions. We require abstractions of the initial condition, as well as of the guards of commands.

The abstraction of the initial conditions consists of the blocks that contain an initial state of the program, i.e. it is the overapproximation $\alpha^\uparrow(\llbracket I \rrbracket)$ of the initial states $\llbracket I \rrbracket$ in terms of blocks:

$$I^\sharp = \{ B \in Q \mid \exists s \in B : \ s \in \llbracket I \rrbracket \} = \alpha^\uparrow(\llbracket I \rrbracket) \ . \tag{6.5}$$

To determine on which blocks a command is enabled, we also need to abstract the guards of commands. The required information goes beyond an overapproximation. This is because we would like to be able to distinguish different cases. Namely, whether a command c is enabled at none, all or some states within a block. Therefore we are interested in an underapproximation $\alpha^\downarrow(\llbracket g_c \rrbracket)$ and an overapproximation $\alpha^\uparrow(\llbracket g_c \rrbracket)$ of the guard g_c of the command

Generally speaking, we need methods to compute the underapproximation $\alpha^\downarrow(\llbracket e \rrbracket)$ and overapproximation $\alpha^\uparrow(\llbracket e \rrbracket)$ of a given Boolean expression e (for a definition of the abstraction functions, please refer to Section 2.2.2).

Abstraction of Commands. The abstraction of a command c consists of a set of abstract transitions. These abstract transitions consist exactly of the abstractions of the concrete transitions in the semantics of the command:

$$\llbracket c \rrbracket^\sharp := \{ (B, \overline{\pi}) \mid \exists s \in B : \ (s, \pi) \in \llbracket c \rrbracket \} \ . \tag{6.6}$$

To construct menu games from programs, we require the infrastructure to abstract expressions and commands which we have just discussed. We explain in the coming sections how it can be realized in practice.

We first formalize in a lemma how abstractions of expressions and commands can be combined to an abstraction of the program:

Lemma 6.7 (Symbolic Abstraction). *Let $P = (X, I, C)$ be a program, and let $\mathcal{M}$ be the semantics of P. The menu game $\widehat{\mathcal{G}}_{\mathcal{M},Q} = ((V, E), V_{init}, (V_1, V_2, V_p), \delta)$ with respect to partition $\mathcal{M}$ and partition Q can be obtained from P as follows:*

- $V_1 = Q \cup \{\star\}$,

- $V_2 = \bigcup_{c \in \mathcal{C}} \{(v_1, a_c) \mid \exists v_p \in V_p : (v_1, v_p) \in [\![c]\!]^{\sharp}\}$,
- $V_p = \bigcup_{c \in \mathcal{C}} \{v_p \mid \exists v_1 \in V_1 : (v_1, v_p) \in [\![c]\!]^{\sharp}\} \cup \{v_p^{\star}\}$,
- $V_{init} = \alpha^{\uparrow}([\![I]\!])$,
- δ is the identity function,
- and the edges are given by:

$$
\begin{aligned}
E = &\bigcup_{c \in \mathcal{C}} \{(v_1, v_2) \mid v_1 \in V_1, v_2 = (v_1, a_c) \in V_2, v_1 \in \alpha^{\uparrow}([\![g_c]\!])\} \\
&\cup \bigcup_{c \in \mathcal{C}} \{(v_2, v_p) \mid \exists v_1 \in V_1 : v_2 = (v_1, a_c) \in V_2, (v_1, v_p) \in [\![c]\!]^{\sharp}\} \\
&\cup \bigcup_{c \in \mathcal{C}} \{(v_2, v_p^{\star}), (v_p^{\star}, \star) \mid \exists v_1 \in V_1 : v_2 = (v_1, a_c) \in V_2, v_1 \notin \alpha^{\downarrow}([\![g_c]\!])\} \\
&\cup \{(v_p, v') \mid v_p \in V_p, v' \in V_1, v_p(v') > 0\} \ .
\end{aligned}
$$

This section describes how to obtain menu games based on abstractions of expressions and commands. Next we explain how to obtain abstractions of expressions and commands based on predicate abstraction.

6.3.2. State Partition

We recall the basic concept of predicate abstraction in this subsection. Our focus is thereby on notation and the state partition induced by predicate abstraction.

A predicate φ is a Boolean expression over the program variables. For example, the program in Figure 4.1 has an integer variable x and the expression $x > 0$ is a predicate. A predicate denotes the set of states $\{s \in S \mid s \vDash \varphi\}$ that satisfy it, e.g., all states for which variable x has value greater than zero.

We fix a finite set $\mathcal{P}$ of predicates:

$$
\mathcal{P} = \{\varphi_1, \ldots, \varphi_n\} \ .
$$

The predicates induce a partition of the state space. Each block of the partition is determined by which predicates hold in it and which ones do not. A block B can thus be represented by a bit vector $(b_1, \ldots, b_n) \in \{0, 1\}^n$ such that B consists of the states defined by a conjunction of literals:

$$
B = [\![b_1 \Leftrightarrow \varphi_1 \wedge \ldots \wedge b_n \Leftrightarrow \varphi_n]\!] \ .
$$

Note that $0 \Leftrightarrow \varphi_i$ is equivalent to the negation $\neg\varphi_i$ and $1 \Leftrightarrow \varphi_i$ is equivalent to φ_i. Therefore the literals in the above conjunction are either negations of predicates or predicates. The partition Q is thus given by

$$
Q = \{[\![b_1 \Leftrightarrow \varphi_1 \wedge \ldots \wedge b_n \Leftrightarrow \varphi_n]\!] \mid b_1, \ldots, b_n \in \{0, 1\}\} \ .
$$

For notational convenience, we will no longer distinguish between a block B and its respective bit-vector representation $(b_1, \ldots, b_n)$, i.e. we write $B = (b_1, \ldots, b_n)$.

Predicate abstraction is thus clearly an instance of partition abstraction, which is described in Section 2.2.2. In the next section, we show how the underapproximating and overapproximating abstraction functions can be computed.

6.3.3. Abstraction of Expressions

This subsection addresses the problem of computing the abstraction of a Boolean expression e with respect to a given set of predicates $\mathcal{P}$. More precisely, we are interested in two abstractions of e: its overapproximation $\alpha^\uparrow(\llbracket e \rrbracket) \subseteq 2^Q$ and its underapproximation $\alpha^\downarrow(\llbracket e \rrbracket) \subseteq 2^Q$ respectively.

To compute these abstractions with SMT solvers, we need an encoding in terms of logic, which we describe now. We begin with overapproximation. The overapproximation $\alpha^\uparrow(\llbracket e \rrbracket)$ contains exactly the blocks $B = (b_1, \ldots, b_n)$ that intersect with $\llbracket e \rrbracket$:

$$\alpha^\uparrow(\llbracket e \rrbracket) = \{(b_1, \ldots, b_n) \mid \exists s: \ s \vDash e \wedge b_1 \Leftrightarrow \varphi_1 \wedge \ldots \wedge b_n \Leftrightarrow \varphi_n\} \ . \tag{6.7}$$

The naive approach to compute $\alpha^\uparrow(\llbracket e \rrbracket)$ is to enumerate all bit vectors in $\{0,1\}^n$ and to check for each one if the constraint $e \wedge b_1 \cdot \varphi_1 \wedge \ldots \wedge b_n \cdot \varphi_n$ in Equation 6.7 is satisfiable. However, this would entail $|Q| = 2^n$ calls to a decision procedure independent of the input expression e.

It is often more efficient to only enumerate the blocks that are actually in $\alpha^\uparrow(\llbracket e \rrbracket)$. The preferred approach is to express the elements of $\alpha^\uparrow(\llbracket e \rrbracket)$ by a single constraint from which the blocks can be enumerated as satisfying assignments without checking all possible bit vectors [Lahiri et al., 2006].

To this end, we use a fresh Boolean variable b^φ for each predicate φ. As a whole, these Boolean variables encode the bit-vector representation of blocks. To express the binding between these Boolean variables and predicates, we employ the following constraint:

$$\mathcal{B} := \bigwedge_{\varphi \in \mathcal{P}} (b^\varphi \Leftrightarrow \varphi) \tag{6.8}$$

which expresses that each Boolean variable is logically equivalent to the respective predicate.

Obtaining the underapproximation of a given Boolean expression can be reduced to obtaining the overapproximation of its negation. Overall, the abstraction of expressions works according to the following lemma:

Lemma 6.8. *Let e be a Boolean expression and $\mathcal{B}$ as defined above. Then over- and underapproximation of e can be expressed as follows:*

- $\alpha^\uparrow(\llbracket e \rrbracket) = \{(b_1, \ldots, b_n) \mid b_1, \ldots, b_n \vDash \exists X. \ e \wedge \mathcal{B}\}$
- $\alpha^\downarrow(\llbracket e \rrbracket) = Q \setminus \alpha^\uparrow(\llbracket \neg e \rrbracket)$

For a proof, we refer to [Flanagan and Qadeer, 2002]. At the level of expressions, we leverage standard operations of conventional predicate abstraction. Methods that carry out the described under- and overapproximations of expressions have been investigated extensively [Lahiri et al., 2006]. The non-standard, probabilistic aspect comes into play when we compute abstractions of commands.

6.3.4. Abstraction of Commands

In this section, we describe how the abstraction of a command can be computed with respect to a given set of predicates. Formally, we need to compute the set of abstract transitions:

$$\llbracket c \rrbracket^\sharp = \{(B, \overline{\pi}) \mid \exists s \in B : (s, \pi) \in \llbracket c \rrbracket\} \ .$$

This can be realized in a similar way as the abstraction of expressions. We formulate the problem in terms of abstract transition constraints that involve instances of the program variables and Boolean variables, which encode the abstract transitions. The abstract transitions can then be enumerated using an SMT solver. Here the same principal machinery is used as for the abstraction of expressions, albeit with a different encoding.

Abstract transition constraints. We have discussed transition constraints that describe the semantics of a command symbolically. To obtain abstract transitions, we introduce an abstract counterpart, abstract transition constraints. The constraints are determined by a given command and a set of predicates.

From now on, let us assume that a command c is given. Without loss of generality, this command has k probabilistic alternatives with corresponding probabilities $p_1, \ldots, p_k$. An abstract transition in the abstraction of c can be characterized in terms of $k + 1$ blocks $B_0, \ldots, B_k \in Q$. An abstract transition is a tuple $(B_0, \bigoplus_{i=1}^k p_i : B_i)$ consisting of present block B_0 and distribution $\bigoplus_{i=1}^k p_i : B_i$. At the encoding level, we consider Boolean variables b_i^φ for all predicates $\varphi \in \mathcal{P}$ and all $i \in \{0, \ldots, k\}$. Variable b_i^φ represents the value of predicate φ at time i, where $i = 0$ refers to the present and values of i larger than zero refer to the respective probabilistic alternative.

For a given command c, an abstract transition constraint is a symbolic representation of the abstraction $\llbracket c \rrbracket^\sharp$:

Definition 6.9 (Abstract Transition Constraint). *Let c be a command and k the number of its probabilistic alternatives. Further, let $\mathcal{R}_c$ be its transition constraint. Let $\mathcal{P}$ be a set of predicates. The abstract transition constraint with respect to $\mathcal{P}$ is defined by:*

$$\mathcal{R}_c^\sharp := \exists X_0 \ldots X_k : \ \mathcal{R}_c \wedge \bigwedge_{i=0}^k \mathcal{B}_j \tag{6.9}$$

where

$$\mathcal{B}_j := \bigwedge_{\varphi \in \mathcal{P}} (b_j^\varphi \Leftrightarrow \varphi[X/X_j])$$

is the instantiation of the formula $\mathcal{B}$ (see Equation 6.8) for the respective instance X_j of the program variables and the Boolean variables respectively with $j \in \{0, \ldots, k\}$.

An abstract transition constraint encodes the abstract transitions $[\![c]\!]^\sharp$ as Boolean assignments to the variables b_i^φ:

Lemma 6.10 (Correctness). *Let c be a command then:*

$$[\![c]\!]^\sharp = \{(B_0, \bigoplus_{i=1}^{k} p_i : B_i) \mid (B_0, \ldots, B_k) \vDash \mathcal{R}_c^\sharp\} \ .$$

Proof. We begin with the inclusion $\subseteq$. Let $(B, \pi^\sharp) \in [\![c]\!]^\sharp$. Then there exists a pair $(s, \pi) \in [\![c]\!]$ with $\overline{\pi} = \pi$. By definition there must be states $s_0, \ldots, s_k \in S$ with $s_0 = s$ and $\pi = \bigoplus_{j=1}^{k} p_j : s_j$ which fulfill the transition constraint $\mathcal{R}_c$, i.e. $(s_0, \ldots, s_k) \vDash \mathcal{R}_c$. Therefore, the blocks $(B_0, \ldots, B_k)$ with $B_0 = B$ and $B_j = \overline{s_j}$ (for all $j \in \{1, \ldots, k\}$) fulfill the constraint $\mathcal{R}_c^\sharp$.

We show the inclusion $\supseteq$. Let $B_0, \ldots, B_k$ be blocks such that $(B_0, \ldots, B_k) \vDash \mathcal{R}_c^\sharp$. There exist states $s_0, \ldots, s_k \in S$ such that $s_j \vDash \mathcal{B}_j$ (for all $j \in \{1, \ldots, k\}$) which fulfill R_c. Therefore, we have $s_j \in B_j$ (for all $j \in \{1, \ldots, k\}$) and $(s_0, \pi = \bigoplus_{j=1}^{k} p_j : s_j) \in [\![c]\!]$. This immediately implies $(B_0, \bigoplus_{j=1}^{k} p_j : B_j) \in [\![c]\!]^\sharp$. ∎

Abstract transition constraints contain $k + 1$ instances of the program variables: the present-state instance plus the instances of the probabilistic alternatives.

Next we give a simplified form of transition with fewer variables. The method is a straightforward extension of Dijkstra's weakest preconditions [Dijkstra, 1976] to our setting. Intuitively, we can express transition constraints where only the present-state instances X_0 are involved. This is possible because each transition (s, π) in the semantics of a command is already fully determined by the state s. The states in the distribution π are the result of evaluating the respective assignment E_j in state s.

Since we only enumerate abstract transitions and not concrete transitions, we can syntactically quantify out the next-state instances of program variables X_j with $j > 0$. We do so by replacing the corresponding variables with the update formulas that determine their value in the respective probabilistic alternative.

The modified abstract transition constraints replace the transition constraint $\mathcal{R}_c$ by applying syntactic weakest preconditions to the formulas $\mathcal{B}_j$ instead. Syntactic weakest preconditions replace the variable instances X by the expressions defined in the assignments of the respective probabilistic alternative j, i.e. $\mathcal{B}_j[X_j/E_j]$. The resulting expression is an expression over X. However, we would like to have an expression over X_0. Therefore we additionally apply the substitution $[X/X_0]$. This yields the following definition.

Definition 6.11 (Simplified Abstract Transition Constraint). *Let c be a command. The simplified abstract transition constraint of c is defined by:*

$$\mathcal{R}_c^{\sharp,wp} := \exists X_0 : \ g[X/X_0] \wedge \mathcal{B}_0 \wedge \bigwedge_{j=1}^{k} \mathcal{B}_j[X_j/E_j][X/X_0] \qquad (6.10)$$

For illustration, consider command c

```
[a] x > y -> 0.5: (x'=x-1)+ 0.5: (x'=y);
```

where x and y are integer variables.

We construct the simplified abstract transition constraint $\mathcal{R}_c^{\sharp,wp}$ for this command with respect to predicates $\{x < 0, x \geq 0\}$:

$$(x_0 > y_0) \wedge (b_0^{x<0} \Leftrightarrow x_0 < 0) \wedge (b_0^{x\geq0} \Leftrightarrow x_0 \geq 0)$$
$$\wedge \, (b_1^{x<0} \Leftrightarrow x_0 < 1) \wedge (b_1^{x\geq0} \Leftrightarrow x_0 \geq 1)$$
$$\wedge \, (b_2^{x<0} \Leftrightarrow y_0 < 0) \wedge (b_2^{x\geq0} \Leftrightarrow y_0 \geq 0) \, .$$

We also need to make sure that simplified transition constraints yield the correct abstraction, which is stated in the following proposition:

Proposition 4. *Let c be a command then:*

$$[\![c]\!]^{\sharp} = \{(B_0, \bigoplus_{j=1}^{k} p_j : B_j) \mid (B_0, \ldots, B_k) \vDash \mathcal{R}_c^{\sharp,wp}\} \, .$$

Proof. The formulas $\mathcal{R}_c^{\sharp,wp}$ and $\mathcal{R}_c^{\sharp}$ are logically equivalent. ∎

This completes the description of SMT-based predicate abstraction and the technical material of this chapter. We conclude the chapter with a discussion of different abstraction techniques for probabilistic models and of related work.

6.4 Related Work

Predicate abstraction [Graf and Saïdi, 1997] has been successfully used for software verification. Tools like SLAM [Ball and Rajamani, 2002], BLAST [Henzinger et al., 2005a] and MAGIC [Clarke et al., 2005] have been applied to low-level operating system code written in C. Further applications of predicate abstraction are the verification of hardware circuits [Clarke et al., 2003] and hybrid systems [Alur et al., 2006].

The first practical application of predicate abstraction to infinite-state probabilistic models has been presented in [Wachter et al., 2007]. Previous abstraction techniques aimed at finite probabilistic models. Our work differs in that:

- computing abstractions of infinite-state models typically requires reasoning at the language level. We presented one of the first applications of SMT techniques to probabilistic models.

- compared to predicate abstraction for non-probabilistic models, probabilistic models have a transition structure involving probabilistic choice, which makes the abstraction process more complex.

The predicate-abstraction method described in this chapter is an improved version of our initial work. In [Wachter et al., 2007] we used a quotient construction that maps to MDPs [D'Argenio et al., 2002]. The improvement consists in the use of games, which admit the computation of lower and upper bounds [Wachter and Zhang, 2010].

Currently, the only other application of predicate abstraction to probabilistic models is [Kattenbelt et al., 2009]. They consider C programs with probabilistic choice and extend the machinery of a C software-model checker [Clarke et al., 2005] with game-based abstraction [Kwiatkowska et al., 2006].

The work in [Kattenbelt et al., 2009] focuses on sequential programs, while we consider concurrent programs. Game-based abstraction [Kattenbelt et al., 2009] can be exponentially more expensive than menu-based abstraction in presence of concurrency.

We now give a detailed comparison of different techniques that have been used in conjunction with predicate abstraction of probabilistic models:

- MDP-based abstraction [D'Argenio et al., 2001, D'Argenio et al., 2002],
- game-based abstraction [Kwiatkowska et al., 2006],
- and menu-based[2] abstraction [Wachter and Zhang, 2010].

We illustrate these abstractions and their differences with a concrete example program. We discuss precision, complexity and size of the obtained abstractions in the general case, as well as practical aspects of implementation.

Size

In our discussion of size, we assume that all abstractions operate over the same partition.

Among the three abstractions, MDP-based abstraction is a special case because it maps to MDPs rather than games. Thus there are obviously no player 2 vertices, unlike in menu-based abstraction and game-based abstraction. On the other hand, abstract MDPs feature the same probability distributions as game-based and menu-based abstractions. This means that MDP-based abstraction yields strictly smaller abstractions.

We now concentrate on the comparison of game-based with menu-based abstraction. Note that the number of player 1 vertices and of probabilistic vertices is the same in both cases (up to the star vertex). It remains to compare the difference in the number of player 2 vertices.

For menu-based abstraction, the number of player 2 vertices $|V_2|$ is given by the number of enabled actions. Formally, we have

$$|V_2| = \sum_{v_1 \in V_1} |En(v_1)|$$

where $|En(v_1)|$ is the number of enabled actions at a block. Therefore, the worst-case number of player 2 vertices is $|V_1| \cdot c$ where c is a constant that gives the maximal number of actions enabled at any block.

---

[2]In [Wachter and Zhang, 2010], we have used the term "parallel abstraction" instead of menu-based abstraction.

```
module main
s    : [0..2];    // control flow
x,y  : int;       // integer variables
[a] s=0 -> 1.0:(s'=1)&(x'=y);
[b] s=0 & x>10 -> 0.5:(s'=0)+ 0.5:(s'=2);
endmodule
init
s = 0 & x > 0
endinit
```

Figure 6.2.: Example program.

For game-based abstraction [Kwiatkowska et al., 2006], the number of player 2 vertices is determined by the behaviors of states distinguishable under abstraction:

$$|V_2| = \sum_{v_1 \in V_1} \left| \{ \overline{Distr(s)} \mid s \in v_1 \} \right|$$

where $\overline{Distr(s)}$ is the abstraction of the distributions available at state s. Each player 2 vertex corresponds to a *subset* of V_p. Therefore, in the worst case, the number of player 2 vertices lies in the order of $|V_1| \cdot 2^{|V_p|}$. The number can be significantly larger than the bound $|V_1| \cdot c$ of menu-based abstraction.

Summary. Menu-based abstraction can be exponentially smaller than game-based abstraction for the same partition and it is easier to implement. Compared to MDP-based, menu-based abstraction additionally stores player 2 vertices.

The difference between game-based and menu-based abstraction has a strong impact on implementation aspects, as we shall see next.

Implementation

From a practical point of view, game-based abstraction is complex to implement in presence of concurrency. Player 2 vertices result from the combined effect of different commands. Therefore, in general, commands enabled on the same block cannot be abstracted in isolation. SMT-based procedures have to consider compounds of commands [Kattenbelt et al., 2008], which can be expensive. In contrast, menu-based and MDP-based abstraction can be computed by considering each command in isolation. This simplifies the implementation and may help to reduce the number of SMT-solver calls.

Let us illustrate the differences with an example.

Example. *This example illustrates differences between MDP-based, menu-based and game-based abstraction using the example program from Figure 6.2. We show how the different abstractions look like given the set of predicates* $\{ s = 0 \ldots 2, x < 0, x = 0, x > 0 \}$.

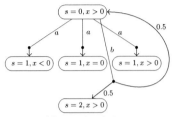

(a) MDP-based abstraction

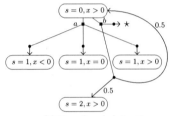

(b) Menu-based abstraction

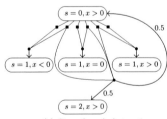

(c) Game-based abstraction

Figure 6.3.: Example of menu-based, MDP-based and game-based abstraction.

Figure 6.3a depicts the MDP-based abstraction. Let us first focus on action a and block $\{s = 0, x > 0\}$. *In the command corresponding to action a, variable x is assigned the value of y. The abstraction has no information about variable y. Therefore there are three possibilities:*

- *either y is less than zero, in which case action a goes to block* $\{s = 1, x < 0\}$,
- *y is zero, in which case action a goes to block* $\{s = 1, x = 0\}$,
- *or y is larger than zero, in which case action a goes to block* $\{s = 1, x > 0\}$.

Action b is not enabled on all states in block $\{s = 0, x > 0\}$. *An abstract transition is anyway added such that the behavior of the program is overapproximated.*

The menu game is shown in Figure 6.3b and has two player 2 vertices, one for each enabled action. These vertices indicate which distribution is induced by action a and which one by action b. The player 2 vertices of the game capture the enabled actions. The abstract distributions are the same as for MDP-based abstraction with one exception. As action b is not enabled on the states in $\{s = 0, x > 0\}$ *with $x \leq 10$, there is special star vertex to indicate this.*

The game-based abstraction is shown in Figure 6.3c. The abstract distributions are the same as for MDP-based abstraction. Further, there are six player 2 vertices. The vertices reflect the different behaviors of states within block $\{s = 0, x > 0\}$. *For each of the six player 2 vertices, there is a state in block* $\{s = 0, x > 0\}$ *that behaves according to the abstract distributions connected with the player 2 vertex. For example, for state $s = 0, x = 9$, only action a is enabled and goes to a state in block* $\{s = 1, x > 0\}$. *For state $s = 0, x = 11$, actions a and b are enabled. With action a, the transition goes to a state in block* $\{s = 1, x > 0\}$ *and with action b probabilistically to* $\{s = 2, x > 0\}$ *and* $\{s = 0, x > 0\}$.

Precision

Theorem 6.3 shows that menu-based abstraction is at most as precise as game-based abstraction for the same partition. There are examples where menu-based abstraction has the same precision. For example, the game-based abstraction in Figure 5.3 yields the same intervals as the menu-based abstraction of Figure 6.1 for both minimal and maximal reachability. The following example shows that menu-based abstraction can be strictly less precise.

Example. *Consider Figure 6.4a. The depicted MDP has three states* $\{s_0, s_1, s_2\}$. *State s_2 is the goal state. There are two actions a and b. At state s_0 only action a is enabled and goes to directly to the goal state s_2. Likewise, at state s_1, action b goes to state s_2. Hence the reachability probability (minimal and maximal) of states s_0 and s_1 is 1.*

We consider the partition that merges the states s_0 and s_1. The game-based abstraction is shown in Figure 6.4b. This game yields maximal reachability probabilities [1, 1]. *However, the menu-based abstraction, shown in Figure 6.4b, yields interval* [0, 1]. *The reason is that, unlike game-based abstraction, menu-based abstraction does not track that block* $\{s_0, s_1\}$ *corresponds to states where at least one of the two actions is enabled.*

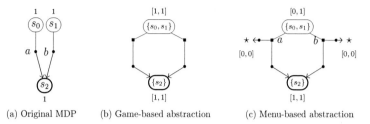

| (a) Original MDP | (b) Game-based abstraction | (c) Menu-based abstraction |

Figure 6.4.: Example where game-based is more precise than menu-based abstraction.

These examples show that, on the same partition, menu-based abstraction can be as precise as game-based abstraction or significantly less precise. On the other hand, there always exists a finer partition where menu-based abstraction achieves the same precision.

Theorem 6.12. *Any finite partition Q can be refined to a finite partition Q' on which menu-based abstraction is at least as precise as the best transformer on Q.*

Proof. The partition Q' can be obtained by splitting the blocks in Q' according to the equivalence classes used in the proof of Theorem 5.9. ∎

Note that the observation in Theorem 6.12 would be trivial, if we did not require partition Q' to be finite. This concludes the comparison of the abstractions.

Summary. For the same partition, being a valid abstraction, menu-based abstraction is at most as precise as game-based abstraction, the best transformer. There are examples where menu-based abstraction is less precise and examples where it has the same precision. There always exist a refined partition on which menu-based abstraction yields the same precision as game-based abstraction. However, this refined partition may take away the size advantage of menu-based abstraction over game-based abstraction.

6.5 Conclusion

In this chapter we have presented menu-based abstraction for concurrent probabilistic programs which yields both lower and upper bounds on reachability probabilities. Menu-based abstraction can be exponentially smaller than game-based abstraction for the same partition and is easier to implement. On the other hand, it may lose information with respect to game-based abstraction. We have also described how to compute menu-based abstraction of programs automatically using SMT solvers. In Chapter 7, we will give refinement techniques that produce suitable predicates in case the obtained abstraction is not fine enough to prove or refute a given property.

7

Refinement

In order to obtain efficient and precise analyses, the abstract domain needs to be customized to the given program and the property of interest. In our case, suitable predicates need to be found. Abstraction refinement automates the process of finding suitable predicates. Starting with a coarse abstraction, which admits efficient computations, automatic abstraction refinement iteratively refines the abstraction as needed.

Counterexample-guided abstraction refinement (CEGAR) has been used very successfully in both software and hardware verification. In Section 7.1, we present probabilistic CEGAR, the first CEGAR technique for infinite-state probabilistic models. Probabilistic CEGAR checks whether the probability to reach a set of goal states is below a given threshold. Probabilistic CEGAR produces both proofs and refutations of such properties. Refutations are of significant interest for the sake of error diagnosis.

We also present an alternative approach, called backward refinement. Backward refinement solves a quantitative verification problem and does not require the specification of a threshold. Backward refinement successively approximates the reachability probability to a given set of goal states. The analysis terminates as soon as the difference between lower and upper bound is smaller than the user-specified precision. Backward refinement is especially useful if the user wants to know the reachability probability in the first place, rather than aiming to establish a particular threshold.

This chapter presents the material of [Hermanns et al., 2008, Wachter and Zhang, 2010] in depth with algorithms, proofs and examples.

7.1 Probabilistic CEGAR

In conventional verification, a program is safe if it cannot reach a bad state. Typically bad states are states in which a runtime error may occur. The verification task consists in checking if there is an execution path of the program that reaches a bad state. In probabilistic verification, we are interested in the probability of reaching certain states. If the probability of reaching bad states remains below a certain threshold, the program can be considered as "safe". The verification problem then consists in proving or refuting probabilistic reachability properties of the following form:

Definition 7.1. *Let P be a concurrent probabilistic program and $e \in BExpr_I$ a Boolean expression over its program variables.*

We consider probabilistic reachability properties which we write as $Reach_{\leq p}(e)$ where $p \in [0, 1]$ is a probability value, and the Boolean expression e describes the states to be reached. Let $\mathcal{M} = \llbracket P \rrbracket$ be the MDP semantics of P.

For an adversary η in $\mathcal{M}$, we denote by

$$P_s^\eta(\rightsquigarrow e) := P_s^\eta(\{\beta \in Path_s^\eta(\mathcal{M}) \mid \exists i \in \mathbb{N} : \beta[i] \in \llbracket e \rrbracket\})$$

the probability to reach a state in $\llbracket e \rrbracket$.

Property $Reach_{\leq p}(e)$ is satisfied by a state s, denoted by $s \vDash Reach_{\leq p}(e)$, if $P_s^\eta(\rightsquigarrow e) \leq p$ for all adversaries η. In other words, a state fulfills $Reach_{\leq p}(e)$ if its maximal reachability probability $p^+(\llbracket e \rrbracket)$ is bounded by p, i.e., $p^+(\llbracket e \rrbracket)(s) \leq p$.

The program P satisfies $Reach_{\leq p}(e)$ if all of its initial states $s \in I$ satisfy $s \vDash Reach_{\leq p}(e)$.

The proof of a property consists in an abstraction which fulfills the property. A refutation consists in a concrete counterexample that shows that the program violates the property.

We discuss how counterexample-guided abstraction refinement can be developed in this probabilistic setting. The core challenge lies in the notion and analysis of counterexamples. In the traditional setting, an abstract counterexample is a single finite path (to some bad state) and counterexample analysis consists in checking if the concrete model exhibits a corresponding error path. In contrast, a counterexample against a probabilistic reachability property can be viewed as a finite Markov chain [Chatterjee et al., 2005] which generally contains cycles. Due to these cycles, probabilistic counterexample analysis is not directly amenable to conventional methods. We tackle this problem by preprocessing the abstract counterexample using the notion of strongest evidence [Han and Katoen, 2007]. Namely, we generate a finite set $\mathcal{C}_{real}$ of abstract finite paths that together carry enough abstract probability mass. Then we formulate the problem of computing the realizable probability mass of $\mathcal{C}_{real}$ in terms of a weighted MAX-SMT problem [Papadimitriou and Yannakakis, 1991]. The set $\mathcal{C}_{real}$ is built incrementally in an *on-the-fly* manner, until either enough probability is realizable, or $\mathcal{C}_{real}$ cannot be enriched with sufficient probability mass to make the probability threshold realizable. In the latter case, the counterexample is spurious.

These ingredients result in a theory for probabilistic CEGAR. We have evaluated the approach on various case studies. Indeed, CEGAR entirely mechanizes the verification process: predicates are added mechanically on demand based on counterexample analysis. To this end, our implementation employs interpolation [McMillan, 2006] to generate new predicates from spurious paths.

Challenge

The obvious idea for refinement is to follow the established CEGAR approach: start with a coarse abstraction and successively refine it using predicates learned from spurious counterexamples until either a realizable counterexample is found or the abstract model is precise enough to establish the property. In order to put counterexample-guided refinement to work for probabilistic models, several questions of both principal and practical nature need to be answered:

(i) We need to identify what an abstract counterexample constitutes.

(ii) We need to lift abstract counterexamples to the concrete system.

(iii) We have to determine if it is spurious.

(iv) Ultimately, we need to identify appropriate predicates to refine the abstraction.

Outline of Section 7.1

The section on CEGAR is structured as follows:

Section 7.1.1 We discuss abstract probabilistic counterexamples and their analysis.
Section 7.1.2 We describe how to synthesize predicates from abstract counterexamples.
Section 7.1.3 We give the probabilistic CEGAR algorithm.
Section 7.1.4 We formalize the progress achieved by a refinement iteration.
Section 7.1.5 We conclude the section on CEGAR.

7.1.1. Counterexamples

We fix a program $\mathcal{P}$, its MDP semantics $\mathcal{M}$, a partition Q and the reachability property $Reach_{\leq p}(\mathbf{e})$. We consider the menu-based abstraction of $\mathcal{P}$ and the stochastic game $\mathcal{G}$ defined by it (see Section 6.2).

Abstract Counterexamples. An abstract counterexample witnesses the violation of the property in the abstract game. It consists of a resolution of non-determinism in the abstract game which achieves a probability above the threshold. Formally, an abstract counterexample is a tuple $(B, (\sigma_1, \sigma_2))$ consisting of an initial block B and strategies for the two players. The game strategies induce a Markov chain $\mathcal{G}^{\sigma_1, \sigma_2}$ in the abstract setting. In this Markov chain, the probability to reach an $\mathbf{e}$-state from a block B is given by:

$$P_B^{\sigma_1, \sigma_2}(\leadsto \mathbf{e}) := P_B(\{\beta \in Path_B(\mathcal{G}^{\sigma_1, \sigma_2}) \mid \exists i \in \mathbb{N} : \beta[i] \cap [\![\mathbf{e}]\!] \neq \emptyset\}) .$$

Definition 7.2 (Abstract Counterexample). *A counterexample for $Reach_{\leq p}(\mathbf{e})$ is a pair $(B_0, \eta^\sharp)$ where $B_0 \in V_{init}$ is an initial block and $\eta^\sharp = (\sigma_1, \sigma_2)$ is a pair of game strategies such that*

$$P_B^{\eta^\sharp}(\leadsto \mathbf{e}) > p .$$

In this case, $\eta^\sharp$ is called a counter-strategy.

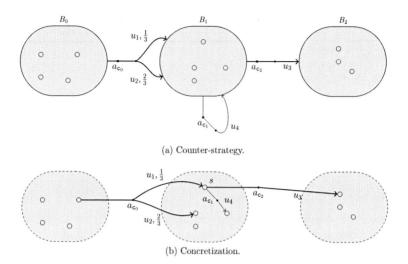

(a) Counter-strategy.

(b) Concretization.

Figure 7.1.: Concretization of a counter-strategy.

Spurious Counterexamples. In the non-probabilistic setting, a counterexample is an abstract path. Such an abstract path is called spurious if there does not exist a corresponding concrete path. We now introduce spurious counterexamples in our probabilistic setting.

Concretization of Counter-strategies. The concrete counterpart of a game strategy is an adversary in the MDP. Correspondingly, the concretization of a counter-strategy $\eta^\sharp = (\sigma_1, \sigma_2)$ is an adversary in the concrete MDP $\mathcal{M}$. Given a state s, this adversary $\gamma(\eta^\sharp)$ chooses an action so that the choice is compatible with $\eta^\sharp$. The adversary $\gamma(\eta^\sharp)$ is defined as follows:

$$\gamma(\eta^\sharp)(s) := \begin{cases} a_c & ; \text{ if } \sigma_1(\bar{s}) = (\bar{s}, a_c) \text{ and } \sigma_2(\sigma_1(\bar{s})) = \overline{\pi_{s,a_c}} \\ \mathcal{D}_\delta & ; \text{ otherwise} \end{cases}.$$

The case distinction and the formal definition can be explained as follows:

- Recall that $\bar{s}$ denotes the block that contains s. For this block, the player 1 strategy σ_1 chooses a player 2 vertex $v_2 := \sigma_1(\bar{s})$. Player 2 vertex v_2 consists of a tuple $(\bar{s}, a_c)$ where the first component is block $\bar{s}$ and the second component is an action a_c. The choice of the player 2 strategy at v_2 is given by $v_p := \sigma_2(\sigma_1(\bar{s}))$.

  Adversary $\gamma(\eta^\sharp)$ returns a_c if the probabilistic vertex v_p chosen at v_2 is the abstraction of the distribution π_{s,a_c} that we get with action a_c at state s.

- In case of $\gamma(\eta^\sharp)(s) = \mathcal{D}_\delta$, the adversary $\eta^\sharp$ has chosen an action which is not enabled at s, i.e., state s does not satisfy the guard $\mathbf{g_c}$ associated with c. Thus, we let $\gamma(\eta^\sharp)$ stop at state s.

For illustration, consider the fragment of the MDP and its corresponding abstract game depicted in Figure 7.1. If the strategy $\eta^\sharp$ chooses action a_{c_2} at state B_1, the concretization $\gamma(\eta^\sharp)$ chooses action a_{c_2} at state s.

Concretization of Counterexamples.

Now consider a counterexample $(B, \eta^\sharp)$. Its concretization, denoted by $\gamma(B, \eta^\sharp)$, is the set:

$$\gamma(B, \eta^\sharp) = \{(s, \eta) \mid \eta = \gamma(\eta^\sharp) \wedge s \in (I \cap \gamma(B))\} .$$

The pairs (s, η) in the concretization share the same adversary. They differ in terms of the initial state s. The concretization can thus contain many (even infinitely many) elements, depending on the cardinality of the set of initial states.

Each pair (s, η) induces a Markov chain and a corresponding reachability probability $p_s^\eta(F)$. Different elements $(s, \eta) \in \gamma(B, \eta^\sharp)$ in the concretization may thus result in different probabilities.

An abstract counterexample $(B, \eta^\sharp)$ is realizable if its concretization contains a pair (s, η) that exceeds the probability threshold. Otherwise the abstract counterexample is called spurious. In other words, a spurious counterexample does not induce any concrete Markov chain in which the probability to reach e is above the specified threshold.

Definition 7.3 (Spurious and Realizable Counterexamples). *Let $(B, \eta^\sharp)$ be a counterexample for $Reach_{\leq p}(e)$ in $\mathcal{G}$. Then, the counterexample $(B, \eta^\sharp)$ is called* realizable *if there exists a pair $(s, \eta) \in \gamma(B, \eta^\sharp)$ such that $p_s^\eta(F) > p$. Otherwise we say that the counterexample is* spurious.

Consider again Figure 7.1 and property $Reach_{\leq 0.07}(B_2)$. The goal states are contained in block B_2. With the given adversary, the probability of reaching the goal states is $\frac{1}{3}$, more than the threshold 0.07. The depicted abstract counterexample is therefore realizable.

Checking Counterexamples

Checking realizability of counterexamples is a key element of the refinement procedure: if a counterexample turns out to be realizable, the property is refuted. A concrete counter-adversary η then witnesses the violation and may be useful for debugging purposes. If the counterexample is spurious, the abstract model is too coarse. Additional predicates need to be added to eliminate the false negative.

Overall Idea. In the non-probabilistic setting, an abstract counterexample is a single finite abstract path $\sigma^\sharp$ starting in an abstract initial state. Its concretization is a set of corresponding paths in the concrete model, each of which starts in some concrete initial state and respects the concrete transition relation. This set might be infinite. If it is empty, the counterexample is spurious.

It is common practice to check if an abstract path is spurious by checking satisfiability of its corresponding path formula [Henzinger et al., 2002]. The path formula expresses the behavior enforced on the concrete program by the abstract path. If the formula is satisfiable, the path's concretization is non-empty. In this case, we have found a concrete counterexample violating the property. Hence the counterexample is realizable. Otherwise, it is spurious, and additional predicates can be extracted from the path $\sigma^\sharp$.

In the probabilistic setting, however, the situation is much more involved. What makes the counterexample $(B, \eta^\sharp)$ realizable is a concrete initial state $s \in (I \cap \gamma(B))$ and an adversary η such that the probability of reaching an e-state in the induced concrete Markov chain exceeds the given threshold p. All candidates (s, η) are contained in the concretization $\gamma(B, \eta^\sharp)$. But this concretization might be an infinite set.

We deal with this problem by preprocessing the abstract counterexample using the notion of strongest evidence [Han and Katoen, 2007]. Han and Katoen have devised a method that, for a given Markov chain, can be used to construct the smallest set of paths reaching e-states with an accumulated probability measure above p. This fits well to our needs.

The abstract counterexample $(B, \eta^\sharp)$ induces an abstract Markov chain. To this Markov chain, we can apply the algorithm from [Han and Katoen, 2007] to obtain *a finite* set of *finite paths* starting from state B with probability measure larger than p. Each of these paths directly corresponds to a play of the game $\mathcal{G}$.

To check if the counterexample is spurious, our goal is then to compute how much measure out of this set of paths can be reproduced in $\mathcal{M}$. In other words, we are interested in the highest probability that a pair $(s, \eta) \in \gamma(B, \eta^\sharp)$ in the concretization can achieve. If a pair (s, η) indeed achieves a probability larger than the threshold p, the abstract counterexample is realizable. Otherwise we may be able to conclude that it is spurious, or conclude that more work is needed, as we will explain below.

Spuriousness of Abstract Paths. Before we come to adversaries, we first explain how to determine whether a single abstract path is realizable or spurious. The idea is that a logical formula, called path formula, represents the (potentially empty) concretization of an abstract path. Checking realizability (or emptiness of the concretization) then reduces to checking the satisfiability of the path formula. This is a standard approach in software verification [Ball et al., 2001, Henzinger et al., 2002], which we adapt to the probabilistic setting.

We fix a counterexample $(B_0, \eta^\sharp)$ and consider a path in the induced Markov chain $\beta^\sharp$. The path corresponds to a play in the game. Thus it contains a sequence of player 1, player 2 and probabilistic choices in the abstract game $\mathcal{G}$. The player 1 decisions are given by player 2 vertices, i.e. pairs of blocks and actions (B_i, a_i), which admit to identify the command responsible for the transition.

For simpler notation, we abbreviate player 2 vertices (B_i, a_i) by their action a_i. In the context of a path, the block B_i is already determined by the respective player 1 vertex B_i. In turn, the player 2 decisions are represented by probabilistic vertices $v_{p,i}$, as usual. The probabilistic alternative within a command can be identified with a label u_i. Thus a path has the form:

$$\beta^\sharp = (B_0, a_0, v_{p,0}, u_0)(B_1, a_1, v_{p,1}, u_1) \dots B_k .$$

The actions together with these labels allow to trace back each step within an abstract path to points in the program.

Before focusing on entire paths, we look at an individual step from one block B_i to the next B_{i+1} within a path. The action a_i uniquely identifies the command c and the label u_i the particular probabilistic alternative within command c responsible for the step. Recall that transition constraints (see Section 4.3) give a formula that describes the transitions induced by a command. Taking into account the particular probabilistic choice, the semantic effect is thus determined by the assignment E_{u_i}. This gives rise to the step formula:

$$\mathcal{R}_{c, u_i}(\mathtt{X}_i, \mathtt{X}_{i+1}) = g[\mathtt{X}/\mathtt{X}_i] \wedge (\mathtt{X}_{i+1} = E_{u_i}[\mathtt{X}/\mathtt{X}_i]) \tag{7.1}$$

It is not necessary to check realizability of an individual step within an abstract path. Thanks to how we construct abstractions, an abstract step in the path always corresponds to a concrete step in the MDP. However, the fact that each abstract step has a corresponding step in the concrete does not necessarily imply that the path as a whole is realizable, as can be seen in Figure 7.1. Abstract transitions only guarantee local reachability (there always exist matching concrete transitions), yet they generally do not give a guarantee of transitive reachability (there exists a corresponding concrete *path*) when combined to abstract paths. Therefore an abstract path has to be checked as a whole using a logical formula that involves the conjunction of the formulas for the individual steps. Next we develop this formula.

The concretization $\gamma(\beta^\sharp)$ of an abstract path $\beta^\sharp$ is a set of finite paths in $\mathcal{M}$ with consistent states, and the same update and action labels, i.e.

$$\gamma(\beta^\sharp) = \{(s_0, a_0, u_0) \dots s_k \mid (s_0, \dots, s_k) \models TF(\beta^\sharp)\} .$$

Thereby $TF(\beta^\sharp)$ denotes the path formula. The path formula is defined as a conjunction of the initial condition $\mathtt{I}$, the blocks along the path and the constraints for the individual steps (Equation 7.1):

$$TF(\beta^\sharp) = \mathtt{I}(\mathtt{X}_0) \wedge \left(\bigwedge_{i=0}^{k} B[\mathtt{X}/\mathtt{X}_i] \right) \wedge \left(\bigwedge_{i=0}^{k-1} \mathcal{R}_{c_i, u_i}(\mathtt{X}_i, \mathtt{X}_{i+1}) \right) . \tag{7.2}$$

The path $\beta^\sharp$ is called *realizable* if its concretization is non-empty, $\gamma(\beta^\sharp) \neq \emptyset$, otherwise it is called *spurious*. An abstract path is realizable if its path formula is satisfiable

---

Algorithm 1 WP of an abstract path $\beta^\sharp$

$\quad$ **procedure** $\mathrm{WP}(\beta^\sharp = (B_0, a_0, v_{p,0}, u_0)(B_1, a_1, v_{p,1}, u_1) \dots B_k)$
$\qquad exp_{\beta^\sharp} \leftarrow F(B_k)$
$\qquad$ **for** $(j = k - 1, \dots, 0)$ **do**
$\qquad\qquad exp_{\beta^\sharp} \leftarrow \mathsf{g}_{c_j} \wedge F(B_j) \wedge \mathrm{WP}_{u_j}(exp_{\beta^\sharp})$
$\qquad$ **end for**
$\qquad$ **return** $exp_{\beta^\sharp} \wedge I$
$\quad$ **end procedure**

---

or, equivalently, its weakest precondition, which is analogous to the non-probabilistic setting [Henzinger et al., 2002, Ball and Rajamani, 2002].

Intuitively, the weakest precondition of an abstract path describes a constraint on the initial states, so that an initial state has a corresponding concrete path if and only if it fulfills the weakest precondition of that abstract path. The benefit of weakest preconditions is that they only refer to one instance of the program variables, as opposed to path formulas. The weakest precondition of an abstract path is computed by Algorithm 1 as the repeated application of the standard *syntactic weakest precondition* $\mathrm{WP}_E(e)$ where $\mathrm{WP}_E(e) := e[\mathtt{X}/E(\mathtt{X})]$ for an expression e and an update $\mathtt{X}' = E$.

Lemma 7.4. *For an abstract path $\beta^\sharp$, the following statements are equivalent:*

(i) The weakest precondition $\mathrm{WP}(\beta^\sharp)$ of path $\beta^\sharp$ is satisfiable.

(ii) The path formula $TF(\beta^\sharp)$ of $\beta^\sharp$ is satisfiable.

(iii) The path $\beta^\sharp$ is realizable, i.e. $\gamma(\beta^\sharp) \neq \emptyset$.

Proof. Path formulas, as given by Equation 7.2, correspond to sequential straight-line programs. In this setting, Dijkstra's work on weakest preconditions [Dijkstra, 1976] applies and directly yields the claims. $\blacksquare$

Checking Realizability. The counterexample $(B, \eta^\sharp)$ is guaranteed to be realizable if it has a concretization with sufficiently high measure. We would like to check realizability of the counterexample by analyzing abstract paths. The following lemma guarantees that abstract paths carry the same probability mass as their concretizations.

Lemma 7.5. *The paths in the concretization of an abstract path $\beta^\sharp$ have the same probability as $\beta^\sharp$.*

Proof. Consider an abstract path $\beta^\sharp = (B_0, a_0, v_{p,0}, u_0)(B_1, a_1, v_{p,1}, u_1) \dots B_k$. The measure of $\beta^\sharp$ under $(B, A^\sharp)$ is $\prod_{i=0}^{k-1} \delta(v_{p,i})(u_i, B_{i+1})$. Let $\beta = (s_0, a_0, u_0) \dots s_k$ be a path in the concretization of $\beta^\sharp$, i.e., $\beta \in \gamma(\beta^\sharp)$. The measure of β with respect to the corresponding cylinder set $Cyl(\beta)$ under $(s, \eta) \in \gamma(B, \eta^\sharp)$ is given by $\prod_{i=0}^{k-1} \pi_{s_i, a_i}(u_i, s_{i+1})$ if $s = s_0$. This is the same as the probability of $\beta^\sharp$ because distribution $\delta(v_{p,i})$ is the abstraction of distribution π_{s_i, a_i}, i.e., $\delta(v_{p,i}) = \overline{\pi_{s_i, a_i}}$. $\blacksquare$

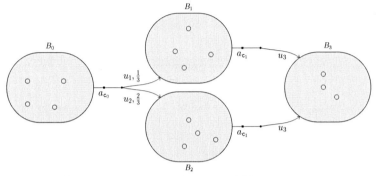

(a) Two realizable abstract paths whose probability sums up to 1.

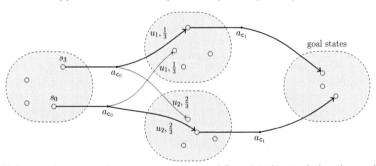

(b) However the corresponding concrete paths start in different initial states. In fact, the actual maximal reachability probability is $\frac{2}{3}$.

Figure 7.2.: Why summing up probabilities of abstract paths is insufficient to determine realizable probability mass.

A naive counterexample analysis would sum up the probability of realizable paths and check if the probability is lower than the threshold p. However, there may be multiple initial states. Corresponding concrete paths may start in different initial states, so that the probability in the concrete model is possibly lower. Which is why the naive counterexample analysis is incorrect, unless there is only a single initial state.

For illustration, consider Figure 7.2. The two abstract paths in Figure 7.2a are both realizable, as can be seen from the two paths in Figure 7.2b. Further, the probabilities of the two abstract paths sum up to 1. Yet the concrete reachability probability is only the maximum of the path probabilities $\frac{1}{3}$ and $\frac{2}{3}$, not their sum.

For a set $\mathcal{C}$ of abstract paths respecting $(B, \eta^\sharp)$, we let $\gamma(\mathcal{C}) = \bigcup_{\beta^\sharp \in \mathcal{C}} \gamma(\beta^\sharp)$ denote the union of the concretizations. As shown, the probability mass of $\mathcal{C}$ does not necessarily correspond to the same amount of concrete probability. The realizable probability of $\mathcal{C}$ is given by the maximal probability measure of the concretization $\gamma(\mathcal{C})$ under some concretization of $\gamma(B, \eta^\sharp)$.

Thus the problem of determining the realizable probability can be reduced to an optimization problem. We need to find a subset of the paths $\mathcal{C}$ with maximal probability that share a common initial state, i.e., an initial state from which there exist corresponding concrete paths. To characterize the start states of abstract paths we use their weakest preconditions, as computed by Algorithm 1.

Reduction to MAX-SMT. We formulate the problem of computing the realizable probability mass of a set of abstract paths in terms of a weighted MAX-SMT problem. MAX-SMT [Papadimitriou and Yannakakis, 1991] takes a collection of weighted expressions and returns the maximal subset whose logical conjunction is satisfiable. In our case, the expressions are given by the weakest preconditions of the paths weighted with the path probability. MAX-SMT returns a solution such that the total weight of the satisfied expressions is maximal. Such a solution then corresponds to a particular initial state, which is able to follow the abstract paths achieving maximal probability. The weight of the solution is exactly the realizable probability of the abstract paths.

For $\mathcal{C} = \{\beta_1^\sharp, \ldots, \beta_n^\sharp\}$, let $exp_1, \ldots, exp_n$ denote the weakest preconditions returned by $\mathrm{WP}(\beta_i^\sharp)$. Moreover, for each of them, the probability measure of path $\beta_i^\sharp$ is given as a weight, denoted by p_i, which corresponds to the probability of the set $\gamma(\beta_i^\sharp)$ under the condition that we start from some state characterized by expression exp_i. Formally, the MAX-SMT problem is defined by:

$$\mathrm{MaxSmt}(exp_1, \ldots, exp_n) = \max \left\{ \sum_{i=1}^{n} [\![exp_i]\!]_s \cdot p_i \mid s \in [\![\mathrm{I} \wedge F(B)]\!] \right\} .$$

The following lemma gives necessary conditions that admit to decide whether an abstract counterexample is realizable. As discussed, the decision is based on reducing the problem of determining realizable probability mass to a MAX-SMT problem.

Lemma 7.6 (Realizability of a Counterexample). *Let $(B, \eta^\sharp)$ be a counterexample for $Reach_{\leq p}(e)$, and let $\mathcal{C} = \{\beta_1^\sharp, \ldots, \beta_n^\sharp\}$ be a set of abstract paths with measure greater than p. It holds:*

(i) $\text{MAXSMT}(exp_1, \ldots, exp_n) > p$ implies that $(B, \eta^\sharp)$ is realizable,

(ii) $\text{MAXSMT}(exp_1, \ldots, exp_n) + P_B^{\eta^\sharp}(\leadsto e) - P_B^{\eta^\sharp}(\mathcal{C}) \leq p$ implies that the counterexample $(B, \eta^\sharp)$ is spurious.

Proof. Part (i). We assume that $\text{MAXSMT}(exp_1, \ldots, exp_n) > p$ and show that this implies the existence of a concrete counterexample.

Let state $s \in B \cap I$ be a solution of the MAX-SMT problem, i.e., state s fulfills $\text{MAXSMT}(exp_1, \ldots, exp_n) = \sum_{i=1}^n [\![exp_i]\!]_s \cdot p_i$. We choose a subset $J \subseteq \{1, \ldots, n\}$ of the indices where $J := \{i \in \{1, \ldots, n\} \mid [\![exp_i]\!]_s = 1\}$. By construction, we have $\text{MAXSMT}(exp_1, \ldots, exp_n) = \sum_{j \in J} p_j$. The abstract paths $\{\beta_j^\sharp \mid j \in J\}$ have realizable probability mass $\sum_{j \in J} p_j$. The conjunction $\bigwedge_{j \in J} TF(\beta_j^\sharp)$ must be satisfiable.

There are concrete paths $(\beta_j)_{j \in J}$, starting in state s such that $\beta_j \in \gamma(\beta_j^\sharp)$. Let $\eta = \gamma(\eta^\sharp)$ be the concretization of $\eta^\sharp$. Observe that $(s, \eta) \in \gamma((B, \eta^\sharp))$.

By definition, the paths β_j are in the Markov chain induced by adversary η and all start in s. Therefore the pair (s, η) achieves a reachability probability $P_s^\eta(\leadsto e) > p$. Thus the abstract counterexample $(B, \eta^\sharp)$ is realizable, which concludes the proof of (i).

Part (ii). Let $\leadsto e := \{\beta \in Path_B(\mathcal{G}^{\sigma_1, \sigma_2}) \mid \exists i \in \mathbb{N} : \beta[i] \cap [\![e]\!] \neq \emptyset\}$ denote the set of abstract paths to a goal block in the game. Slightly abusing notation, we also denote the set of concrete paths to a goal state by $\leadsto e$. The distinction will be clear from context.

Let us assume that $\text{MAXSMT}(exp_1, \ldots, exp_n) + P_B^{\eta^\sharp}(\leadsto e \setminus \mathcal{C}) \leq p$ holds. Observe that $P_B^{\eta^\sharp}(\leadsto e \setminus \mathcal{C}) = P_B^{\eta^\sharp}(\leadsto e) - P_B^{\eta^\sharp}(\mathcal{C})$ because $P_B^{\eta^\sharp}$ is a measure. Our claim is that $(B, \eta^\sharp)$ is a spurious counterexample. To prove that $(B, \eta^\sharp)$ is spurious, we show that, for every $(s, \eta) \in \gamma((B, \eta^\sharp))$, the following inequality holds:

$$P_s^\eta(\leadsto e) \leq \text{MAXSMT}(exp_1, \ldots, exp_n) + P_B^{\eta^\sharp}(\leadsto e \setminus \mathcal{C}) . \tag{7.3}$$

By assumption, the right-hand side of Inequality 7.3 is smaller or equal to p. In combination, this gives $P_s^\eta(\leadsto e) \leq p$ for every (s, η). Thus proving Inequality 7.3 is indeed sufficient to establish the claim.

We prove Inequality 7.3. Let $(s, \eta) \in \gamma(B, \eta^\sharp)$. The set $\leadsto e$ can be partitioned into two disjoint subsets M_1 and M_2. The set M_1 of paths that are prefixes of a concretization of a path in $\mathcal{C}$, i.e., $M_1 := \{\beta \mid \exists \beta^\sharp \in \mathcal{C} : \beta \leq \gamma(\beta^\sharp)\}$ and its complement $M_2 := \leadsto e \setminus M_1$. The probability $P_s^\eta(\leadsto e) = P_s^\eta(M_1) + P_s^\eta(M_2)$ is the sum of the probability of these two sets. To prove the claim, we establish suitable upper bounds of these two summands $P_s^\eta(M_1)$ and $P_s^\eta(M_2)$ respectively.

- The probability $P_s^\eta(M_1)$ is given by the sum of the probabilities of the abstract paths (see cylinder sets in Section 3.2) that have concretization starting in s.

Therefore, we have:

$$P_s^\eta(M_1) \leq \mathrm{MAXSMT}(exp_1, \ldots, exp_n) \ . \tag{7.4}$$

The inequality can be strict as there might be an initial state achieving a higher probability than s.

- For each path β in M_2, there exists a path in $\leadsto e \backslash \mathcal{C}$ that concretizes to β. Therefore, we have:

$$P_s^\eta(M_2) \leq P_B^{\eta^\sharp}(\leadsto e \setminus \mathcal{C}) \tag{7.5}$$

Combining Inequalities 7.4 and 7.4 yields Inequality 7.3 and we are done. ∎

Let $\varepsilon = P_B^{\eta^\sharp}(\leadsto e) - P_B^{\eta^\sharp}(\mathcal{C})$ denote the probability of the set of abstract paths which violate the property $Reach_{\leq p}(e)$, but are not part of the set $\mathcal{C}$. The lemma indicates that the decision algorithm is only partial: if the value $\mathrm{MAXSMT}(exp_1, \ldots, exp_n)$ lies in the interval $(p - \varepsilon, p]$, we are not sure whether the counterexample $(B, \eta^\sharp)$ is spurious or realizable. Obviously, counterexample analysis based on the MAX-SMT criterion is a heuristic rather than a complete decision procedure. In the next section, we show that an algorithm that provides a complete decision procedure cannot exist.

Checking Realizability is Undecidable. We now show that there exists no general algorithm that decides whether for a program P and a property $Reach_{\leq p}(e)$, a given abstract counterexample $(B, \eta^\sharp)$ against the property is realizable.

To prove undecidability of the general problem, we employ a reduction to the halting problem for two-counter machines [Minsky, 1967]. A two-counter machine has two counter variables ranging over the integers and consists of a sequence of instructions $l_1, \ldots, l_h$. Computation begins at l_1 and halts at l_h. Instructions $l_1, \ldots, l_{h-1}$ are of the following form:

- the jump-if-zero instruction l_j: jz l_k c checks if the value of counter c is zero. The machine jumps to instruction l_k if c is zero. Otherwise the machine goes to instruction l_{j+1}.
- the decrement instruction l_j: dec c decrements the value of counter c by one and the machine goes to instruction l_{j+1}.
- the increment instruction l_j: inc c increments the value of counter c by one and the machine goes to instruction l_{j+1}.

In the initial state of a two-counter machine, the value of both counters is zero and the program counter of the machine is at l_1. The halting problem for two-counter machines asks if a given counter machine reaches the halting instruction l_h when started in its initial state.

For every two-counter machine, we can construct a program P, a property $Reach_{\leq p}(e)$ and a corresponding abstract counterexample $(B, \eta^\sharp)$ such that the abstract counterexample is realizable if and only if the two-counter machine halts. Two-counter machines are Turing-complete [Minsky, 1967]. Therefore their halting problem is undecidable.

Based on this argument, we show that checking realizability of abstract counterexamples is undecidable.

Lemma 7.7. *Checking realizability of abstract counterexamples is undecidable.*

Proof. Let us first construct a concurrent probabilistic program $P = (X, I, C)$. We choose variables $X = \{pc, c_1, c_2\}$ where the program counter is modeled by variable pc and the counters by variables c_1 and c_2. The initial condition I is defined by the expression $pc = l_1 \wedge c_1 = 0 \wedge c_2 = 0$.

For each of the instructions in the counter machine, we introduce corresponding commands in the program. For some instructions, we introduce multiple commands.

For an instruction of the form l_j: jz l_k c, we introduce three guarded commands. One command creates a probabilistic branch:

$$[a_j] \; \texttt{pc = j -> 0.5: } (\texttt{pc'} = l_j^{true}) \texttt{ + 0.5: } \texttt{pc'} = l_j^{false})); \, , \qquad (7.6)$$

and the other two commands check if counter c is zero. The first of these commands goes to l_k if c is zero:

$$[a_j^{true}] \; \texttt{pc } = l_j^{true} \texttt{ \& c=0 -> } (\texttt{pc'} = l_k); \, , \qquad (7.7)$$

and the second command goes to l_{j+1} if c is not zero:

$$[a_j^{false}] \; \texttt{pc } = l_j^{false} \texttt{ \& c} \neq \texttt{0 -> } (\texttt{pc'} = l_{j+1}); \, . \qquad (7.8)$$

For a decrement instruction l_j: dec c, we introduce a guarded command

$$[a_j] \; \texttt{pc=} l_j \texttt{ -> } (\texttt{pc'} = l_{j+1}) \texttt{ \& } (\texttt{c'=c-1}); \, . \qquad (7.9)$$

For an increment instruction l_j: dec c, we introduce a guarded command

$$[a_j] \; \texttt{pc=} l_j \texttt{ -> } (\texttt{pc'} = l_{j+1}) \texttt{ \& } (\texttt{c'=c+1}); \, . \qquad (7.10)$$

We choose property $Reach_{\leq 0}(pc = l_h)$. We consider the set of predicates $\mathcal{P}$ where $\mathcal{P} = \{pc = l_j, pc = l_j^{true}, pc = l_j^{false} \mid 1 \leq j \leq h\}$. Since the predicates are mutually exclusive, we can denote blocks by only referring to a single predicate, e.g., we have block $\{pc = l_1\}$.

Regarding the property, we obtain an abstract counterexample $(B_0, \eta^\sharp)$. It consists of the block $B_0 = \{pc = l_1\}$ and the counter-strategy $\eta^\sharp$. For a given block $\{pc = l_j\}$ the counter-strategy chooses action a_j. For a block $\{pc = l_j^{true}\}$, it chooses action a_j^{true}. Analogously, for block $\{pc = l_j^{false}\}$, action a_j^{false} is chosen. For a player-2 vertex (B, a), we get $\eta^\sharp((B_0, \{pc = l_j\})) = \{pc = l_{j+1}\}$ if action a corresponds to an increment instruction, decrement instruction or $a = a_j^{false}$ for some j. If action a corresponds to a probabilistic branch (case 7.6), we get

$$\eta^\sharp((B_0, \{pc = l_j\})) = 0.5 : \{pc' = l_j^{true}\} + 0.5 : \{pc' = l_j^{false}\})) .$$

Otherwise we have $a = pc = l_j^{true}$ and the underlying command jumps to some l_k (case 7.7), Then we get $\eta^\sharp((B_0, \{pc = l_k\}))$.

The counterexample witnesses the non-zero probability to reach block $\{pc = l_h\}$. If there is no realizable path among the paths of the induced Markov chain, the counterexample is spurious. Otherwise the counterexample is realizable. If the counter machine halts there exists a realizable path. Conversely a realizable path corresponds to a halting run of the counter machine. ∎

In the proof, we have reduced the halting problem for two-counter machines to checking realizability of an abstract probabilistic counterexample. We have used a reduction to a property of the form $Reach_{\leq 0}(\mathsf{e})$. By slightly adapting the construction, the halting problem can be reduced to realizability problem with a property $Reach_{\leq p}(\mathsf{e})$ for any $0 \leq p < 1$. For the case $p = 1$, the problem is trivially decidable.

Despite this undecidability result, our notion of probabilistic counterexamples admits to design effective counterexample analysis techniques. The idea is to use a heuristic based on Lemma 7.6 which may fail to decide realizability. However, whenever realizability cannot be established, at least a predicate is returned to refine the abstraction. In this way, the overall refinement algorithm can then continue with a potentially better abstraction. In the next section, we discuss methods to obtain such predicates.

7.1.2. Predicate Synthesis

In our discussion of counterexample analysis in Section 7.1.1, we have identified two potential sources of imprecision: spurious abstract paths and a too coarse abstraction of the initial states. We describe methods to remove imprecision by generating fresh predicates. This constitutes one more step towards a CEGAR algorithm.

Predicates to Remove Spurious Paths. Let $(B, \eta^\sharp)$ be a counterexample in $\mathcal{G}$. Let $\beta^\sharp$ be a path in the induced Markov chain that starts in B and ends in a goal vertex, i.e., $\beta^\sharp[0] = B$ and $last(\beta^\sharp) \cap [\![\mathsf{e}]\!] \neq \emptyset$. Assume that $\beta^\sharp$ is spurious. We would like to find predicates to eliminate the spurious abstract path. The abstract path resolves both non-deterministic choice between different commands, and probabilistic choice between different updates. That enables us to use standard techniques developed in the non-probabilistic setting to find predicates. Here we employ interpolation and apply it to the path formulas along the lines of well-known abstraction refinement techniques [Henzinger et al., 2004] in software verification.

In a nutshell, interpolation admits to find compact expressions that reflect the reason why a path is spurious. By adding such expressions as predicates, spurious paths can be removed from the abstraction.

The idea is that a spurious path of length k can be split into two parts. There is a cut point, an index $j \in \{0, \ldots, k-1\}$. The path is split into a prefix that incorporates all steps until the cut point and a postfix consisting of the rest of the path. The reason why the path is spurious is reflected by the fact that *none* of the states at step j, the states reachable with the prefix, can execute the remaining postfix of the path.

We denote the prefix formula by ψ_j^- and the postfix formula by ψ_j^+. Using the notation for path formulas (Formula 7.2), we get prefix:

$$\psi_j^- := \mathrm{I}(\mathrm{X}_0) \wedge \left(\bigwedge_{0 \leq i \leq j} B[\mathrm{X}/\mathrm{X}_i] \right) \wedge \left(\bigwedge_{0 \leq i < j} \mathcal{R}_{c_i, u_i}(\mathrm{X}_i, \mathrm{X}_{i+1}) \right)$$

and postfix:

$$\psi_j^+ := \left(\bigwedge_{j < i \leq k} B[\mathrm{X}/\mathrm{X}_i] \right) \wedge \left(\bigwedge_{j \leq i < k} \mathcal{R}_{c_i, u_i}(\mathrm{X}_i, \mathrm{X}_{i+1}) \right) .$$

Obviously, since $TF(\beta^\sharp) = \psi_j^- \wedge \psi_j^+$ for every cutpoint $j \in \{0, \ldots, k-1\}$, the formulas $\psi_j^- \wedge \psi_j^+$ are unsatisfiable if the path is spurious.

An interpolant for the pair ψ_j^- and ψ_j^+ splits the states that can be reached with the prefix from the states that can execute the postfix.

In the general case, an interpolant of a pair of mutually exclusive formulas (ψ^-, ψ^+) is an expression in the common variables of ψ^- and ψ^+ that over-approximates ψ^- but is still mutually exclusive with ψ^+. Because an interpolant only contains common variables of both expressions, it provides a smaller witness of unsatisfiability of the conjunction $\psi^- \wedge \psi^+$ than ψ^- itself. For example, the expression $x > 0$ is an interpolant of the pair $(x = y \wedge y = 2, x \leq 0)$. To see this, observe that $x = y \wedge y = 2$ logically implies $x = 2$ and thus $x > 0$. Further the expressions $x \leq 0$ and $x > 0$ are mutually exclusive.

Definition 7.8 (Interpolant). *Let $\psi^- \in BExpr_I$ and $\psi^+ \in BExpr_I$ be Boolean expressions over the program variables. Assume that the conjunction of ψ^- and ψ^+ is unsatisfiable. An interpolant ϕ is an expression $\phi \in BExpr_I$ such that:*

- *ψ^- logically implies ϕ,*
- *the conjunction of ϕ and ψ^+ is unsatisfiable*
- *ϕ contains only variables that appear in both ψ^- and ψ^+.*

Interpolants fit nicely with predicate synthesis from path formulas. The shared variables of the prefix formula ψ_j^- and the postfix formula ψ_j^+ consists only in a single instance of the program variables, namely X_j, the instance of the program variables at time j. After substituting the variable instances, we obtain a well-formed predicate over the program variables X.

Observe that a single cut point j is in general not sufficient to eliminate a spurious path. To ensure elimination of a spurious path in the refined abstraction, we go through all cut points $j \in \{0, \ldots, k-1\}$, as proposed in [Henzinger et al., 2004].

Predicates to Separate Initial Blocks. Observe the case where no path in $\mathcal{C}$ is spurious but the realizable probability of the paths is lower than the probability threshold p, i.e., $\text{MAXSMT}(exp_1, \ldots, exp_n) \leq p$. In this case, the initial block B_0 may be too coarse. To this end, we choose the maximal solution obtained from MAXSMT. Let ψ^- denote the conjunction of non-satisfied exp_i, and ψ^+ denote the conjunction of satisfied exp_i. Obviously, $\psi^- \wedge \psi^+$ is not satisfiable. Hence interpolants can be found to refine the abstraction of the initial states.

7.1.3. Algorithm

Now we combine the ideas discussed in Section 7.1 thus far and come to one of the central results of this chapter: the probabilistic CEGAR algorithm.

Probabilistic CEGAR is an abstraction refinement technique that aims to decide if a given program fulfills a reachability property of the form $Reach_{\leq p}(\mathsf{e})$ (Definition 7.1). The pseudo-code is given by procedure CEGAR (Algorithm 2). Procedure CEGAR takes, as arguments, the program P to be verified, the specification of the goal states e, the probability threshold p and a set of initial predicates $\mathcal{P}$. The procedure returns *true* if it succeeds to prove the property. If the property could be refuted, it returns *false*. However, the general problem to check $Reach_{\leq p}(\mathsf{e})$ is undecidable, as proved in Lemma 7.10. Therefore the procedure may not terminate on certain problem instances.

The algorithm revolves around a refinement loop which terminates when the property has either been proved or refuted. First of all, an abstraction of the program is constructed (line 3) using the predicate-abstraction techniques of Chapter 6. From the obtained abstraction, we compute lower and upper bounds along with the corresponding strategies (lines 4 and 5).

Then the algorithm iterates over the different initial blocks to check the property (line 7). If the lower bound for an initial block is larger than the threshold p (condition in line 8), the property is refuted. On the other hand, if the upper bound is larger than p (condition in line 10), we continue (line 11) and select a counterexample (line 12).

After the iteration over the initial blocks, we check the Boolean flag *done* which indicates whether all initial blocks satisfy the property (condition in line 16). If they do, we can report that the property holds (line 17). Otherwise counterexample analysis is invoked (line 19) calling procedure CEXANALYSIS. If the counterexample is realizable (line 20), we have refuted the property and can report a violation (line 21).

Counterexample Analysis. The counterexample-analysis procedure CEXANALYSIS (Algorithm 3) tries to decide whether the counterexample is realizable or spurious. The arguments are the abstract game $\mathcal{G}$, an initial block B, a counterstrategy $\eta^\sharp$, the probability threshold p to be checked, the upper-bound valuation w^u and a reference to the current set of predicates $\mathcal{P}$. It may fail to decide realizability of a given counterexample due to the limit on the number of spurious paths. Unless CEXANALYSIS reports the counterexample to be realizable, it always adds predicates to the set $\mathcal{P}$ as a side effect.

Algorithm 2 Probabilistic CEGAR

1: **procedure** CEGAR(P, e, p, $\mathcal{P}$)
2:     **loop**   ▷ Refinement loop
3:         $\mathcal{G} \leftarrow$ ABSTRACT(P, $\mathcal{P}$, e)
4:         $(w^l, \sigma_1^l, \sigma_2^l) \leftarrow$ VALITER($\mathcal{G}, l$)   ▷ Lower bound
5:         $(w^u, \sigma_1^u, \sigma_2^u) \leftarrow$ VALITER($\mathcal{G}, u$)   ▷ Upper bound
6:         $done \leftarrow true$
7:         **for all** $v_{init} \in V_{init}$ **do**
8:                 **if** $w^l(v_{init}) > p$ **then**
9:                         **return** "False"
10:                **else if** $w^u(v_{init}) > p$ **then**
11:                         $done \leftarrow false$
12:                         $(B, \eta^\sharp) \leftarrow (v_{init}, (\sigma_1^u, \sigma_2^u))$ ▷ Pick a counterexample
13:                         **break**
14:                 **end if**
15:         **end for**
16:         **if** $done$ **then**
17:                 **return** "True"   ▷ Propery satisfied in $\mathcal{G}$
18:         **end if**
19:         $result \leftarrow$ CEXANALYSIS($\mathcal{G}, B, \eta^\sharp, p, w^u, \mathcal{P}$)
20:         **if** $result$ is "Realizable" **then**
21:                 **return** "False"
22:         **end if**
23:     **end loop**
24: **end procedure**

The basic idea of our counterexample analysis is the following. We maintain a sequence $\mathcal{C} = \langle \beta_1^\sharp, \beta_2^\sharp, ..., \beta_n^\sharp \rangle$ of abstract paths reaching an e-state in the Markov Chain induced by $(B, \eta^\sharp)$. An additional set $\mathcal{C}_{real} \subseteq \mathcal{C}$ contains realizable paths in $\mathcal{C}$. As illustrated in the diagram below, sequence $\mathcal{C}$ is ordered by decreasing probability mass – a longer bar means higher probability measure of the path; $\mathcal{C}$ is computed incrementally by a variant of best first search [Dechter and Pearl, 1985] in a weighted graph obtained from the Markov Chain, along the ideas of strongest evidence [Han and Katoen, 2007]. Initially $\mathcal{C}$ contains only the path with the highest probability, path $\beta_1^\sharp$.

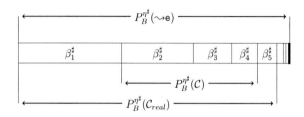

First we check if path $\beta_1^\sharp$ is realizable using Lemma 7.4 (in the diagram we assume $\beta_1^\sharp$ is spurious), and, if so, we add $\beta_1^\sharp$ to the set of confirmed paths $\mathcal{C}_{real}$. If enough "alleged" probability mass has already accumulated in $\mathcal{C}_{real}$ to exceed the threshold, i.e. $P_B^{\eta^\sharp}(\mathcal{C}_{real}) > p$, we check how much of that probability is actually realizable using Lemma 7.6. If the realizable probability mass exceeds the threshold, the property is refuted, since we can report a realizable counterexample. Otherwise we repeat the process with path $\beta_2^\sharp$, which has the second highest probability. We add $\beta_2^\sharp$ to $\mathcal{C}$, and check if it is realizable. If realizable, we add $\beta_2^\sharp$ to $\mathcal{C}_{real}$. We continue in this way until either we can refute the property, find out that the counterexample is spurious or bail out due to the spurious-path limit. In any of the latter cases, we proceed to predicate generation. The spurious-path limit $maxsp$ is set by the user, in the diagram we have $maxsp = 2$. If needed, predicates are generated from spurious paths or from weakest preconditions. Then the next iteration of the algorithm commences.

The pseudo-code is structured around an outer loop which enumerates paths with best-first search. The loop condition (line 5) checks if there still exists a path to enumerate. In the loop body, a path is generated (line 6) and added to the current set of abstract paths $\mathcal{C}$ (line 7). To decide if the current path is realizable, a path formula is constructed and checked for satisfiability (line 8).

If the path is realizable, it is added to $\mathcal{C}_{real}$ (line 9). We then check if the probability mass of the realizable paths already exceeds the threshold p (line 10). If this is not the case, we proceed to the next iteration of the outer loop (line 5). If it is the case, the MAXSMT procedure is used to determine the actual probability mass $mass$ (line 11). If the actual probability mass exceeds the threshold p (condition in line 12), we can report a realizable counterexample (line 13). If the actual probability is below, we generate predicates for the initial states (line 15), as described in Section 7.1.2. We then apply the spuriousness criterion of Lemma 7.6 (Lemma 16) to determine if the counterexample is spurious (line 17). If the criterion does not apply (line 19), the algorithm gives up (line 17). Note that the algorithm does not terminate "empty-handed" in this case, i.e., it generates a non-empty set of predicates.

If the path is spurious (line 23), the algorithm generates predicates in order to remove the path. To this end, we apply interpolation to the path formula. The loop over the different indices (line 24) applies interpolation to different cutpoints (line 25), as described in Section 7.1.2. Then we check if there is still enough probability to exceed the threshold value after subtracting the probability of the spurious paths $\mathcal{C} \setminus \mathcal{C}_{real}$ (line 27). If not, the counterexample is reported to be spurious (line 28). Otherwise we check if the number of spurious paths has been exceeded (line 29). If their number exceeds $maxsp$, we report that realizability of the counterexample could not be decided (line 30).

In the remainder of Section 7.1, we show correctness of the probabilistic CEGAR algorithm and explain why termination can in general not be guaranteed due to fundamental undecidability results.

Correctness

We prove correctness of probabilistic CEGAR (Algorithm 2) and its underlying counterexample analysis (Algorithm 3). Further, we prove that our counterexample analysis always terminates. Although the counterexample analysis cannot provide a complete decision procedure to check realizability of counterexamples, it always terminates with a useful result at any rate. Whenever the counterexample is either classified as spurious or gives up ("Don't know"), the counterexample analysis generates predicates to refine the abstraction. The overall probabilistic CEGAR algorithm cannot terminate on every input since the underlying verification problem is undecidable, which we also prove in this section.

Counterexample Analysis. The counterexample analysis inspects abstract counterexamples and reports whether or not they are realizable. The correctness of the realizability check hinges on Lemma 7.6:

Proposition 5 (Correctness of Counterexample Analysis). *If* CEXANALYSIS *returns "spurious" ("realizable") the counterexample* $(B, \eta^\sharp)$ *is spurious (realizable).*

Proof. The invariant of the outer loop is that variable $\mathcal{C}_{real}$ contains a set of abstract paths in the induced Markov chain. Paths added to the set $\mathcal{C}_{real}$ in line 7 are obtained by best-first search in the induced Markov chain (line 6). Hence the invariant is preserved.

The algorithm returns that the counterexample is realizable (line 12) under the condition that $\mathrm{MAXSMT}(TF(\beta^\sharp) \mid \beta^\sharp \in \mathcal{C}_{real}) > p$. Case (i) of Lemma 7.6 guarantees that this answer is correct. The value $\mathrm{MAXSMT}(TF(\beta^\sharp) \mid \beta^\sharp \in \mathcal{C}_{real})$ corresponds to $\mathrm{MAXSMT}(exp_1, \ldots, exp_n)$ in the lemma where the expressions $\mathbf{e}_i$ are the formulas $TF(\beta^\sharp)$ for $\beta^\sharp \in \mathcal{C}_{real}$.

Algorithm 3 Counterexample Analysis

1: **procedure** CEXANALYSIS$(\mathcal{G}, B, \eta^\sharp, p, w^u, \mathcal{P})$
2: $\quad maxsp \leftarrow 0$
3: $\quad \mathcal{C} \leftarrow \emptyset$
4: $\quad \mathcal{C}_{real} \leftarrow \emptyset$
5: $\quad$ **while** EXISTSPATH$(\mathcal{G}, \eta^\sharp, \mathcal{C})$ **do**
6: $\quad\quad \beta^\sharp \leftarrow$ NEXTPATH$(\mathcal{G}, \eta^\sharp, \mathcal{C})$
7: $\quad\quad \mathcal{C} \leftarrow \mathcal{C} \cup \{\beta^\sharp\}$
8: $\quad\quad$ **if** SAT$(TF(\beta^\sharp))$ **then** $\hfill \triangleright$ Realizable Path
9: $\quad\quad\quad \mathcal{C}_{real} \leftarrow \mathcal{C}_{real} \cup \{\beta^\sharp\}$
10: $\quad\quad\quad$ **if** $P_B^{\eta^\sharp}(\mathcal{C}_{real}) > p$ **then**
11: $\quad\quad\quad\quad mass \leftarrow$ MAXSMT$\{TF(\beta) \mid \beta \in \mathcal{C}_{real}\}$
12: $\quad\quad\quad\quad$ **if** $mass > p$ **then**
13: $\quad\quad\quad\quad\quad$ **return** "Realizable"
14: $\quad\quad\quad\quad$ **else**
15: $\quad\quad\quad\quad\quad \mathcal{P} \leftarrow \mathcal{P} \cup \{\text{INTERPOLANT}(\psi^-, \psi^+)\}$ $\hfill \triangleright$ Separate initial blocks
16: $\quad\quad\quad\quad\quad$ **if** $mass + w^u(B) - P_B^{\eta^\sharp}(\mathcal{C}_{real}) \leq p$ **then**
17: $\quad\quad\quad\quad\quad\quad$ **return** "Spurious"
18: $\quad\quad\quad\quad\quad$ **else**
19: $\quad\quad\quad\quad\quad\quad$ **return** "Don't know"
20: $\quad\quad\quad\quad\quad$ **end if**
21: $\quad\quad\quad\quad$ **end if**
22: $\quad\quad\quad$ **end if**
23: $\quad\quad$ **else** $\hfill \triangleright$ Spurious Path
24: $\quad\quad\quad$ **for all** $j \in \{1, \ldots, |\beta^\sharp| - 1\}$ **do**
25: $\quad\quad\quad\quad \mathcal{P} \leftarrow \mathcal{P} \cup \{\text{INTERPOLANT}(\psi_j^-, \psi_j^+)\}$ $\hfill \triangleright$ Remove spurious path
26: $\quad\quad\quad$ **end for**
27: $\quad\quad\quad$ **if** $w^u(B) - P_B^{\eta^\sharp}(\mathcal{C} \setminus \mathcal{C}_{real}) \leq p$ **then**
28: $\quad\quad\quad\quad$ **return** "Spurious"
29: $\quad\quad\quad$ **else if** $|\mathcal{C}| - |\mathcal{C}_{real}| = maxsp$ **then**
30: $\quad\quad\quad\quad$ **return** "Don't know"
31: $\quad\quad\quad$ **end if**
32: $\quad\quad$ **end if**
33: $\quad$ **end while**
34: $\quad$ **return** "Spurious"
35: **end procedure**

The algorithm reports that the counterexample is spurious under the condition that $mass + w^u(B) - P_B^{\eta^\sharp}(\mathcal{C}_{real}) \leq p$. Variable $mass$ equals $\text{MAXSMT}(TF(\beta^\sharp) \mid \beta^\sharp \in \mathcal{C}_{real}))$. Case (ii) of Lemma 7.6 guarantees correctness. Note that the upper bound $w^u(B)$ equals the probability $P_B^{\eta^\sharp}(\leadsto e)$ in the lemma.

If condition $w^u(B) - P_B^{\eta^\sharp}(\mathcal{C} \setminus \mathcal{C}_{real}) \leq p$ (line 27) is fulfilled the algorithm reports the counterexample to be spurious. The justification is that, for every $(s, \eta) \in \gamma((B, \eta^\sharp))$, we have $P_s^{\eta}(\leadsto e) \leq w^u(B) - P_B^{\eta^\sharp}(\mathcal{C} \setminus \mathcal{C}_{real})$. ∎

Counterexample analysis involves a non-trivial loop which enumerates paths of the induced Markov chain. Thus the question of termination arises, since the number of paths in a Markov chain may be infinite. The following proposition establishes termination of Algorithm CEXANALYSIS. Within probabilistic CEGAR, counterexample analysis is only invoked if the probability mass in the induced Markov chain is strictly larger than the threshold. Therefore we can use this assumption.

Proposition 6 (Termination of Counterexample Analysis). *Assume that the probability mass in the induced Markov chain is strictly larger than the threshold. Then Algorithm* CEXANALYSIS *terminates after finitely many steps.*

Proof. Consider the paths in the induced Markov chain. If the set of these paths is finite, the algorithm clearly terminates. Without loss of generality, we can therefore assume that there are infinitely many paths $\beta_0, \beta_1, \beta_2, \ldots$ which are indexed by natural numbers and ordered by descending probability mass.

We have $w^u(B) = \lim_{j \to \infty} \sum_{0 \leq i \leq j} P_B^{\eta^\sharp}(\beta_i)$. The probability $w^u(B)$ to reach the goal block in the induced Markov chain is larger than p. Thus there exists a $J \in \mathbb{N}$ such that $\sum_{0 \leq i \leq J} P_B^{\eta^\sharp}(\beta_i) > p$ (see also [Han, 2009, Lemma 3.6]).

We now define two constants K and L to carry out the termination proof.

Let $K \in \mathbb{N} \cup \{\infty\}$ be the smallest index such that the sum of the realizable paths β_i with $i \leq K$ is larger than the threshold p:

$$K := \min\{j \in \mathbb{N} \mid \sum_{\substack{0 \leq i \leq j \\ \beta_i \text{ realizable}}} P_B^{\eta^\sharp}(\beta_i) > p\} .$$

We set $K = \infty$ if and only if the sum of the *realizable* paths always remains smaller than p, so that K is well-defined even if the minimum does not exist.

For any given index $j \in \mathbb{N}$, let $M_j := \{\beta_i \mid 0 \leq i \leq j : \beta_i \text{ spurious}\}$ denote the set of spurious paths with index smaller equal to j.

Let $L \in \mathbb{N} \cup \{\infty\}$ be the minimal index such that there exist at least *maxsp* spurious paths with index smaller than L:

$$L := \min\{j \in \mathbb{N} \mid |M_j| \geq maxsp\} .$$

We define $L = \infty$ if and only if the number of *spurious* paths is smaller than *maxsp*. We distinguish different cases regarding the values of K and L.

Case $K \leq L$: If $K < \infty$ holds, condition $P_B^{\eta^\sharp}(\mathcal{C}_{real}) > p$ (line 10) becomes true after at most J paths and then $P_B^{\eta^\sharp}(\mathcal{C}_{real}) = \sum_{\beta \in \mathcal{C}_{real}} P_B^{\eta^\sharp}(\beta)$. Once this condition holds, the algorithm is guaranteed to terminate with either of the return statements in line 15, line 17 or line 19.

If $K = \infty$ holds, we have $L = \infty$ by the assumption that $K \leq L$. From $L = \infty$, it follows immediately that the number of spurious paths among the set of paths $\{\beta_i \mid i \in \mathbb{N}\}$ must be smaller than $maxsp$ and thus clearly finite. We denote the spurious paths by $M := \{\beta_i \mid i \in \mathbb{N} : \beta_i \text{ spurious}\}$. For sufficiently large n (where n is larger than the index of the last spurious path), we get:

$$\sum_{\substack{0 \leq i \leq n \\ \beta_i \text{ realizable}}} P_B^{\eta^\sharp}(\beta_i) = \sum_{0 \leq i \leq n} P_B^{\eta^\sharp}(\beta_i) - P_B^{\eta^\sharp}(M) . \qquad \boxed{7.11}$$

The right-hand side of Equation 7.11 converges and we get the limit:

$$w^u(B) - P_B^{\eta^\sharp}(M) = \lim_{n \to \infty} \sum_{0 \leq i \leq n} P_B^{\eta^\sharp}(\beta_i) - P_B^{\eta^\sharp}(M) . \qquad \boxed{7.12}$$

Because $K = \infty$ the left-hand side of Equation 7.11 is smaller or equal to p. Therefore, in combination with Equation 7.12, we get that:

$$w^u(B) - P_B^{\eta^\sharp}(M) \leq p . \qquad \boxed{7.13}$$

After several steps of the algorithm, we get $M = \mathcal{C} \setminus \mathcal{C}_{real}$ and the condition $w^u(B) - P_B^{\eta^\sharp}(\mathcal{C} \setminus \mathcal{C}_{real}) \leq p$ (line 27) becomes true thanks to Inequality 7.13.

Case $K > L$: The admissible number of spurious paths $maxsp$ is exceeded before enough probability mass can be accumulated to attain p. Therefore the condition in line 29 eventually becomes true and the algorithm terminates.

■

Probabilistic CEGAR.   If probabilistic CEGAR terminates, it correctly reports whether the reachability probability of a given program is bounded by the given threshold p:

Theorem 7.9 (Correctness of probabilistic CEGAR). *If Algorithm 2 returns "true", the program P satisfies the property $Reach_{\leq p}(e)$ and the property is violated if "false" is returned.*

Proof. We consider the different positions at which the algorithm reports property satisfaction or violation respectively. The proof obligation is to show that these answers are indeed correct.

To this end, we use Lemma 6.7, which shows that our program abstraction computes the menu-based abstraction of the program. In turn, Theorem 6.3 guarantees that menu-based abstraction yields lower and upper bound on the concrete reachability probability of the program. In addition, we need Proposition 5 which establishes the correctness of counterexample analysis.

- At line 9, the algorithm reports a property violation. The justification is that the lower bound computed from the game, already exceeds the threshold. Therefore the program violates the property.

- At line 17, the algorithm reports that the property holds if the upper bound obtained from the game is lower than the threshold. By correctness of the program abstraction, the actual reachability probability of the program must also be less or equal to p, Thus the property is indeed satisfied.

- At line 21, the algorithm reports a property violation. The counterexample analysis reports that the current counterexample is realizable. We can conclude that the answer is correct as a corollary of Lemma 5.

■

Termination of probabilistic CEGAR

Regarding termination of probabilistic CEGAR, observe that establishing thresholds on reachability probabilities is an undecidable problem as shown in Lemma 7.10. Therefore probabilistic CEGAR cannot terminate on every problem. We discuss a weaker progress property in Section 7.1.4.

Lemma 7.10. *The verification problem to check $Reach_{\leq p}(e)$ for any given program P and any probability threshold $p \in [0, 1)$ is undecidable.*

Proof. We re-use the construction of Lemma 7.7 which gives us a probabilistic program that simulates a two-counter machine. Recall that the program has a program counter pc. The predicate $pc = l_h$ corresponds to the halting state of the counter machine. The two-counter machine then halts if and only if the program violates the property $Reach_{\leq 0}(pc = l_h)$. Again it is easy to adapt the construction so that we reduce to a property of the form $Reach_{\leq p}(pc = l_h)$ for $p > 0$. ■

7.1.4. Progress

In this section, we discuss the progress achieved by a single step of the refinement loop.

The counterexample analysis either reports the counterexample to be realizable or produces predicates (provided that $maxsp > 0$). For a spurious path, an interpolant is computed from the path formula. In case of a realizable path, the algorithm may either be able to prove that the counterexample is realizable or the considered initial block can be split.

The addition of a predicate that splits a spurious path is guaranteed to eliminate the spurious path. The algorithm never inspects a spurious path more than once. First of all, the path-enumeration algorithm [Dechter and Pearl, 1985] produces pair-wise distinct paths in the Markov chain. Second, after a refinement iteration, predicates added to eliminate spurious guarantees that this path cannot re-occur:

Lemma 7.11 (Elimination of Spurious Paths). *Assume we are in the situation of Algorithm 3 line 23. Let $\beta^\sharp$ be the spurious path with*

$$\beta^\sharp = (B_0, a_0, u_0, \pi_0^\sharp)(B_1, a_1, u_1, \pi_1^\sharp) \ldots B_k .$$

Let $\mathcal{G}'$ be the refined game in the next iteration of probabilistic CEGAR. Then there exists no path:

$$\beta'^\sharp = (B_0', a_0, u_0, \pi'^\sharp_0)(B_1', a_1, u_1, \pi'^\sharp_1) \ldots B_k' .$$

with $B_i' \subseteq B_i$.

Proof. [Henzinger et al., 2004, Theorem 1] shows that the interpolants obtained from the path formula of a spurious path makes the best transformer precise enough to eliminate the path in the abstract (they call the best transformer "abstraction of the strongest postcondition"). Since we are computing best transformers for the individual commands, this is a sufficiently strong condition and the claim follows as a special case of this theorem.

■

Observe that the loop, which iterates over the different prefix and postfix pairs (ψ_j^-, ψ_j^+) in line 24 of Algorithm 3 is essential to ensure progress, as it is in general not sufficient to compute only the interpolant of a single pair to ensure elimination of a spurious path in the refined abstraction [Henzinger et al., 2004].

As a corollary of Lemma 7.11, a given counterexample cannot induce a spurious path that has previously been eliminated. If an initial block has been split, the next counterexample starts in a different block from which certain combinations of paths are not possible. The counterexamples therefore induce different Markov chains. In this sense, a given counterexample is eliminated by refinement.

In summary, the progress achieved by probabilistic CEGAR amounts to spurious-path elimination and splitting of initial blocks.

7.1.5. Conclusion

This section presented probabilistic CEGAR. We address for the first time the interplay of abstract and concrete counterexamples. Our solution to counterexample analysis involves MAX-SMT and other nontrivial components. The resulting approach constitutes the first running CEGAR implementation, and also works for infinite models. Like for predicate abstraction in software verification, the refinement loop of probabilistic CEGAR is not guaranteed to terminate due to undecidability of the verification problem. However, counterexample analysis is more involved than for conventional nonprobabilistic abstraction refinement. Checking realizability of counterexamples alone turns out to be an undecidable problem since counterexamples correspond to programs with loops.

7.2 Backward Refinement

Probabilistic CEGAR checks thresholds on reachability probability – it solves a decision problem. However, probability thresholds may not always be given. Instead, one may want to compute reachability probabilities of initial states of the program without giving a threshold beforehand. The backward refinement algorithm we present in this section approximates these probabilities successively. It takes as argument a desired precision ϵ and refines the partition until the bounds differ by less than ϵ.

The refinement algorithm is based on probability bounds and game strategies. Backward refinement splits blocks such that states that behave according to the lower-bound strategy are separated from those that behave according to the upper-bound strategy.

Outline of Section 7.2

This section is structured as follows:

Section 7.2.1 We describe how blocks are refined in backward refinement.

Section 7.2.2 We describe the complete refinement algorithm and give an example where we illustrate backward refinement.

Section 7.2.3 We formalize what is achieved by a single refinement iteration.

Section 7.2.4 We conclude the section.

7.2.1. Refining Blocks

Problem Statement. Assume that we have computed a menu game $\mathcal{G}$. Analysis of the game produces lower and upper bounds w^l and w^u respectively for the reachability probabilities w.r.t. to goal states F. Furthermore, there exist two pairs of corresponding optimal player 1 and player 2 strategies for the lower bound σ_1^l, σ_2^l and for the upper bound σ_1^u, σ_2^u respectively. We can assume that all these strategies are maps from vertices to vertices (they are memoryless and do not use randomization). For example, for $v_1 \in V_1$, we get $\sigma_1^l(v_1) \in V_2$ and $\sigma_1^l(v_2) \in V_p$.

The interesting case occurs when the bounds are too imprecise for some initial vertex $v_{init} \in V_{init}$, i.e., we have $w^u(v_{init}) - w^l(v_{init}) > \epsilon$. Then there is need to refine the abstraction. Technically backward refinement selects blocks where precision gets lost and refines them.

Pivot blocks. We call the blocks which are candidates for refinement *pivot blocks*. The question is which blocks should be refined to increase precision, i.e., to decrease the difference between lower bound and upper bound.

An initial idea would be to refine blocks where the difference between the bounds is large. Yet that alone is not a good criterion. For example, consider a block B where all neighboring blocks B' have trivial bounds, i.e., lower bound $w^l(B') = 0$ and upper bound $w^u(B') = 1$. The bounds for B are then also $[0, 1]$ independent of the behavior of B. Refining B would not increase precision, not even the bounds at block B. The actual cause for the deviation of the bounds does not lie at the block B itself but rather at its successor blocks. So what is a good criterion to select pivot blocks?

Our criterion to select pivot blocks is based on differences between the strategy for the lower bound from the upper-bound strategy. Game strategies admit to diagnose the cause for the deviation between the lower and the upper bound at a block.

However, we have to be careful which strategies we use. There can generally be many strategies that yield the same probability in a given stochastic game. For instance, there may be multiple strategies that achieve the upper-bound valuation in $\mathcal{G}$. Obviously, the differences between *these* strategies do not indicate where precision is lost.

This problem of unnecessary differences between strategies can be fixed by imposing constraints on the considered strategies. Without loss of generality, we can assume that the lower-bound and upper-bound strategies only take different choices if necessary, i.e., the upper-bound strategies σ_i^u only differ from the lower-bound strategies σ_i^l if the probability value for the lower-bound choice yields a smaller value [Chatterjee et al., 2006], i.e., $w^u(\sigma_i^l(v)) < w^u(v)$ for some game vertex $v \in V_i$. If there are deviations between the choices of *such* strategies, the strategies had to resolve the uncertainty introduced by abstraction in a different way to achieve the different bounds. To guarantee our assumption about game strategies in practice, strategies have to be computed in a proper way. We describe a suitable algorithm in Appendix B.

Remember that player 2 corresponds to the uncertainty introduced by abstraction. The criterion for a pivot block is that the optimal player 2 decisions differ.

Definition 7.12 (Pivot block). *Let $v \in V_1$ be a block that is reachable from some initial block. Let $v_2^l = \sigma_1^l(v)$ and $v_2^u = \sigma_1^u(v)$ be the player 1 decisions at v. Block v is a pivot block if the player 2 decisions $\sigma_2^l(v_2^l) \neq \sigma_2^u(v_2^u)$ are different.*

Clearly a sensible criterion for pivot blocks needs to be defined so that pivot blocks always exist whenever the precision of the abstraction is too low. The following lemma guarantees that this is indeed the case.

Lemma 7.13 (Existence of pivot blocks). *If the lower and upper bound deviate for an initial block v_{init} of the abstract game, i.e., $w^u(v_{init}) - w^l(v_{init}) > 0$, then there exists a pivot block v_{pivot} (in the sense of Definition 7.12).*

Proof. For the sake of contradiction, let us assume that there exists no pivot block. Then the game strategies agree. Since the strategies are optimal, the lower and upper bounds then are also the same. Contradiction! ∎

How to obtain predicates from pivot blocks. We define a function REFBLOCK that takes a pivot block as an argument and returns a set of predicates to refine the block. The predicate synthesis is based on the game strategies. Function REFBLOCK has a subroutine which works on player 2 vertices. This means that the subroutine refines the abstraction of commands. We compute predicates as follows:

$$\mathrm{REFBLOCK}(v_{pivot}) := \mathrm{REFBLOCK}(\sigma_1^l(v_{pivot})) \cup \mathrm{REFBLOCK}(\sigma_1^u(v_{pivot})) \,.$$

Note that $\sigma_1^l(v_{pivot})$ and $\sigma_1^u(v_{pivot})$ are player 2 vertices.

Now we define function REFBLOCK for player 2 vertices. Let $v_2 \in V_2$ be a player 2 vertex and let a_c be the action of the vertex v_2, i.e., $v_2 = (., a_c)$. As a shorthand, we let $v_p^l := \sigma_2^l(v_2)$ and $v_p^u := \sigma_2^l(v_2)$ denote the choices of the player 2 strategies for $v_2 \in V_2$. If there is no uncertainty from abstraction at v_2, i.e., if $v_p^l = v_p^u$ holds, we return the empty set of predicates. We set $\mathrm{REFBLOCK}(v_2) = \emptyset$.

If v_p^l or v_p^u is the star vertex $v_p^\star$, it is not clear from the abstraction whether or not the given command is enabled. In this case, REFBLOCK returns the guard of command c.

Otherwise, both v_p^l and v_p^u are ordinary distributions over blocks. By assumption that v_{pivot} is a pivot block, we know that the vertices v_p^l and v_p^u are distinct. The weights in the distributions must be the same, since the distributions are induced by command c. Being distinct and equipped with the same weights, the abstract distributions v_p^l and v_p^u must have different blocks in their support set. Hence there exists a probabilistic alternative i in the command a such that the corresponding blocks v_1 and v_1' differ, i.e., $v_p^l((a_c, i), v_1) = v_p^u((a_c, i), v_1') > 0$ (see Definition 4.4 and Definition 6.5). The two blocks are different and hence there is a predicate $\varphi \in \mathcal{P}$ where $v_1(\varphi) \neq v_1'(\varphi)$ (see Section 6.3.2). We return the weakest precondition of φ under the update $u = (a_c, i)$ of command a. Overall we have:

$$\mathrm{REFBLOCK}(v_2) := \begin{cases} \emptyset & ; \text{ if } v_p^l = v_p^u \\ \{\mathsf{g_c}\} & ; \text{ if } v_p^l = v_p^\star \text{ or } v_p^l = v_p^\star \\ \{\mathsf{WP}_u(\varphi)\} & ; \text{ if } v_p^l(u, v_1) = v_p^u(u, v_1') > 0 \text{ and } v_1(\varphi) \neq v_1'(\varphi) \end{cases}$$

where $v_p^l = \sigma_2^l(v_2)$ and $v_p^u = \sigma_2^u(v_2)$.

Proposition 7. *For a pivot block v_{pivot}, the set of predicates synthesized by REFBLOCK is non-empty:*

$$\mathrm{REFBLOCK}(v_{pivot}) \neq \emptyset \,.$$

Proof. Let $v_2^l = \sigma_1^l(v_{pivot})$ and $v_2^u = \sigma_1^u(v_{pivot})$ be the player 1 decisions at v_{pivot}. Because v_{pivot} is a pivot block the probabilistic vertices $\sigma_2^l(v_2^l) \neq \sigma_2^u(v_2^u)$ are different. If $v_2^l = v_2^u$ holds, we are done because a predicate will be synthesized from the chosen distributions. Let us assume that $v_2^l \neq v_2^u$. For at least one of the player 2 vertices v_2^l and v_2^u the choice of the optimal distribution differs, i.e., it cannot hold that $\sigma_2^l(v_2^l) = \sigma_2^u(v_2^l)$ and $\sigma_2^l(v_2^u) = \sigma_2^u(v_2^u)$. Otherwise $w^l(v_{pivot}) = w^u(v_{pivot})$ and therefore v_{pivot} cannot be a pivot. Hence predicates will be generated for at least one of the player 2 vertices. ∎

Algorithm 4 Backward refinement

1: **procedure** BACKREFINE($\mathsf{P}, \mathsf{e}, \epsilon, \mathcal{P}$)
2:     **repeat**
3:         done := false
4:         $\mathcal{G} :=$ ABSTRACT($\mathsf{P}, \mathcal{P}, \mathsf{e}$)
5:         $(w^l, \sigma_1^l, \sigma_2^l) :=$ VALITER($\mathcal{G}, l$)
6:         $(w^u, \sigma_1^u, \sigma_2^u) :=$ VALITER($\mathcal{G}, u$)
7:         **if** $\forall v_{init} :\ w^u(v_{init}) - w^l(v_{init}) < \epsilon$ **then**
8:             *done := true*
9:         **else**
10:             $v_{pivot} :=$ PIVOT($w^l, \sigma_1^l, \sigma_2^l, w^u, \sigma_1^u, \sigma_2^u$)
11:             $\mathcal{P} := \mathcal{P} \cup$ REFBLOCK(v_{pivot})
12:         **end if**
13:     **until** *done*
14:     **return** (w^l, w^u)
15: **end procedure**

7.2.2. Algorithm

The pseudo-code of the backward-refinement algorithm, procedure BACKREFINE, is shown in Algorithm 4. The procedure takes as input the program P to be analyzed, the expression that specifies the goal states e, the desired precision ϵ, and a set of initial predicates $\mathcal{P}$.

First the abstract game is constructed from the program using subroutine ABSTRACT. Then value iteration VALITER is executed for both the lower and the upper bound. Along with the bounds, the corresponding optimal strategies are computed. Then BACKREFINE checks if the desired precision has already been achieved. If so, the refinement loop is terminated. Otherwise a pivot block is computed using subroutine PIVOT. Thanks to Lemma 7.13, a pivot block exists. Then predicates are synthesized by REFBLOCK. The procedure starts with the next iteration of the refinement loop.

In the following example, we illustrate the backward-refinement algorithm.

Example. *Consider the program in Figure 4.1. We are interested in the maximal probability to reach $e := (m = 2)$. We set the desired precision to $\epsilon := 10^{-4}$.*

We start with predicates $m = 0$, $m = 1$, $m = 2$, $m = 3$ and $x \geq 1$. The corresponding program abstraction is shown in Figure 7.3a. The probability bounds computed by value iteration are annotated as intervals next to the blocks. To improve readability, singleton intervals are denoted by a single value, e.g., we write the singleton interval $[0.09, 0.09]$ as 0.09.

For the initial block in the game of Figure 7.3a, the lower bound is 0 and the upper bound is 0.3. The difference between lower and upper bound is higher than ϵ. Refinement has to be invoked. We now describe the refinement steps from the initial abstraction to the termination of the procedure. Pivot blocks are highlighted with a thick border and a gray *background:*

- *Step 1: Consider block $B = \{m = 1, x \geq 1\}$ in Figure 7.3a. The choices of the optimal strategy witness that B is a pivot. These choices are annotated next to the game vertices using the notation of Definition 7.12. Note that the player 1 vertices selected by the optimal strategies are equal in this example, which essentially means that the same command command is selected for both the lower and the upper bound. For block B, the strategies for player 2 however choose different distributions. More precisely, the difference in the chosen distributions lies in the probabilistic successor with weight 0.3 and update $x'=x-1$. The distribution corresponding to the lower bound goes to block $\{m = 1, x \geq 1\}$ and the distribution corresponding to the upper bound to block $\{m = 1, x < 1\}$. The blocks differ with respect to predicate $x \geq 1$. The weakest precondition of $x \geq 1$ with respect to update $x'=x-1$ is $\varphi := x \geq 2$. The predicate is added and we re-compute the abstraction. This leads to the abstract game in Figure 7.3b.*

- *Step 2: In the refined game, the pivot block from the previous iteration is split into blocks $\{m = 1, 1 \leq x < 2\}$ and $\{m = 1, x \geq 2\}$ with bounds $[0.3, 0.3]$ and $[0, 0.09]$ respectively. The latter block is a pivot and with a similar approach as for the previous step, we obtain predicate $\{x \geq 3\}$ and obtain the refined game in Figure 7.3c.*

Figure 7.3c shows the final game on which backward refinement terminates. The probability bounds of the initial block are $[0.09, 0.09]$. There are still blocks in the game with imprecise bounds. However, they do not influence the result for the initial block because we are considering maximal reachability and the bounds $[0, 0.027]$ of block $\{m = 1, x \geq 3\}$ show that this part of the state space contributes a lower probability. Therefore there is no need to refine these blocks.

7.2.3. Progress

We now discuss the progress achieved by a single iteration of backward refinement.

After a refinement step, the pivot block is split into several blocks. We formalize the progress of backward refinement at the state level. Within a pivot block, we consider the different states and their transitions. Given the lower and upper bounds, we can compute bounds for individual states within the block. This corresponds to two steps within the best transformer: a concretization of the abstract bounds is followed by the concrete transformer. From this point of view, we are then in the situation before the abstraction step, i.e., we obtain lower and upper bounds for the individual states. Backward refinement separates states achieving different bounds. This is the intuition behind the progress property, which we formalize and prove now.

Theorem 7.14 (Progress). *Let Q be the current partition. Let v_{pivot} be a pivot block. Assume that we have computed predicates $\text{REFBLOCK}(v_{pivot})$ and that Q' is the resulting partition that refines Q.*

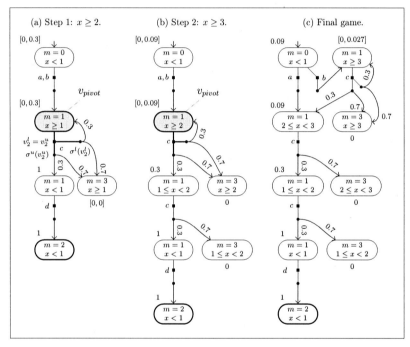

Figure 7.3.: Illustration of backward refinement.

Let w_Q^l and w_Q^u be the lower and upper bounds respectively with respect to partition Q. For any action a, we denote the concrete transformer for action a by pre_a. Further, we abbreviate by $w_a^l := (pre_a \circ \gamma_Q)(w_Q^l) \in [0,1]^S$ and $w_a^u := (pre_a \circ \gamma_Q)(w_Q^u) \in [0,1]^S$ the image of the lower and upper bounds, respectively, under function $pre_a \circ \gamma_Q$.

There exist states $s, s' \in p_{pivot}$ and action $a \in En(p_{pivot})$ such that

- $w^l(p_{pivot}) = w_a^l(s) < w_a^l(s')$ or $w^u(p_{pivot}) = w_a^u(s) > w_a^u(s')$
- s and s' are contained in distinct blocks of Q'.

Proof. Let $v_2^l = \sigma_1^l(v_{pivot})$ and $v_2^u = \sigma_1^u(v_{pivot})$ be the player 1 decisions at v. By assumption that v_{pivot} is a pivot block, the player 2 decisions $\sigma_2^l(v_2^l) \neq \sigma_2^u(v_2^u)$ are different. There are states $V_l \subseteq v_{pivot}$ in block v_{pivot} that behave according to $\sigma_2^l(v_2^l)$:

$$V_l := \left\{ s \in v_{pivot} \mid \sigma_2^l(v_2^l) = \overline{\pi_{s,a}} \right\},$$

and states $V_u \subseteq v_{pivot}$ behaving according to $\sigma_2^u(v_2^u)$:

$$V_u := \left\{ s' \in v_{pivot} \mid \sigma_2^u(v_2^u) = \overline{\pi_{s',a}} \right\}.$$

By construction, neither of the sets V_l and V_u is empty. Further, the states $s \in V_l$ fulfill $w_a^l(s) = w^l(p_{pivot})$, while the states $s \in V_u$ fulfill $w_a^l(s') = w^u(p_{pivot})$.

If $v_2^l = v_2^u$ holds, there is an action a picked by both the lower and the upper bound strategy, in the sense that $v_2^l = (v_{pivot}, a)$ and $v_2^u = (v_{pivot}, a)$. A predicate φ is synthesized with respect to action a. Without loss of generality[1] the states $\llbracket \varphi \rrbracket \subseteq S$ represented by predicate φ contain V_l and are disjoint with V_u, i.e., $V_l \subseteq \llbracket \varphi \rrbracket$ and $V_u \cap \llbracket \mathcal{P} \rrbracket = \emptyset$. This is a basic property of weakest preconditions. Adding the predicate means that states in V_l are not in the same block as states from V_u in the refined partition.

Let us assume that $v_2^l \neq v_2^u$. For at least one of the player 2 vertices v_2^l and v_2^u the choice of the optimal distribution differs, i.e., it cannot hold that $\sigma_2^l(v_2^l) = \sigma_2^u(v_2^l)$ and $\sigma_2^l(v_2^u) = \sigma_2^u(v_2^u)$ (otherwise $w^l(v_{pivot}) = w^u(v_{pivot})$ and therefore v_{pivot} cannot be a pivot). We can apply a similar argument as above to this player 2 vertex. ∎

Termination for Special Classes of Programs. In each refinement steps, blocks are split. For finite-state programs, backward refinement must therefore terminate. Beyond finite-state programs, termination of backward refinement can be shown for the more general class of programs with a finite bisimulation quotient. Let us sketch the proof, which works along the lines of [Henzinger et al., 2005b].

Bisimulation for MDPs is defined in [Baier, 1998]. It is easy to see that backward refinement splits only states that are not bisimilar. Furthermore, the progress property guarantees that at least one block is split per iteration of the refinement algorithm. Therefore, backward refinement must terminate if the bisimulation quotient is finite.

Regarding finite-state programs, the progress property of probabilistic CEGAR also guarantees termination, which can be proved with an analogous argument.

---

[1]There is also the symmetric case.

7.2.4. Conclusion

We have presented backward refinement, a refinement technique to approximate reachability probabilities of concurrent probabilistic programs. Backward refinement supports both minimal and maximal reachability probabilities. Backward refinement refines blocks where the abstraction loses precision, so-called pivot blocks.

The preceding Section 7.1 discussed a refinement technique to check reachability properties of the form $Reach_{\leq p}(\mathsf{e})$. The backward refinement algorithm can also be used to check such properties. The idea is to exchange the counterexample analysis in the probabilistic CEGAR algorithm with pivot-based backward refinement. The algorithm thus obtained is not able to refute properties based on counterexamples anymore. However, the lower bounds from the game can still be used for refutation.

Conversely, probabilistic CEGAR cannot replace backward refinement because it requires a threshold and it is constrained to maximal reachability properties.

A summary of the differences between probabilistic CEGAR and backward refinement will be given in Section 7.5.

7.3 Extension to Until Formulas

The presented refinement methods are geared towards probabilistic reachability. Beyond reachability, temporal logics admit to express more complex properties. We leave full support of logics like PCTL [Hansson and Jonsson, 1994, Bianco and de Alfaro, 1995] for future work. Instead we focus on a modest extension in this section. We discuss how abstraction refinement can be adapted to until formulas.

Compared to probabilistic reachability, an until formula is a stronger type of reachability. An until formula is of the form $\mathsf{e}_1 \, \mathcal{U} \, \mathsf{e}_2$ where e_1 and e_2 are predicates over the program variables. The semantics is that a path must eventually reach a goal state e_2 and, in the meantime, expression e_1 must hold until an e_2-state is reached. Formally, the until formula describes the paths:

$$\{\beta \in Path_B(\mathcal{M}) \mid \exists i \in \mathbb{N} : \beta[i] \in [\![\mathsf{e}_2]\!] \wedge \forall j \in \{0, \ldots, i-1\} : \beta[i] \in [\![\mathsf{e}_1]\!]\} \ .$$

Thus a reachability property $\leadsto \mathsf{e}$ corresponds to the until formula $true \, \mathcal{U} \, \mathsf{e}$.

Like for reachability, we can reason about the probability of this set of paths. Until formulas can be verified by a simple model transformation, whose correctness follows directly from the semantics of the until operator [Manna and Pnueli, 1995]. Before applying refinement, we remove all blocks that do not satisfy either of the predicates e_1 and e_2 from the game. In this way, the reachability probability in the modified game is exactly the probability of the paths specified by $\mathsf{e}_1 \, \mathcal{U} \, \mathsf{e}_2$ in the original game.

7.4 Related Work

We summarize related work in the area of probabilistic counterexamples and abstraction refinement for probabilistic models.

Probabilistic Counterexamples

There are two major temporal logics: linear temporal logic (LTL) [Pnueli, 1977] and computation-tree logic. Counterexamples witness that a property is violated and may be helpful in error diagnosis. Beside model checking algorithms, counterexample generation has been studied extensively in model checking of temporal logic [Clarke, 2008].

There are different notions and ways to represent counterexamples. What mathematical structure constitutes a counterexample largely depends on the kind of properties under consideration. For example, a counterexample for a safety property is a finite path that reaches an error state. For a liveness property, a counterexample is an infinite path that shows non-termination of a system. More sophisticated properties of temporal logic sometimes require more complex structures than paths, e.g. trees for the universal fragment of Computation-Tree Logic (CTL) [Clarke et al., 2002].

Extending classical temporal logics, probabilistic temporal logics have evolved. Among these there are probabilistic CTL (PCTL) [Hansson and Jonsson, 1994] and probabilistic LTL (PLTL) [Vardi, 1985]. Probabilistic temporal properties involve probabilistic operators that impose thresholds on the probability that a sub-formula is fulfilled.

In the probabilistic setting, the notion of a counterexample is quite involved, as it is not sufficient to show the presence or absence of a certain behavior – counterexamples need to convey information about probability mass. For example, in PCTL, one can specify that the probability to reach certain goal states is higher or lower than a certain threshold p. Unlike for safety or liveness properties in the non-probabilistic setting, single paths are not adequate as counterexamples, even for simple reachability properties. In general, a single path to a goal state typically does not carry enough probability mass to either prove or refute a probability threshold.

Probabilistic counterexamples are a relatively young and highly active area of research. We summarize several works in this area and outline the relationship to this thesis.

Counterexamples for Reachability Properties. Aljazzar *et al.* gave algorithms to obtain counterexamples against (timed) probabilistic reachability properties of continuous-time and discrete-time Markov chains [Aljazzar et al., 2005, Aljazzar and Leue, 2006]. The algorithms generate sets of paths by applying explicit-state search algorithms. The state exploration is thereby guided by heuristics that drive the search faster to a goal state.

PCTL Counterexamples. Han and Katoen studied counterexamples for a certain class of PCTL properties [Han and Katoen, 2007]. They propose to guide counterexample generation by probability mass. The paths that make up a counterexample are enumerated according to their significance, i.e., paths with higher probability first. This guarantees that the sets of paths are in some sense minimal counterexamples, while this is in general not the case for the approach in [Aljazzar et al., 2005, Aljazzar and Leue, 2006]. Han showed that, for Markov chains and reachability properties, the path-generation problem corresponds to a single-source shortest path problem [Eppstein, 1998]. Han *et al.* extended the strongest evidence idea to bounded reachability properties and gives more compact representations of paths by regular expressions [Han et al., 2009]

The notion of strongest evidence provides the first approach to generate minimal counterexamples for reachability properties of Markov chains. Probabilistic CEGAR employs this strongest evidence idea within counterexample analysis to enumerate abstract paths.

Chada and Viswanathan consider counterexamples against safe and live PCTL formulas [Chadha and Viswanathan, 2010]. In presence of nested formulas, Markov chains or sets of paths are insufficient representations for counterexamples. The authors propose that counterexamples should be MDPs as well. A counterexample is then some minimal sub-model of the original MDP that still violates the property. They give an algorithm that computes counterexamples. The algorithm iteratively reduces the MDP by non-deterministically choosing transitions to be deleted from the MDP. Depending on the non-deterministic choices, the reduction algorithm may produce different results.

Ábrahám *et al.* propose a PCTL model-checking algorithm for Markov chains which is able to produce counterexamples [Ábrahám et al., 2010]. Due to loops in Markov chains, the number of paths representing a counterexample can be very large. Therefore their algorithm takes into account strongly connected components (SCCs) in the Markov chain and uses Tarjan's SCC algorithm [Tarjan, 1972] to compute these SCCs. When counterexamples are returned the parts of a path within an SCC are folded. The algorithm can unfold these parts on demand. It would be interesting to investigate how folded counterexamples can be employed for counterexample analysis in the context of abstraction.

PLTL Counterexamples. Andres *et al.* study PLTL counterexamples in the style of Han and Katoen [Andrés et al., 2008], only for LTL rather than PCTL. Schmalz *et al.* address the challenge that counterexamples for a certain type of properties may not have a finite representation [Schmalz et al., 2009]. To circumvent this problem, the authors propose an interactive game between the user and the model checker that illustrates the cause of the violation to the user.

Counterexample Generation Using BMC. Traditionally, Bounded Model Checking (BMC) [Biere et al., 2003] aims at bounded properties, such as "no error state is reachable within k steps". Technically, to check if an error state is reachable, BMC constructs a formula by unrolling the transition relation of the model up to depth k. The formula is then checked using a SAT solver.

[Wimmer et al., 2009] proposes bounded model checking (BMC) of finite-state Markov chains. The approach targets bounded reachability properties, i.e., the probability to reach a set goal states within a certain step limit. While [Han and Katoen, 2007] assumes that the Markov chain is given by an explicit graph representation, Wimmer *et al.* start from a symbolic representation of the model. The paths are enumerated with a SAT solver. Here an off-the-shelf SAT solver is used which is not aware of probabilities. The approach thus cannot guarantee minimal counterexamples. To improve efficiency in the presence of loops, several optimizations are described that admit more compact representation of paths.

Summing up, bounded model checking admits counterexample generation for bounded reachability properties. The employed SAT-based enumeration has benefits if the state space is very large and an explicit graph representation of Markov chain as assumed in [Han and Katoen, 2007] is not available.

The question arises if BMC for Markov chains can be used in our setting, e.g., to carry out counterexample analysis. First of all, regarding efficiency, graph algorithms are more efficient for path enumeration than the techniques from [Wimmer et al., 2009] as induced Markov chains are already given explicitly as graphs. Regarding expressive power, Wimmer's BMC approach only supports a single initial state and paths of a fixed length. Further, their implementation is based on a SAT solver so that only finite-state models can be encoded. Overall, more work would be needed before BMC for Markov chains could be used in the context of probabilistic CEGAR.

Stochastic SMT. Satisfiability Modulo Theory solvers [Ganzinger et al., 2004] are decision procedures for formulas that involve Boolean combinations of quantifier-free terms in a decidable theory. SMT solvers are a very effective technique in the context of bounded model checking of software [Ganai and Gupta, 2007].

Fränzle and Teige present stochastic SMT, a technique that enables bounded-model-checking of probabilistic hybrid systems [Fränzle et al., 2008]. The backbone of the approach is a decision procedure for a stochastic logic. Stochastic SMT formulas consist of Boolean combinations of quantifier-free terms *and* randomized quantifiers. Randomized quantifiers associate sub-formulas with a certain probability.

By unrolling the transition relation of a given stochastic hybrid system, bounded-model-checking problems can be encoded as stochastic SMT formulas. The formulas are submitted to a stochastic SMT solver. The solver combines a theory solver for the arithmetic ground theory with a probabilistic variant of DPLL [Littman et al., 2001]. In this way, the approach generalizes conventional SMT solvers, which employ a Boolean DPLL engine [Ganzinger et al., 2004].

Summing up, stochastic SMT admits model checking for probabilistic hybrid systems up to a depth bound.

Regarding the use of stochastic SMT for counterexample analysis in our setting, several challenges arise. Due to the bounded nature of the approach, stochastic SMT can only be directly applied to acyclic Markov chains. For cyclic Markov chains, the depth bound could be increased incrementally. An interesting challenge would be to extend stochastic SMT with interpolation, in order to also generate predicates from spurious counterexamples.

Summary

The works mentioned in this section provide concepts and algorithms to deal with probabilistic counterexamples. None of these works consider counterexamples in the context of abstraction. We have discussed how these approaches could be fruitfully combined with probabilistic CEGAR to analyze abstract counterexamples. This may open up a new application domain for probabilistic counterexamples. In the next section, we discuss abstraction-refinement techniques for probabilistic models.

Abstraction Refinement

State explosion is a major challenge in (probabilistic) verification. Abstraction refinement has the potential to deal with large state spaces without sacrificing automation. Automatic abstraction refinement of probabilistic models is a vibrant area of research that has made tremendous progress in the last years. We summarize the different approaches and explain how they relate to our work.

Abstraction and Refinement of Probabilistic Systems. D'Argenio *et al.* introduced abstractions of MDPs. These abstractions admit to compute lower bounds on minimal and upper bounds on maximal reachability probabilities [D'Argenio et al., 2001, D'Argenio et al., 2002]. Technically, a quotient MDP is built from a given MDP and a state partition. The resulting MDP is analyzed to get the desired bounds.

In addition to quotient MDPs, initial ideas for refinement strategies are described. The authors explain that refining certain blocks cannot improve precision. The selection of blocks is left open as an implementation decision. In later refinement algorithms, this selection is guided by diagnostic information. Diagnostic information is thereby obtained from abstract counterexamples [Hermanns et al., 2008] or deviations between probability bounds [de Alfaro and Roy, 2007, Kattenbelt et al., 2009, Wachter and Zhang, 2010].

Their quotient construction also appears in subsequent works [Wachter et al., 2007, Hermanns et al., 2008, Chadha and Viswanathan, 2010]. In this thesis, however, we use an abstraction based on stochastic games (see Chapter 6) so that lower *and* upper bounds can be obtained for both minimal and maximal reachability probabilities.

Counterexample-Guided Planning. Chatterjee *et al.* develop abstraction refinement in the context of certain planning problems which map to reward properties of stochastic games [Chatterjee et al., 2005]. The approach supports discounted rewards and long-run average rewards.

As a basis for the abstraction of stochastic games, the paper proposes a quotient construction that maps stochastic games to a quotient stochastic game based on a state partition. The quotient construction guarantees that if player 1 has a strategy to achieve a reward with value r in the abstract game, player 1 can also achieve reward r in the original game. The abstraction thus yields lower bounds on rewards.

The paper describes an abstraction refinement algorithm that applies to two-player stochastic games with rewards. The goal is to check the property whether player 1 can achieve at least reward r. The algorithm takes as input a stochastic game and a real value r. If player 1 can achieve value r in the abstract, the property is fulfilled. Otherwise an abstract spoiling strategy for player 2 exists. If the abstract spoiling strategy is realizable, i.e. corresponds to a concrete strategy, the property can be refuted. The algorithm checks if the abstract counterexample is realizable. The abstract game is refined if no concrete strategy can be synthesized. The check if a counterexample is realizable is based on an explicit graph representation of the original stochastic game. It is not explained how to extend this to a symbolic approach for large or even infinite-state spaces. Further the method has yet to be evaluated in practice.

Wrapping up, counterexample-guided planning is an abstraction refinement method for finite stochastic games with rewards.

To handle infinite-state games with rewards, it may be interesting to extend our abstract refinement approach to MDPs with rewards or even games with rewards.

Magnifying-Lens Abstraction. Magnifying-lens abstraction is an abstraction refinement algorithm for finite-state MDPs which computes lower and upper bounds on reachability probabilities [de Alfaro and Roy, 2007]. The algorithm also directly computes safety probabilities. Safety probabilities can also be obtained by computing corresponding reachability probabilities (this follows, e.g., from determinacy results for games [de Alfaro and Majumdar, 2004]). Therefore safety does not add expressive power. The algorithm maintains a partition of the state space. For each block in the partition, the algorithm saves a lower and an upper probability bound. Blocks are refined if the difference between lower and upper bound exceeds a user-specified amount. To recompute the probability bounds after a refinement step, the algorithm carries out a so-called magnification step. Magnification concretizes the states in a block and traverses their transitions – either explicitly [de Alfaro and Roy, 2007] or using decision diagrams [Roy et al., 2008]. Using the transitions and the probability bounds of neighboring blocks, the probability bounds are computed in a local fixed-point computation (fixed-point computation is needed due to loops). Due to the magnification step, the algorithm is limited to finite-state MDPs. The magnifying-lens algorithm has $\sqrt{8 \cdot |S|}$ as a lower bound on the space complexity where $|S|$ is the cardinality of the state space.

Magnifying lens abstraction provides a memory-saving alternative to conventional value-iteration algorithms for finite-state MDPs. Conventional value iteration tends to be faster if the MDP and the iteration vector fit into main memory.

Abstraction Refinement for Probabilistic Software. Kattenbelt *et al.* propose an abstraction-refinement technique for probabilistic C programs [Kattenbelt et al., 2009].

Their technique is based on game-based abstraction [Kwiatkowska et al., 2006], predicate abstraction and backward refinement. We have already discussed the relationship between their and our predicate-abstraction technique in Section 6.4. Section 7.2 was inspired by their backward refinement procedure [Kattenbelt et al., 2009]. A major difference is that we consider concurrent programs where different commands can be simultaneously enabled. We limit refinement to a particular command.

In their line of work, the notion of progress has not yet been addressed. We conjecture that backward refinement for game-based abstraction admits a stronger progress property than in presence of menu-based abstraction (Section 7.2.3).

Both their and our backward-refinement methods do not produce or use counterexamples. Probabilistic CEGAR, on the other hand, is based on counterexamples and can thus provide diagnostic information explaining the cause of violation.

Abstraction Refinement for Probabilistic Timed Automata. Extending the game-based abstraction approach, Kwiatkowska also propose an abstraction refinement technique that aims at probabilistic timed automata [Kwiatkowska et al., 2009]. Analogously to game-based abstraction for MDPs [Kwiatkowska et al., 2006], the abstraction of probabilistic timed automata maps to stochastic games, so that lower and upper bounds on reachability probabilities can be obtained from the abstraction. The state-space abstraction is given by clock constraints, the special type of predicates commonly used in the context of timed automata. Abstraction refinement potentially introduces fewer clock constraints than the full region abstraction.

The idea of game-based abstraction is combined with the region abstraction for timed automata. The refinement strategy works along the lines of game-based predicate abstraction for probabilistic software [Kattenbelt et al., 2009].

The state-space abstraction based on clock constraints is only a covering rather than a disjoint partition, as clock constraints may overlap. It may be interesting to extend our framework so that general coverings are supported.

Counterexample-Guided Abstraction Refinement Framework for MDPs. Aiming at MDPs, Chada and Viswanathan consider abstraction refinement for safe PCTL. They use the MDP-based quotient construction [D'Argenio et al., 2001] as abstract models. Refinement relies on the construction of a probabilistic simulation relation between states of the concrete MDP and the abstract counterexample MDP. Constructing such a simulation relation could be rather expensive and precludes treatment of infinite-state models. The method has yet to be implemented and evaluated in practice.

As already discussed, Chada and Visnwanathan investigate counterexamples for MDPs and fragments of PCTL. They leverage counterexamples for an abstraction-refinement algorithm for finite MDPs and safe PCTL.

finite-state techniques		
technique	input models	properties
[D'Argenio et al., 2002]	finite MDP	$p^-(F) \geq p,\, p^+(F) \leq p$
[Chatterjee et al., 2005]	finite stoch. game	$r^{+-} \geq p$
[de Alfaro and Roy, 2007]	finite MDP	$p^{\{-,+\}}(F)$
[Chadha and Viswanathan, 2010]	finite MDP	safe PCTL
infinite-state techniques		
technique	input models	properties
[Hermanns et al., 2008]	concur. programs	$p^+(F) \leq p$
[Kattenbelt et al., 2009]	seq. programs	$p^{\{-,+\}}(F),\, r^{\{-,+\}}$
[Kwiatkowska et al., 2009]	PTA	$p^{\{-,+\}}(F)$
Probabilistic CEGAR (Section 7.1)	concur. programs	$p^+(F) \leq p$
Backward Refinement (Section 7.2)	concur. programs	$p^{\{-,+\}}(F)$

Legend:

$p^-(F)$	minimal reachability probability (to goal states F)
$p^+(F)$	maximal reachability probability (to goal states F)
r^-	minimal reward
r^+	maximal reward

Figure 7.4.: Overview of abstraction-refinement methods for probabilistic models.

Summary

Let us outline the distinguishing aspects of our work. The refinement techniques presented in this chapter are the first ones applicable to infinite-state concurrent probabilistic programs. A further novelty is the use of counterexample-guided abstraction for infinite-state probabilistic programs. This admits both proof and refutation of properties supplemented with diagnostic information.

To wrap up the section, Figure 7.4 gives an overview of all the probabilistic abstraction-refinement techniques. The techniques can be put into different categories according to which models (column: models) and properties they support (column: properties).

1. **models**: The types of models include finite MDPs, stochastic games, probabilistic timed automata, sequential probabilistic programs and concurrent probabilistic programs. The abstraction-refinement techniques limited to finite MDPs and stochastic games rely on the construction of the original model. This, however, precludes the treatment of infinite-state systems such as sequential and concurrent programs. The alternative symbolic approach consists in constructing the abstraction at the language level using decision procedures.

2. **properties**: Probabilistic reachability, denoted by reachability in Figure 7.4, is the pre-dominant kind of property. [de Alfaro and Roy, 2007] additionally supports probabilistic safety, the dual of probabilistic reachability. [Chatterjee et al., 2005]

and [Kattenbelt et al., 2009] consider rewards.

All techniques are based on state partitioning. Partitions are represented in different ways. The finite-state methods represent block by storing the individual states either explicitly or in variants of binary decision diagrams [Bryant, 1985]. To support larger state spaces, predicate abstraction is used in our work and [Kattenbelt et al., 2009]. For timed systems, region abstraction can be employed [Kwiatkowska et al., 2009].

7.5 Conclusion

In this chapter, we have explored abstraction refinement for concurrent probabilistic programs. We have both investigated foundational questions, e.g., what constitutes an abstract probabilistic counterexample, and presented two refinement techniques that automatically verify reachability properties.

The first refinement technique, probabilistic CEGAR, verifies thresholds on *maximal* reachability probabilities producing either proofs or refutations. Probabilistic CEGAR is based on probabilistic counterexamples, which correspond to a potentially cyclic Markov chain or infinitely paths, unlike in the non-probabilistic setting, where a counterexample is typically a single path. This makes counterexample analysis very difficult: we have proved that the problem of checking realizability for probabilistic counterexamples is undecidable using a reduction to two-counter machine.

To deal with probabilistic counterexamples, probabilistic CEGAR enumerates paths with decreasing probability mass and extracts predicates from spurious paths. In this way, predicates are obtained and properties are refuted by computing lower bounds on the reachability probability. Although realizability is undecidable, we obtain an effective refinement procedure: if the analysis detects a spurious counterexample *or* fails to decide realizability, a predicate to refine the abstraction is returned in any case.

The other refinement technique, backward refinement, computes lower and upper bounds for *both* minimal and maximal reachability probabilities without requiring a threshold. Rather than considering paths, backward refinement inspecting the game strategies and identifies pivot blocks where the abstraction loses information. Pivot blocks are split according to predicates obtained from weakest preconditions. Backward refinement does not employ a full-fledged counterexample analysis, it only produces predicates but no refutations or more precise bounds. Diagnostic information and bounds follow directly from local inspection of the abstract game.

There are significant differences between the two refinement techniques. Probabilistic CEGAR is restricted to maximal probabilistic reachability, whereas backward refinement supports both minimal and maximal reachability. Thus backward refinement can be used to check thresholds on the maximal reachability probability instead of probabilistic CEGAR. However, backward refinement relies entirely on bounds obtained from the abstract game, so that probabilistic CEGAR may produce refutations faster based on potentially tighter lower bounds obtained from counterexample analysis.

Regarding computational cost, probabilistic CEGAR employs a heavy-weight counterexample analysis, which analyzes a potentially very large number of abstract paths and combines information about paths using non-trivial MAX-SMT procedures. In comparison, backward refinement discovers predicates with a light-weight analysis that runs in linear time with respect to the abstract game.

The remainder of the thesis investigates how effective the two refinement techniques are in practice and how they compare to each other. In the next chapter, we describe their implementation and give an experimental evaluation.

8

Abstraction in Practice

To provide effective tool support for the analysis of concurrent probabilistic programs, the machinery proposed in previous chapters has been implemented in the tool PASS, which stands for Predicate Abstraction for Stochastic Systems. In this section, we present the tool including implementation details and optimizations. Then we report on experiments that assess the proposed abstraction refinement techniques. We have applied PASS to verify network protocols. Some of the considered case studies are entirely beyond the reach of previous methods due to infinite state spaces.

Part of this material has appeared in previous publications [Hermanns et al., 2008, Wachter and Zhang, 2010]. In [Hahn et al., 2010b], we have published a description of PASS. The tool and the case studies are available at:

http://d.cs.uni-saarland.de/tools/pass/

Outline. The chapter is structured as follows:

Section 8.1 We introduce PASS including its input language and architecture.

Section 8.2 We describe case studies from the area of network protocols.

Section 8.3 We present present experimental results.

Section 8.4 We conclude the chapter and summarize results.

8.1 PASS

This section describes our implementation PASS. First, we cover the input language and properties. Then we give an overview of the architecture of the tool and describe its components one by one in more detail.

Input Language. One of the largest collections of case studies in the area of probabilistic verification is probably the PRISM repository [Kwiatkowska et al., 2010]. Therefore the input language of PASS strives for compatibility with the PRISM language, i.e., it offers modules, synchronization, guarded commands, variable declarations and declaration of formulas. Regarding variable types, PASS admits unbounded integer variables and real variables, in addition to the bounded integers in the PRISM language. On the other hand, process algebra operators are currently not implemented in PASS. The full language is internally reduced to the core language of concurrent probabilistic programs presented in Chapter 4. More details of this reduction are given in the description of the PASS front end.

Properties.   PASS verifies probabilistic reachability properties and more general until[1] formulas. We now describe the property language in more detail and explain how the different properties map to the refinement techniques inside the tool.

Properties are denoted in the syntax of Probabilistic Computation-Tree Logic (PCTL) [Hansson and Jonsson, 1994, Bianco and de Alfaro, 1995], although the tool does not support full PCTL. Thereby paths are characterized by until formulas, which specify the goal states by an expression e_2 and additionally require that another expression e_1 is fulfilled along the way to the goal states. Internally, PASS reduces the verification problem for until properties to a probabilistic reachability problem using the method sketched in Section 7.3. Like for probabilistic reachability, there is a minimal and a maximal variant. Thus properties are specified by until formulas of the form:

$$Pmin_{\lhd p}(e_1 \; \mathcal{U} \; e_2) \tag{8.1}$$

$$Pmax_{\lhd p}(e_1 \; \mathcal{U} \; e_2) \; . \tag{8.2}$$

where $Pmin$ refers to minimal and $Pmax$ to maximal reachability. Operator $\lhd p$ either imposes a bound or represents a query to compute this probability:

- if $\lhd \; = \leq$, an upper bound is to be checked,
- if $\lhd \; = \geq$, a lower bound is to be checked,
- similarly for the strict inequalities.
- if $\lhd \; = ?$, this corresponds to a query.

For the queries $Pmin_{=?}(e_1 \; \mathcal{U} \; e_2)$ and $Pmax_{=?}(e_1 \; \mathcal{U} \; e_2)$, PASS computes probabilities rather than giving a Boolean answer.

Backward refinement is available for all of these variants of until formulas. Technically it computes probability intervals for the initial vertices. The user provides a precision ε. For the Boolean queries, PASS terminates as soon as the lower and upper bounds are precise enough to decide the property up to the given precision. For qualitative queries, PASS terminates as soon as the lower and upper bounds differ by less than ε.

Probabilistic CEGAR is available for properties of the form $Pmax_{\leq p}(e_1 \; \mathcal{U} \; e_2)$. Note that these properties subsume reachability properties of the reachability properties of form $Reach_{\leq p}(e)$ treated in Section 7.1. Probabilistic CEGAR terminates as soon as it is either able to refute or prove the property.

---

[1] As we have shown in Section 7.3, the presented refinement techniques easily generalize from probabilistic reachability to until formulas.

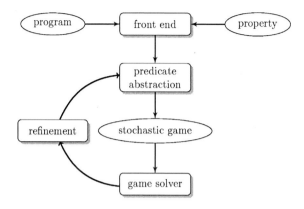

Figure 8.1.: Architecture of PASS.

Architecture

The architecture of PASS revolves around a refinement loop, which is depicted in Figure 8.1. In the remainder of Section 8.1 we explain the different analysis phases:

Section 8.1.1 The front end reads in program and property performing several transformations. The resulting verification problem is passed to the analysis engine.

Section 8.1.2 The first analysis step is to compute the abstraction of the program with respect to the current set of predicates. Initially predicates are extracted from the property and the guards. The abstraction of a program is a stochastic game.

Section 8.1.3 To obtain lower and upper bounds, we solve the stochastic game. Along with the bounds, corresponding optimal game strategies are computed.

Section 8.1.4 If the bounds are too imprecise, the abstraction-refinement techniques from Section 7 are used to refine the abstraction. Refinement is based on the probabilities and game strategies obtained by solving games.

8.1.1. Front End

The front end of PASS consists of a parser and program transformations, which are described in this section.

Reduction to Core Language. Input programs are typically structured into different modules. To arrive at concurrent probabilistic programs, the front end flattens the model, i.e., it transforms the module structure into a single module. To this end, synchronization between different commands is resolved.

We use a model transformation that follows the semantics of synchronization in the PRISM language. That is, when commands synchronize on the same event all of these commands fire simultaneously. In the transformation, these commands are then combined into a single combined command. Commands in the same module that synchronize on the same event induce non-determinism, i.e., one command is chosen non-deterministically per module. As a result, a synchronization may induce different combined commands corresponding to the possible combinations of synchronizing commands from different modules.

The guard of a combined command consists of the conjunction of the guards of the synchronizing commands that induce it. PASS checks the satisfiability of this guard and discards the command if the guard is unsatisfiable. The satisfiability checks for combined commands are discharged by the default SMT solver, YICES.

Implementation. We implemented the front end in C++. The parser of the front end is automatically generated from a context-free grammar using the GNU parser generator Bison [GNU, 1998]. The front end has been tested on a large number of examples including many examples from the PRISM website and it is also used in the sister tools of PASS: INFAMY [Hahn et al., 2009] and PARAM [Hahn et al., 2010a]. We did not re-use the parser in the PRISM model checker as it is written in Java and is tailored to PRISM's backend engines.

8.1.2. Program Abstraction

As described in Section 6.3, we obtain predicate abstractions by SMT-based enumeration. In this section, our focus is on efficient representation of the abstraction, implementation details and optimizations.

To speed up SMT-based enumeration, we leverage incremental SMT solving. This means that lemmas and constraints are kept while a command or an expression is being abstracted, rather than re-starting from scratch after having enumerated an abstract transition or block. To this end, PASS is linked against the SMT solver engine, so that the SMT solver can retain its state during the abstraction process.

In addition to incremental SMT solving, we employ problem-specific optimizations to reduce the number of enumeration steps. One of the underlying observations is that, although n predicates define a partition with 2^n blocks, many of those blocks are not interesting because they are unreachable from the initial blocks and thus do not have an impact on the reachability probability of initial blocks. Therefore, PASS computes the abstraction on the fly starting with initial blocks and adds layers of blocks in a breadth-first manner. Thus only abstract transitions of reachable blocks are added. In this way, the program is abstracted to a game which is constructed from these abstract transitions (see Section 6.3.4). As a post-processing step, we also remove blocks which are reachable from the initial blocks but cannot reach a goal block. This can be implemented by a backward reachability analysis from the goal blocks.

We use the CUDD library [Somenzi, 2009] to compactly store sets of reachable blocks, abstract transitions and games in binary decision diagrams (BDDs) [Bryant, 1985]. BDDs lend themselves as a representation, since blocks are defined by Boolean predicate valuations. Thus each predicate corresponds to a BDD variable. After a refinement step, new BDD variables are created for the fresh predicates. Since we also need to store distributions, there is a fixed number of Boolean variables that encode probabilistic choices within a distribution. Additionally, non-deterministic choices resulting from both the abstraction and the non-determinism in the original program are encoded by Boolean variables. Our encoding of games is an extension[2] of the MDP encoding proposed in [de Alfaro et al., 2000].

In the next section, we discuss how lower and upper bounds are computed from the obtained games.

8.1.3. Solving Games

In this section, we discuss how we solve games in order to obtain lower and upper bounds as well as game strategies.

Stochastic games can be solved by strategy iteration [Chatterjee et al., 2006]. Strategy iteration improves an initial game strategy until an optimal strategy has been found. To assess the current strategy, strategy iteration analyzes the Markov chain induced by it and computes reachability probabilities in that Markov chain. Overall, strategy iteration yields an exact method, if we use an exact method to obtain reachability probabilities for Markov chains, e.g., linear programming. However, instead of strategy iteration, PASS employs a more efficient approximate method, called value iteration, like other probabilistic verification tools [Katoen et al., 2009, Hinton et al., 2006].

Value iteration is an iterative method to approximate fixed points of valuation transformers. For a given valuation transformer f and a start valuation w, value iteration performs Kleene iteration, i.e. it computes the sequence $w_i := f^i(w)$. However, since the lattice of valuation is infinitely high, Kleene iteration is not guaranteed to terminate. PASS takes as a parameter a precision δ and stop the fixed-point iteration as soon the difference between old iteration vector and new iteration vector differ by less than δ.

Convergence properties of value iteration for games and correctness of the obtained game strategies are proved in [Chatterjee et al., 2006]. Although the employed methods to solve games are well-known in probabilistic verification, we briefly sketch the algorithms implemented in PASS in Appendix B for the sake of completeness.

Wrapping up, we obtain bounds and strategies by value iteration. These results are subsequently used by the refinement phase, which we describe in the next subsection.

---

[2] Except that we use BDDs rather than MTBDDs. The reason is that probabilities are determined by the commands. Hence there is no reason to store them with each abstract transition.

8.1.4. Refinement

In this section, we discuss how refinement is implemented in PASS.

Probabilistic CEGAR. Probabilistic CEGAR involves path analysis. Interpolation is used to obtain predicates from spurious paths. To that end, PASS interfaces with the MATHSAT SMT solver [Bruttomesso et al., 2008]. Further, counterexample analysis combines information from different paths using MAXSMT procedures. The required machinery is implemented in the YICES SMT solver [Dutertre and de Moura, 2006].

Backward Refinement. Now we discuss implementation choices regarding backward refinement and present an enhancement of backward refinement which uses path-analysis techniques in the style of probabilistic CEGAR. This enhancement can lead to much better performance in practice.

In general, a game can contain multiple blocks that qualify as a pivot. PASS does not refine all of them at once. Instead it uses a policy to choose from these blocks. We choose with maximal deviation between lower and upper bound. We have experimented with criteria involving the distance of the pivot block from the goal vertices. However, no significant differences could be observed. We leave the exploration of more sophisticated criteria to future work.

We have already discussed an optimization for program abstraction that deals with unreachable blocks. Yet, even (abstractly) reachable blocks may not contain a single reachable *state*, meaning that there exists no concrete path to any of the states in a block. We call a block that does not contain any reachable *state* a dead block. In the abstract game, dead blocks may be reachable from an initial block via an abstract path, so that a dead block can become a pivot block.

By default a dead pivot block is split. However, it seems preferable to refine the abstraction so that a dead block becomes unreachable in the refined abstract game as well. This requires a modification that deviates from the pure backward refinement algorithm.

The reachability check for a given block corresponds to safety verification and is thus undecidable in general. Therefore, we employ a semi-decision procedure that is able to identify certain blocks containing reachable states but is not guaranteed to discover all of them. To this end, we construct a path from the initial block to the pivot block. We check if this abstract path is realizable. Technically, we construct the path formula (as in Section 7.1.1) and check its satisfiability. If the path is realizable, the block is definitely not dead. If the path is spurious, the block may be dead. Note that there could nevertheless be a state in the block that is reachable via a different path than the selected path. At any rate, we obtain predicates like in probabilistic CEGAR.

The verification tool for probabilistic C programs described in [Kattenbelt et al., 2009] also employs dead-block elimination.

8.1.5. Conclusion

PASS uses external libraries for SMT solving, interpolation and symbolic data structures. The code base of PASS consists of about 18.000 lines of C++ source code. In this section, we have discussed the abstract refinement loop within PASS and several optimizations. In the coming section, we will evaluate PASS based on case studies from the area of network protocols.

8.2 Case Studies

In this section, we present case studies from the area of network protocols. We briefly wrap up the motivation for studying these models and describe properties of interest to give the reader an idea of the application domain of PASS. The case studies are mostly taken from the PRISM web repository [Kwiatkowska et al., 2010] and have been described in several publications.

IEEE 802.3 CSMA/CD Protocol (CSMA). The CSMA/CD protocol (Carrier Sense Multiple Access with Collision Detection) is an asynchronous access protocol for computers that send messages via a shared transmission medium. The protocol is mainly used in Ethernet networks and is defined in the IEEE standard 802.3.

The protocol works as follows. A station desiring to transmit first senses the medium. If the medium is busy (another station is transmitting), the station defers the transmission. If the medium is sensed free, the station can transmit. There is a chance that a collision occurs, i.e., multiple stations transmit simultaneously because they sensed the medium free and decided to transmit.

If a station would resume the transmission at once after a collision, this could result in another collision immediately. Therefore, stations should defer their transmission by different delays, i.e. they should not send at the same rate.

To this end, a station involved in a collision picks a random number z from the interval $\{0, \ldots, 2^{bc} - 1\}$ where bc (backoff counter) is the number of collisions that have occurred during the current transmission. The station waits for a time span given by z multiplied with the package transmission time, and then sends again if the medium is free.

Since the number of possible delays grows exponentially after each collision, it is very unlikely that collisions occur repeatedly. Nevertheless, a transmission may still fail. CSMA/CD is parameterized with a maximal number of collisions, denoted by BOFF in the model, after which the stations gives up and reports an error. Hard real-time guarantees can therefore not be given. We aim for probabilistic guarantees instead, i.e., the probability of successful delivery for example. The model we analyze was developed in [Duflot et al., 2005]. We consider the following properties. The maximal probability such that:

(p1) both stations deliver.

(p2) the message of any station is eventually delivered before 1 backoff.

and one minimal reachability property:

(pmin) the message of any station is eventually delivered before 1 backoff.

IEEE 802.11 Wireless LAN Protocol (WLAN). The IEEE 802.11 standard for wireless LAN (WLAN) includes a CSMA/CA protocol, which is used as an access protocol. CSMA/CA (Carrier Sense Multiple Access with Collision Avoidance) is an extended version of CSMA/CD tailored to the limitations of wireless hardware. The main limitation is that full-duplex is typically not offered due to cost reasons, i.e., a station cannot send and receive at the same time. Thus stations cannot detect collisions during transmissions as required by CSMA/CD.

Since collisions cannot be detected, a station does not try to send immediately but delays the transmission by a time span of DIFS first (where DIFS is a parameter). This adds an additional waiting phase to the protocol compared to CSMA/CD and lowers the transmission rate, making collisions less likely.

Waiting can be modeled by a clock. The natural modeling formalism is therefore a probabilistic timed automaton. Kwiatkowska *et al.* have modeled the protocol by a probabilistic timed automaton and observed that the resulting probabilistic timed automaton falls into the category of probabilistic timed automata that can be discretized [Kwiatkowska et al., 2002]. Discretization means that the continuous clock can be replaced by digital clocks over an integer domain. We consider the digital-clock model here.

The model has two parameters. Like the CSMA/CD model there is a backoff-counter limit BOFF. Further there is a maximal package send time of T μs.

We analyze the probability that a particular number of collisions occur. To this end, we consider the maximal reachability properties:

(k=3) either station's back-off counter reaches 3.

(k=6) either station's back-off counter reaches 6.

Further we consider the minimal reachability property that

(k=3) either station's back-off counter reaches 3.

Bounded Retransmission Protocol (BRP). The bounded retransmission protocol is a data-link-layer network protocol that retransmits lost or corrupted messages. The BRP sends a file in a number of chunks over a lossy channel, but only a bounded number of retransmissions is allowed per chunk.

The considered model [Helmink et al., 1993, D'Argenio et al., 2001] consists of a sender, a receiver and two channels. One channel is used to transmit data, and the other channel is used to send acknowledgment messages. Both channels lose messages with a certain probability.

The BRP model has two parameters:

- N denotes the length of the file to be transmitted,

- MAX denotes the maximal number of retransmissions.

We consider a variant of the model where parameter N is set to a fixed value and additionally a variant that admits to establish properties of the model for arbitrary file size. In this variant of the model, parameter N is an integer with the additional constraint that the file size is at least 16 (of course this can be changed to some other constant as well).

We have studied the maximal reachability probability that:

(p1) the sender does not report a successful transmission,

(p4) the receiver does not receive any chunk and the sender tried to send a chunk.

The names $p1$ and $p4$ are chosen to match the naming scheme in [D'Argenio et al., 2001].

Sliding Window Protocol (SWP). Sliding window protocols are used in packet-based data transmission protocol like TCP to ensure in-order delivery of packets. Thereby packets are assigned unique consecutive sequence numbers. The receiver uses the sequence number to identify the correct ordering of packets, so that duplicates and lost packets can be detected.

There is no limit on the number of sequence numbers. However the protocol poses limits on the number of pending packets that can be transmitted at any given time. The limits define an admissible window of values. To allow for an unlimited number of packets, the window slides as time passes. Care has to be taken that the window does not limit the effective throughput. Therefore, we are interested in goodput properties which consider the difference between the number of sent and received packets. We want to know the probability that the number of sent packets exceeds the number of received packets by a particular constant.

Acknowledgements are sent by a receiver when a packet has arrived successfully. Timeout occurs if the acknowledgement of a packet has not been received within a specified time frame. We consider a lossy channel where packets get lost with a certain probability. Therefore, we are interested in the probability of a protocol timeout as well.

8.3 Evaluation

To assess the effectiveness of the abstraction-refinement methods developed in this thesis, we apply PASS to various case studies from the area of network protocols including the ones described in Section 8.2. The focus is on precision and efficiency, also relative to competing methods.

PASS features two refinement engines based on probabilistic CEGAR and backward refinement respectively. For clarity, we refer to PASS_C when the probabilistic CEGAR engine is used and to PASS_B when running backward refinement.

When analyzing finite-state concurrent probabilistic programs, we used PRISM 3.1.1 in its default mode, the so-called hybrid engine, to compare the performance with a state-of-the-art probabilistic model checker.

The experiments were carried out on a Linux machine (Ubuntu Linux 9.10) with a Pentium 4 processor at 2.6GHz and 2Gb of main memory. The execution times are given in seconds. Further the timeout limit was set to two hours and the memory limit to one gigabyte. In tables, timeout is indicated by **TO**. The numerical precision for value iteration was set to $\delta = 10^{-6}$ and the precision for the bounds was set to $\varepsilon = 10^{-4}$. For given lower and upper bounds, we say that the bounds are precise as soon as their relative difference is smaller than ε for each initial block.

Outline. The remainder of Section 8.3 is structured as follows:

Section 8.3.1 We focus on the ability of probabilistic CEGAR to prove reachability properties and apply PASS_C to models of network protocols. In addition, we assess the refutation capabilities of PASS_C.

Section 8.3.2 We compare backward refinement with probabilistic CEGAR. We discuss the enhancement of backward refinement with path analysis. Further, we compare with a related tool.

8.3.1. Probabilistic CEGAR

In this section, we apply probabilistic CEGAR to network protocols. We first focus on proving reachability properties and then on refutation.

Proving properties

We assess probabilistic CEGAR in terms of its capability to establish properties. Probabilistic CEGAR checks *upper bounds* on maximal reachability probabilities. In this experiment, we evaluate probabilistic CEGAR on finite and infinite models recording running time, number of refinements steps, number of predicates and number of explored paths. For finite-state models, we are interested in the effect of abstraction on model size and running time. To this end, we compare PASS_C with PRISM, which builds up and analyzes the concrete MDP. To obtain a meaningful comparison, we specify as a threshold the exact maximal reachability probability[3]. Results are summarized in Table 8.1 showing results of PRISM (column "Conventional") next to the ones of PASS_C (column "Abstraction").

The code of the models, except our own SWP model, is taken from the PRISM web repository. The models can be scaled via different parameters. Unconstrained parameters yield infinite-state models (denoted by "∞").

We now go through the different case studies one by one.

---

[3] For finite-state models, these probabilities can be computed by PRISM. For infinite-state models, lower and upper bounds from menu-based abstraction can be used to establish exact probabilities.

Table 8.1.: Statistics. Model parameters and properties studied are shown on the left. On the right we display the number of reachable states/blocks, transitions (non-zero entries in sparse matrix), computation time, number of iterations of the CEGAR loop (refs), of predicates generated (preds), and of abstract paths analyzed (paths). The number of states/blocks and non-zeros are given in thousands, i.e. 34K means 34,000.

Case study			Conventional			Abstraction (PASS_C)					
(parameters)		Property	states	trans	time	states	trans	refs	preds	paths	time
	5 315	k=3	5,195K	11,377K	93	34K	36K	9	120	604	72
WLAN	6 315	k=3	12,616K	28,137K	302	34K	42K	9	116	604	88
(BOFF T)	6 315	k=6	12,616K	28,137K	2024	391K	113K	9	182	582	306
	6 9500	k=6	–	–	TO	391K	113K	9	182	582	311
	3	p1	41K	52K	10	1K	2K	8	58	28	9
CSMA	4	p1	124K	161K	56	6K	9K	14	100	56	38
(BOFF)	3	p2	41K	52K	10	0.5K	0.9K	12	41	28	10
	4	p2	124K	161K	21	0.5K	1.5K	12	41	44	11
	16 3	p1	2K	3K	5.4	2K	3K	9	46	41	9
BRP	32 5	p1	5K	7K	12	5K	7K	9	64	111	21
(N MAX)	64 5	p1	10K	14K	26	10K	14K	8	95	585	91
	>16 3	p4	∞	–	–	0.5K	0.9K	7	26	17	3
	>16 4	p4	∞	–	–	0.6K	1K	7	27	17	4
	>16 5	p4	∞	–	–	0.7K	1K	8	28	18	5
SWP		goodput	∞	–	–	5K	11K	3	40	7	87
		timeout	∞	–	–	27K	44K	3	49	6	89

WLAN. The WLAN model can be scaled by changing the maximal number of backoffs BOFF and the time horizon T of the clocks. Increasing BOFF from 5 to 6 leads to an exponential increase in model size and running time in PRISM, as shown in Table 8.1. For PASS_C and property $k = 3$, the row is identical for BOFF=5 and BOFF=6 because, although states with back-off counter higher than three can reach a goal state (via a reset), they do not lie on paths with maximal probability. Hence refinement never splits blocks with respect to back-offs beyond three. Further, for fixed value of BOFF, PASS_C scales better than PRISM with respect to different values of the time horizon T.

The reduction in state-space size can be explained by looking at the discovered predicates. The predicates are equalities that track the values of control variables and data variables affecting backoff counters. Value ranges of the digital clocks are tracked to depth 6. Variables irrelevant to the property are completely abstracted away, i.e. no predicate tracks their value. For example, a variable that records the slot at which a package is sent is irrelevant for the value of the backoff counter.

CSMA. PASS_C establishes both properties of the CSMA/CD protocol. For both properties, the abstract state space is an order of magnitude smaller than the concrete one, as shown in the table.

The predicates abstract from the values of digital clocks of the sender and the bus. The clocks can influence the backoff counter. However, to establish upper bounds, this abstraction is precise enough. The upper bound is independent of the duration modeled with the clock.

For property p2, the size of the abstraction does not change with respect to the size of BOFF similar to the WLAN case study. However, the number of paths explored increases with BOFF. The reason is that for greater values of BOFF, there is more branching in the probabilistic model, thus in the abstraction there are more abstract paths being explored.

BRP. PRISM outperforms PASS_C when analyzing property p1. The probability directly depends on the file size and the value of the counter i that keep tracks of how many chunks of a file have already been transmitted. Thus there is no opportunity for abstraction, and PASS_C obtains the full MDP semantics after several refinement steps.

Property p4 can be analyzed for an infinite parameter range with PASS_C because the probability for the property is invariant with respect to the file length N. Thus the constraint $N > 16$ allows us to verify the property for any possible file length greater than 16. Notably the analysis of BRP for $N > 16$ can be considered a parametric analysis: p4 is proven for any such N. Thereby two predicates $i < N$ and $i = N$ concern the counter variable i that records the number of transmitted file chunks and the file size N. These predicates track whether all but the last or all file chunks, respectively, have been transmitted. Thus the value domain of the variable i is abstracted.

SWP. The model contains unbounded integers and is thus not amenable to PRISM. The unbounded integer variables model sequence numbers. PASS_C establishes the probability bound on the goodput property. The second property is a qualitative reachability property. The tool has to prove that certain states are unreachable. PASS_C also proves this property. PASS_C is successful because it is sufficient to reason about the differences between variables rather than their concrete value, e.g., the difference between the next sequence number $nextseqnum$ and the offset of the current receive window $base$. Probabilistic CEGAR infers the required difference constraints as predicates, e.g., predicate $base - nextseqnum > 1$, and is thus able to prove the properties.

Running Time

Table 8.2 gives the relative contribution of the different analysis phases to the overall running time of PASS_C (the table lists representative cases).

Overall predicate abstraction tends to be the dominant phase. This is because the number of SMT enumerations can be quite large, e.g., 10000 calls for a command in SWP. Even though each single call to the SMT solver is typically cheap, the accumulated computational cost of all enumerations can thus be high.

In some cases, predicate synthesis incurs the largest fraction of the running time. This happens if a large number of paths has to be enumerated by probabilistic CEGAR before a spurious path is found. Aside from value iteration, predicate abstraction and predicate synthesis, we summarize miscellaneous other computations. Here the dominating factor

Table 8.2.: PASS_C: Relative contribution of analysis phases to overall running time.

	abstraction	value iteration	predicate synthesis	misc
WLAN 5 315 k=3	78%	1%	1%	20%
WLAN 6 315 k=3	80%	1%	1%	18%
WLAN 6 315 k=6	14%	39%	31%	26%
CSMA 4 prop1	47%	17%	19%	17%
BRP 16 3 P1	20%	27%	45%	8%
BRP INF 3 P4	61%	1%	19%	9%
SWP (goodput)	39%	19%	39%	3%
SWP (timeout)	36%	46%	11%	7%

is the conversion of the symbolic representation of the abstraction into an explicit sparse-matrix representation.

Summary

Wrapping up, PASS_C successfully shows properties of infinite-state models, namely of the Sliding Window protocol and of an instance of BRP with parametric file size. In all of these cases, the abstraction yields compact abstract models that are efficiently analyzable. On large finite-state models, we observe a dramatic state space reduction compared to PRISM. For example for the WLAN protocol the size of the abstraction is reduced from several millions to hundreds of thousands. On smaller models PASS_C is not competitive with PRISM. For certain instances of the BRP model, no state space reduction is achieved. The overhead of refinement makes PASS_C slower.

Refutation with CEGAR

While the focus of the first part of Section 8.3.1 is on proving properties, we now concentrate on refutation. By identifying realizable counterexamples, probabilistic CEGAR can refute properties of the form $Pmax_{\leq p}(\mathsf{e}_1 \; \mathcal{U} \; \mathsf{e}_2)$ by establishing a lower bound on the reachability probability that exceeds threshold p. In the process, probabilistic CEGAR analyzes paths in the induced Markov chain.

To assess probabilistic CEGAR with regard to refutation, we look into the number of paths and time needed to confirm a certain amount of probability mass. We check tightness of the upper bounds obtained in Section 8.3.1 and record how much effort is needed to obtain a certain percentage of the probability mass, e.g., half or three quarters. From this data, the effort for particular thresholds p can be derived.

For the parametric version of BRP and property ($p4$), the analysis is trivial, as the induced Markov chain consists in a single path. However, this is an exception.

For the different case studies, we plot the obtained probability mass as a function of the number of analyzed paths in Figures 8.2 to 8.5. The number of paths (x-axis) is thereby counted in thousands (as indicated by the K). To depict the probability mass (y-axis), we use a percentage scale relative to the upper bound rather than the absolute

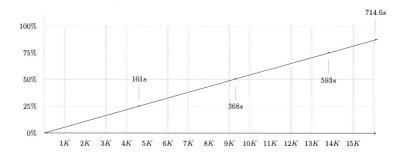

Figure 8.2.: WLAN: counterexample analysis.

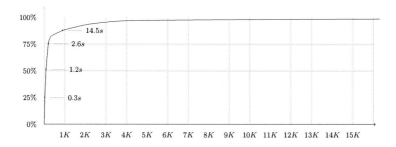

Figure 8.3.: BRP: counterexample analysis.

probability values, so that the upper bound corresponds to 100%. Observe that, in this experiment, this upper bound equals the precise probability and is also chosen as the threshold. At select instants, e.g. when 25% of the probability mass has been achieved, we annotate the running time spent in the current run of probabilistic CEGAR up to that point.

Figure 8.2 shows the curve for the WLAN case study (BOFF=6,T=315,k=3). The points where 25%, 50%, 75% and 87.5 have been reached are marked. 100% of the probability is obtained after 800s. We observe that the probability grows linearly in the number of paths, because these paths have approximately the same probability. The reason is that the Markov chain is acyclic and contains only *uniform* probabilistic choice (corresponding to the different delays of exponential backoff). Although the Markov chain is acyclic, the number of paths is high due to the large fanout of the probability distributions.

In contrast, the curves for BRP with property ($p1$) and CSMA (with property ($p1$)) behave like a geometric series. The geometric series is induced by paths that take

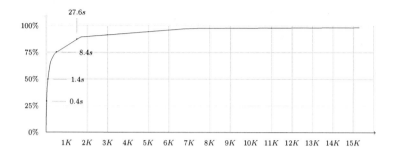

Figure 8.4.: CSMA: counterexample analysis.

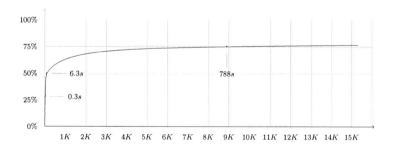

Figure 8.5.: SWP: counterexample analysis.

certain probabilistic choices multiple times due to back-edges in the Markov chain. For an illustration of the mathematical phenomenon on a smaller example, please refer to the Markov chain and the explanation of probabilistic reachability in Section 3.2.

Also concerning BRP and CSMA, we observe that the growth of probabilities is slightly faster in the BRP model than in case of CSMA. This is because the induced Markov chain of the BRP model contains non-uniform distributions (corresponding to the probability of message loss), such that paths that take the alternatives with higher probability have a relatively high probability and thus the curve initially shows a steeper incline.

In case of SWP (goodput property), the probability grows more slowly than for BRP and CSMA. The full probability is achieved in the limit. The induced Markov chain has a cycle and thus corresponds to infinitely many paths. Further, the cycle contains complex probabilistic branching and this induces a large number of paths.

Summary

The experiment shows that non-trivial lower bounds can be computed by counterexample analysis. While the lower bounds obtained from the game are trivial for most case studies, lower bounds from counterexample analysis can be more informative, as indicated by the curves. Yet, the closer to the actual probability the selected threshold is, the more effort is needed. For the finite models considered, determining the exact probability by probabilistic CEGAR is more expensive than analyzing the concrete model. As the number of paths in a counterexample can be quite large, error diagnosis is currently difficult. Thus refutation with probabilistic CEGAR becomes harder and harder the closer the selected threshold is to the actual reachability probability.

8.3.2. Backward Refinement

We assess the quality of the bounds and the efficiency of backward refinement. Further, we compare backward refinement to probabilistic CEGAR and with the abstraction-refinement tool in [Kattenbelt et al., 2009], a model checker for probabilistic C programs.

Backward refinement supports both minimal and maximal reachability. Therefore, in addition to the benchmarks used for probabilistic CEGAR, which targets only maximal reachability properties, we verify minimal reachability properties. Further, backward refinement does not require a threshold probability like probabilistic CEGAR. When running PASS_B, we simply remove the threshold specifications from the properties checked with probabilistic CEGAR. Observe that PASS_B terminates as soon as the bounds are precise, while PASS_C terminates once the upper bound is established.

We first apply the backward-refinement method of Section 7.2. With this method, PASS_C successfully obtains precise bounds for the case studies in Section 8.3.1. However, the number of refinement steps is significantly higher than for probabilistic CEGAR. For example, PASS_C solves the WLAN case study with parameters BOFF=6 T=315 and k=3 in 60 refinement steps and over twenty minutes time. Probabilistic CEGAR requires

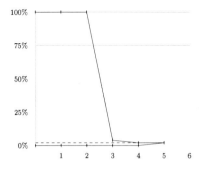

Figure 8.6.: SWP: backward refinement

only 9 steps and 88s time (see Table 8.1) and PRISM is also faster. The situation for the other case studies is similar.

The reason for the higher number of steps is that path analysis with interpolation, as used in probabilistic CEGAR, is superior to precondition-based predicate synthesis of backward refinement. Interpolation discovers predicates in a single run for which backward refinement takes several refinement steps.

The quality of the predicates produced by path analysis is also typically better because backward refinement splits dead blocks (blocks which do not contain reachable states, see Section 8.1). For example, for the SWP case study, backward refinement introduces two predicates resulting from dead blocks, which are not needed to obtain precise bounds.

To this end, the extension of the pure backward-refinement algorithm (see Section 7.2) described in Section 8.1 enhances backward refinement with a path analysis in the style of probabilistic CEGAR that eliminates dead blocks. This significantly improves the efficiency of backward refinement. For example, the mentioned instance of the WLAN case study is solved after 4 iterations within 57s. From now on, we only consider enhanced backward refinement with dead-block elimination as described in Section 8.1.

The charts in Figures 8.6 to 8.9 illustrate the evolution of lower and upper bounds during backward refinement for SWP and CSMA. The y-axis of the charts shows the absolute probability in percent, and the x-axis gives the respective refinement step. The dotted line shows the precise probability, while lower and upper bound, respectively, are shown as solid curves. The lower bound approaches the actual probability from below, while the upper bound descends from above to the actual probability. For example, Figure 8.6 shows the chart for the goodput property of SWP. Initially, the bounds are trivial, but after 5 steps both bounds have reached the actual probability.

Figures 8.7 to 8.9 show the evolution of the bounds for the CSMA case study. For the maximal reachability problems in Figure 8.8 and Figure 8.9, the lower bound tends to remain imprecise for more steps than the upper bound. The situation in case of the

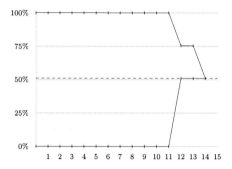

Figure 8.7.: CSMA minimal reachability property: backward refinement

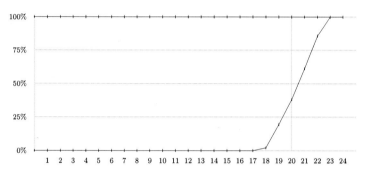

Figure 8.8.: CSMA property 1: backward refinement

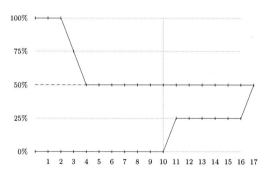

Figure 8.9.: CSMA property 2: backward refinement

Table 8.3.: The table is structured like Table 8.1. Regarding complete entries for PASS_C, we refer to Table 8.1. Model parameters and properties studied are shown on the left. On the right we display the number of reachable states, transitions (non-zero entries in sparse matrix), computation time, the number of iterations of the refinement loop (refs), and the number of predicates generated (preds). The number of blocks and transitions are given in thousands, i.e. 34K means 34,000.

Case study			PASS_C				PASS_B				
(parameters)		Property	blocks	trans	refs	time	blocks	trans	refs	preds	time
	5 315	k=3	34K	36K	9	72	5K	3K	4	107	43
WLAN	6 315	k=3	34K	42K	9	88	5K	3K	4	110	57
BOFF/T	6 315	k=6	391K	113K	9	306	391K	113K	4	140	115
	6 9500	k=6	391K	113K	9	311	391K	113K	3	138	76
	3	p1	1K	2K	8	9	1K	1K	4	73	7
CSMA	4	p1	6K	9K	14	38	3K	4K	5	85	10
BOFF	3	p2	0.5K	0.9K	12	10	148	159	2	60	5
	4	p2	0.5K	1.5K	12	11	188	201	2	56	5
	16 3	p1	2K	3K	9	9	2K	2K	19	51	8
BRP	32 5	p1	5K	7K	9	21	5K	5K	36	68	27
N/MAX	64 5	p1	10K	14K	8	91	10K	10K	69	102	76
	>16 3	p4	0.5K	0.9K	7	3	861	1K	3	34	1
	>16 4	p4	0.6K	1K	7	4	1K	1K	4	35	1
	>16 5	p4	0.7K	1K	8	5	1K	2K	5	36	2
SWP		goodput	5K	11K	4	18	890	1K	8	44	18
		timeout	27K	44K	3	6	831	1K	5	30	2

minimal reachability property of Figure 8.7 is somewhat dual – there the lower bound stabilizes earlier.

Next, we discuss why lower bounds behave in this way, give more performance numbers and compare backward refinement with probabilistic CEGAR.

Comparison with Probabilistic CEGAR

We assess enhanced backward refinement and compare it to probabilistic CEGAR. Results are summarized in Table 8.3. In the table, the entries of PASS_C from Table 8.1 are repeated for direct comparison and better readability. Now we discuss the results obtained in the different case studies, starting with WLAN.

In case of the WLAN case study, backward refinement is faster than probabilistic CEGAR. Probabilistic CEGAR checks hundreds of realizable paths before getting to spurious paths and then synthesizes predicates. Regarding bounds, hundreds of paths explored by probabilistic CEGAR still only amount to lower bounds that may be orders of magnitude below the actual probability, as can be seen in Figure 8.2. Backward refinement, in contrast, focuses on pivot blocks which signify where precision gets lost.

For probabilistic CEGAR, the number of refinement steps is lower for SWP, BRP and CSMA. The reason is that probabilistic CEGAR terminates as soon as an upper bound has been established, while backward refinement also seeks to make the lower bound precise. For the CSMA case study, establishing a tight lower bound requires proving termination of a loop in the program – this requirement is a limitation of the abstraction we are using. A minimal example for this issue is given in Section 7.2.2.

The loop increments a clock variable and models the duration of package transmission. The lower bound becomes precise after the complete value domain of the variable is encoded with predicates up to the loop depth, i.e., $x = 0$, $x = 1$, $x = 2$ and so on.

The phenomenon can be observed in Figure 8.8. The upper bound is tight early and the lower bound becomes precise after several refinement steps. The measurements and the result in the figure are with respect to duration 10. Backward refinement produces lower bounds exclusively based on the abstract game. Therefore the lower bound remains trivial until refinement step 17, as shown in Figure 8.8.

Scaling up the duration, backward refinement produces larger and larger abstractions. With a duration of 31, backward refinement takes 43 refinements and produces an abstraction with $8K$ blocks. With a duration of 100, it times out. Probabilistic CEGAR remains unaffected by the scaling of the duration and always yields the same abstraction. The lower bounds produced by probabilistic CEGAR during refinement achieve up to 50% of the actual probability mass. The explanation is that probabilistic CEGAR unrolls cycles in the induced Markov chain which correspond to realizable paths.

For BRP and property $p1$, PASS_B refines until the concrete model is obtained and the bounds eventually become precise. For the parametric version of BRP and property $p4$, PASS_B obtains precise bounds as well and an abstraction of similar size as probabilistic CEGAR. In these cases, path analysis discovered the predicates and both refinement techniques use a very similar kind of path analysis, which explains this similarity.

For SWP, several predicates involving a timer variable are added by probabilistic CE-GAR but not by backward refinement. These predicates turn irrelevant are in fact irrelevant to the property. As a result, PASS_B produces a smaller abstraction.

As discussed, in addition to maximal probabilistic reachability, we also consider minimal reachability in the context of backward refinement. For minimal reachability properties of the csma and wlan models, PASS_B computes precise probabilities, confirming that backward refinement is also effective for minimal reachability.

Finally, Table 8.10 summarizes the relative running-time contribution of the different analysis phases of PASS_B. Running time in PASS is dominated by the predicate-abstraction phase. Predicate synthesis consumes at most 8% of the running time, significantly less than PASS_C (see Table 8.2). The reason for the discrepancy is that PASS_C analyzes a potentially large set of paths, while PASS_B analyzes a single path per refinement step.

Comparison with other tools.

Kattenbelt *et al.* describe a tool [Kattenbelt et al., 2009] that analyses probabilistic C programs. The tool is an extension of SATABS [Clarke et al., 2005], a software model checker for ANSI C programs based on predicate abstraction. Let us call this tool

	abstraction	value iteration	predicate synthesis	misc
WLAN 5 315 k=3	78	1	1	20
WLAN 6 315 k=3	80	1	1	18
WLAN 6 315 k=6	55	10	1	34
CSMA 4 prop1	80	1	2	17
CSMA 4 prop2	79	1	1	19
BRP 16 3 P1	26	60	2	12
BRP INF 3 P4	64	1	4	31
SWP (goodput)	74	19	2	5
SWP (timeout)	47	40	5	8
Herman	84	0	5	11
ZeroConf	62	6	8	16

Figure 8.10.: PASS$_B$: Relative contribution of analysis phases to overall running time.

SATABS'. Since SATABS' is not publicly available, we compare with the performance numbers published in the paper.

We have translated two C programs from their benchmarks into the input language of PASS, the zeroconf and the herman case study. The other programs cannot readily be translated because they contain features not supported by PASS, e.g., pointers.

The properties[4] in the two case studies involve minimal reachability probabilities. Therefore only PASS$_B$ is applicable. PASS$_B$ successfully solved both verification problems. The tool SATABS' took $1.97s$ and $33.5s$ respectively, on a faster machine, compared to $1.3s$ and $5s$ for PASS$_B$. Throughout their case studies running time is dominated by value iteration. They use a symbolic representation for stochastic games. Value iteration in PASS$_B$ is faster because it uses a sparse-matrix representation for stochastic games.

This completes our technical discussion. Finally, we summarize the results obtained and conclude.

Summary

Path analysis proves effective in both backward refinement or probabilistic CEGAR. Backward refinement tends to be more goal-directed, focusing on pivot blocks. Probabilistic CEGAR enumerates many realizable paths before exploring a spurious one. As a result, predicate synthesis with backward refinement is faster.

Backward refinement can be used to effectively compute lower and upper bounds. However, in presence of loops and counter variables, backward refinement requires loop unrolling, which can blow up the size of the abstraction. Probabilistic CEGAR, on the other hand, is able to leap loops and obtain non-trivial lower bounds before loops have been unrolled in the abstraction.

---

[4]We refer to property A for both the zeroconf and the herman case study in [Kattenbelt et al., 2009].

8.4 Conclusion

In this chapter, we have presented our implementation, case studies and experimental results. We now summarize the obtained results and outline remaining challenges.

The proposed abstraction refinement methods are able to verify infinite-state models. This is possible because predicates involving linear constraints between variables provide sufficient information for these problems. Both refinement techniques are able to outperform the finite-state tool PRISM on larger state spaces. For smaller state spaces, PASS is typically inferior due to its refinement overhead.

Regarding the trade-off between the refinement techniques, we observe that the two techniques have complementary strengths. Probabilistic CEGAR is sometimes able to determine lower bounds earlier than backward refinement. On the other hand, regarding predicate synthesis, probabilistic CEGAR is more expensive since it explores many realizable paths before finding a spurious one.

Our tool PASS is currently the only automatic abstraction tool for concurrent probabilistic programs. PRISM covers the finite-state but not the infinite-state instances. The predicate abstraction tool [Kattenbelt et al., 2009] supports probabilistic C programs but not concurrency.

In the future, it might be worthwhile to leverage both game strategies in probabilistic CEGAR to achieve better guidance. This would fully combine the strengths of backward refinement and probabilistic CEGAR. Further, smaller representations of counterexamples will be needed to facilitate error diagnosis. Finally, backward refinement could be enhanced so that the abstraction is refined simultaneously at different points.

Part III.

Conclusion

9

Summary
and Future Work

State-space explosion and infiniteness limit the scope of probabilistic verification significantly. In the context of non-probabilistic verification, automatic abstraction refinement techniques based on abstract interpretation have been used very successfully to address these issues. Before our work, it was not clear how to develop comparable abstraction techniques in a probabilistic setting and whether they would be effective in practice.

9.1 Summary of Contributions

This thesis has presented automatic abstraction refinement based on abstract interpretation in the context of probabilistic models. Our contributions consist both in theoretical results and in developing effective tool support.

Probabilistic Abstraction

As a foundation for analyses that yield bounds on reachability probabilities, we have presented a *probabilistic abstraction framework* based on abstract interpretation. The framework admits to reason about the relative precision and optimality of analyses. Thanks to its flexibility, we are able to set the dial between precision and efficiency. We have both studied optimal analyses, which mark the limit on the precision achievable by any correct analysis, and approximations, leading to less expensive analyses with potentially lower precision.

Program Abstraction

Based on our probabilistic abstraction framework, we have developed *predicate abstraction* for concurrent probabilistic programs. The resulting abstractions yield lower and upper bounds on reachability probabilities. Effective computation of abstractions for a given set of predicates is enabled by symbolic methods and SMT solvers. Since symbolic methods operate at the language level, we are able to deal with large and even infinite state spaces. Further, by using approximations, we obtain abstractions that are efficiently computable in presence of concurrency.

Refinement

To automate predicate abstraction, we have developed refinement techniques which derive suitable predicates. The challenge is to diagnose where a given abstraction loses precision and to find predicates that improve precision. We have developed *abstraction refinement* techniques for concurrent probabilistic programs which address these challenges. These techniques are based on stochastic games and new notions of abstract probabilistic counterexamples. Ultimately, they enable fully automatic verification of concurrent probabilistic program for the first time.

Implementation

We have presented the tool PASS, which implements abstraction refinement for concurrent probabilistic programs, and we have applied PASS to a number of network protocols from different layers of the protocol stack. The techniques developed in this thesis have shown to be effective in terms of automation and combating state-space explosion. Finite-state programs with large state spaces can be analyzed more efficiently thanks to abstraction. Furthermore, abstraction enables the analysis of infinite-state models, which are entirely beyond the scope of previous methods.

9.2 Conclusions

By combining concepts from the theory of probabilistic models, games, logic and abstract interpretation, we arrive at abstraction techniques that significantly extend the scope of probabilistic verification in terms of the size of the state spaces that can be handled. Our abstraction refinement techniques automatically tailor the abstract domain to the given verification problem and thus completely automate the verification task. This admits to automatically verify probabilistic programs far beyond the reach of any previous method.

9.3 Avenues for Future Work

The work presented in this thesis opens several avenues for future research.

Extensions of Probabilistic CEGAR. The presented CEGAR approach aims at upper bounds on maximal reachability properties. Dually, one might be interested in CEGAR for lower bounds and minimal probabilistic reachability. Algorithms for the generation of abstract paths to refute lower bounds could be adapted from [Han, 2009] where counterexample generation for lower bounds is reduced to counterexample generation for upper bounds. However, the reduction introduces an atomic proposition which refers to strongly-connected components. It could be difficult to cast this graph property back to the concrete model, and thus additional work is needed at this point.

As suggested by our experimental results, exploiting game strategies can be beneficial for refinement. So far, Probabilistic CEGAR only leverages a single game strategy, namely the strategy corresponding to the upper bound. It would be interesting to investigate how to extend Probabilistic CEGAR in such a way that both strategies are used.

Richer Properties. Probabilistic computation-tree logic (PCTL) admits more complex temporal properties [Hansson and Jonsson, 1994, Bianco and de Alfaro, 1995] than probabilistic reachability. An avenue for future research could be to extend the presented work to PCTL. The challenge lies in developing a refinement algorithm that can deal with nested formulas. Due to nesting, sub-formulas may evaluate to an unknown value. To this end, a three-valued interpretation of PCTL formulas and an adaption of the refinement algorithm along the lines of [Shoham and Grumberg, 2004] could be pursued.

Another extension would be to support rewards, costs and expected values. For example, we might ask for the expected number of necessary retransmissions at which a package eventually arrives at a receiver. Presently, the abstract domain admits to represent probabilities between zero and one. To support rewards, the concrete and abstract domains can be extended to real numbers between zero and infinity, e.g., a concrete valuation then becomes a function $S \rightarrow [0, +\infty]$. The concepts of our framework carry over to this setting. The structure and computation of abstract transformers is to be investigated.

Richer Language. MODEST [Bohnenkamp et al., 2006] is a rich modeling language that maps to probabilistic timed automata. Applying PASS to MODEST models seems quite promising. We anticipate that this would admit the verification of models with larger state spaces. PASS currently does not directly support clocks. To support clocks, one could extend PASS with region abstraction [Alur and Dill, 1994] or one can leverage an automatic translation from MODEST models into PRISM models [Hartmanns and Hermanns, 2009] which can in turn be handled by PASS. Our initial experience with the translation approach indicates that clock variables should be handled with a dedicated abstraction-refinement approach for better efficiency. An additional challenging extension would be to handle exponential probability distributions, which are also expressible in MODEST.

Bibliography

[Ábrahám et al., 2010] Ábrahám, E., Jansen, N., Wimmer, R., Katoen, J.-P., and Becker, B. (2010). DTMC Model Checking by SCC Reduction. In *QEST'10: Proceedings of the 7th International Conference on Quantitative Evaluation of Systems.* IEEE Computer Society. to appear.

[Aljazzar et al., 2005] Aljazzar, H., Hermanns, H., and Leue, S. (2005). Counterexamples for Timed Probabilistic Reachability. In *FORMATS'05: Proceedings of the 3rd International Conference on Formal Modeling and Analysis of Timed Systems,* volume 3829 of *Lecture Notes in Computer Science,* pages 177–195. Springer Verlag.

[Aljazzar and Leue, 2006] Aljazzar, H. and Leue, S. (2006). Extended Directed Search for Probabilistic Timed Reachability. In *FORMATS'06: Proceedings of the 4th International Conference on Formal Modeling and Analysis of Timed Systems,* volume 4202 of *Lecture Notes in Computer Science,* pages 33–51. Springer Verlag.

[Alur et al., 2006] Alur, R., Dang, T., and Ivancic, F. (2006). Counterexample-guided predicate abstraction of hybrid systems. *Theoretical Computer Science,* 354(2):250–271.

[Alur and Dill, 1994] Alur, R. and Dill, D. L. (1994). A Theory of Timed Automata. *Theoretical Computer Science,* 126(2):183–235.

[Alur and Henzinger, 1999] Alur, R. and Henzinger, T. A. (1999). Reactive Modules. *Formal Methods in System Design,* 15(1):7–48.

[Andrés et al., 2008] Andrés, M. E., D'Argenio, P. R., and van Rossum, P. (2008). Significant Diagnostic Counterexamples in Probabilistic Model Checking. In *HVC'08: Proceedings of the 4th International Haifa Verification Conference,* volume 5394 of *Lecture Notes in Computer Science,* pages 129–148. Springer Verlag.

[Baier, 1998] Baier, C. (1998). On Algorithmic Verification Methods for Probabilistic Systems. Habilitationsschrift, Universität Mannheim.

[Ball et al., 2001] Ball, T., Podelski, A., and Rajamani, S. K. (2001). Boolean and Cartesian Abstraction for Model Checking C Programs. In *TACAS'01: Proceedings of the 7th International Conference on Tools and Algorithms for the Construction and Analysis of Systems,* volume 2031 of *Lecture Notes in Computer Science,* pages 268–283. Springer Verlag.

[Ball and Rajamani, 2002] Ball, T. and Rajamani, S. K. (2002). The SLAM project: debugging system software via static analysis. In *POPL'02: Proceedings of the 29th Annual Symposium on Principles of Programming Languages,* pages 1–3, New York, NY, USA. ACM Press.

[Bianco and de Alfaro, 1995] Bianco, A. and de Alfaro, L. (1995). Model Checking of Probabilistic and Nondeterministic Systems. In *FSTTCS'95: Proceedings of the 15th*

Conference on Foundations of Software Technology and Theoretical Computer Science, volume 1026 of *Lecture Notes in Computer Science*, pages 499–513. Springer Verlag.

[Biere et al., 2003] Biere, A., Cimatti, A., Clarke, E. M., Strichman, O., and Zhu, Y. (2003). Bounded Model Checking. *Advances in Computers*, 58:118–149.

[Blanchet et al., 2003] Blanchet, B., Cousot, P., Cousot, R., Feret, J., Mauborgne, L., Miné, A., Monniaux, D., and Rival, X. (2003). A static analyzer for large safety-critical software. In *PLDI'03: Proceedings of the ACM SIGPLAN 2003 Conference on Programming Language Design and Implementation*, pages 196–207, New York, NY, USA. ACM Press.

[Bohnenkamp et al., 2006] Bohnenkamp, H. C., D'Argenio, P. R., Hermanns, H., and Katoen, J.-P. (2006). MODEST: A Compositional Modeling Formalism for Hard and Softly Timed Systems. *IEEE Transactions on Software Engineering*, 32(10):812–830.

[Bruttomesso et al., 2008] Bruttomesso, R., Cimatti, A., Franzén, A., Griggio, A., and Sebastiani, R. (2008). The MathSAT 4 SMT Solver. In *CAV'08: Proceedings of the 20th International Conference on Computer Aided Verification*, volume 5123 of *Lecture Notes in Computer Science*, pages 299–303. Springer Verlag.

[Bryant, 1985] Bryant, R. E. (1985). Symbolic manipulation of Boolean functions using a graphical representation. In *DAC'85: Proceedings of the 22nd ACM/IEEE conference on Design automation*, pages 688–694, New York, NY, USA. ACM Press.

[Burch et al., 1990] Burch, J. R., Clarke, E. M., McMillan, K. L., Dill, D. L., and Hwang, L. J. (1990). Symbolic Model Checking: 10^{20} States and Beyond. In *LICS'90: Proceedings of the Fifth Annual IEEE Symposium on Logic in Computer Science*, pages 428–439. IEEE Computer Society.

[Chadha and Viswanathan, 2010] Chadha, R. and Viswanathan, M. (2010). A Counterexample-Guided Abstraction-Refinement Framework for Markov Decision Processes. *ACM Transactions on Computational Logic*. to appear.

[Chatterjee et al., 2004] Chatterjee, K., de Alfaro, L., and Henzinger, T. A. (2004). Trading Memory for Randomness. In *QEST'04: Proceedings of the 1st International Conference on the Quantitative Evaluation of Systems*, pages 206–217. IEEE Computer Society.

[Chatterjee et al., 2006] Chatterjee, K., de Alfaro, L., and Henzinger, T. A. (2006). Strategy Improvement for Concurrent Reachability Games. In *QEST'06: Proceedings of the Third International Conference on the Quantitative Evaluation of Systems*, pages 291–300. IEEE Computer Society.

[Chatterjee et al., 2005] Chatterjee, K., Henzinger, T. A., Jhala, R., and Majumdar, R. (2005). Counterexample-guided Planning. In *UAI'05: Proceedings of the 21st Conference in Uncertainty in Artificial Intelligence*, pages 104–111. AUAI Press.

[Clarke, 2008] Clarke, E. M. (2008). The Birth of Model Checking. In *25 Years of Model Checking*, volume 5000 of *Lecture Notes in Computer Science*, pages 1–26. Springer Verlag.

[Clarke and Emerson, 1981] Clarke, E. M. and Emerson, E. A. (1981). Design and

Synthesis of Synchronization Skeletons Using Branching-Time Temporal Logic. In *LOP'01: Proceedings of the Workshop on Logic of Programs*, volume 131 of *Lecture Notes in Computer Science*, pages 52–71. Springer Verlag.

[Clarke et al., 2000] Clarke, E. M., Grumberg, O., Jha, S., Lu, Y., and Veith, H. (2000). Counterexample-Guided Abstraction Refinement. In *CAV'00: Proceedings of the 12th International Conference on Computer Aided Verification*, volume 1855 of *Lecture Notes in Computer Science*, pages 154–169. Springer Verlag.

[Clarke et al., 2002] Clarke, E. M., Jha, S., Lu, Y., and Veith, H. (2002). Tree-Like Counterexamples in Model Checking. In *LICS'02: Proceedings of the 17th IEEE Symposium on Logic in Computer Science*, pages 19–29. IEEE Computer Society.

[Clarke et al., 2005] Clarke, E. M., Kroening, D., Sharygina, N., and Yorav, K. (2005). SATABS: SAT-Based Predicate Abstraction for ANSI-C. In *TACAS'05: Proceedings of the 11th International Conference on Tools and Algorithms for the Construction and Analysis of Systems,*, volume 3440 of *Lecture Notes in Computer Science*, pages 570–574. Springer Verlag.

[Clarke et al., 2003] Clarke, E. M., Talupur, M., Veith, H., and Wang, D. (2003). SAT-Based Predicate Abstraction for Hardware Verification. In *SAT'03: Proceedings of the 6th International Conference on Theory and Applications of Satisfiability Testing*, volume 2919 of *Lecture Notes in Computer Science*, pages 78–92. Springer Verlag.

[Coletta et al., 2009] Coletta, A., Gori, R., and Levi, F. (2009). Approximating Probabilistic Behaviors of Biological Systems Using Abstract Interpretation. *Electronic Notes in Theoretical Computer Science*, 229(1):165–182.

[Condon, 1992] Condon, A. (1992). The Complexity of Stochastic Games. *Information and Computation*, 96(2):203–224.

[Cousot, 1978] Cousot, P. (1978). *Méthodes itératives de construction et d'approximation de point fixes d'opérateurs monotone sur un treillis, analyse sémantique des programmes*. PhD thesis, Université de Grenoble.

[Cousot, 1981] Cousot, P. (1981). Semantic Foundations of Program Analysis. In Muchnick, S. and Jones, N., editors, *Program Flow Analysis: Theory and Applications*, chapter 10, pages 303–342. Prentice-Hall, Inc., Englewood Cliffs, New Jersey.

[Cousot and Cousot, 1977] Cousot, P. and Cousot, R. (1977). Abstract Interpretation: A Unified Lattice Model for Static Analysis of Programs by Construction or Approximation of Fixpoints. In *POPL'77: Proceedings of the 4th Annual Symposium on Principles of Programming Languages*, pages 238–252, New York, NY, USA. ACM Press.

[Cousot and Cousot, 1992] Cousot, P. and Cousot, R. (1992). Abstract Interpretation and Application to Logic Programs. *Journal on Logic Programming*, 13(2&3):103–179.

[Cousot and Cousot, 2002] Cousot, P. and Cousot, R. (2002). Systematic Design of Program Transformation Frameworks by Abstract Interpretation. In *POPL'02: Proceedings of the 29th Annual Symposium on Principles of Programming Languages*, pages 178–190, New York, NY, USA. ACM Press.

[Dai and Goldsmith, 2007] Dai, P. and Goldsmith, J. (2007). Topological Value Iteration Algorithm for Markov Decision Processes. In *IJCAI'07: Proceedings of the 20th International Joint Conference on Artificial Intelligence*, pages 1860–1865.

[D'Argenio et al., 2001] D'Argenio, P. R., Jeannet, B., Jensen, H. E., and Larsen, K. G. (2001). Reachability Analysis of Probabilistic Systems by Successive Refinements. In *PAPM-PROBMIV'02: Proceedings of the 1st Joint International Workshop on Process Algebras and Performance Modeling and Probabilistic Methods In Verification*, volume 2165 of *Lecture Notes in Computer Science*, pages 39–56. Springer Verlag.

[D'Argenio et al., 2002] D'Argenio, P. R., Jeannet, B., Jensen, H. E., and Larsen, K. G. (2002). Reduction and Refinement Strategies for Probabilistic Analysis. In *PAPM-PROBMIV'02: Proceedings of the 2nd Joint International Workshop on Process Algebras and Performance Modeling and Probabilistic Methods In Verification*, volume 2399 of *Lecture Notes in Computer Science*, pages 57–76. Springer Verlag.

[de Alfaro et al., 2000] de Alfaro, L., Kwiatkowska, M. Z., Norman, G., Parker, D., and Segala, R. (2000). Symbolic Model Checking of Probabilistic Processes Using MTBDDs and the Kronecker Representation. In *TACAS'00: Proceedings of the 6th International Conference on Tools and Algorithms for Construction and Analysis of Systems*, volume 1785 of *Lecture Notes in Computer Science*, pages 395–410. Springer Verlag.

[de Alfaro and Majumdar, 2004] de Alfaro, L. and Majumdar, R. (2004). Quantitative Solution of Omega-Regular Games. *Journal of Computer and System Sciences*, 68(2):374–397.

[de Alfaro and Roy, 2007] de Alfaro, L. and Roy, P. (2007). Magnifying-Lens Abstraction for Markov Decision Processes. In *CAV'07: Proceedings of the 19th International Conference on Computer Aided Verification*, volume 4590 of *Lecture Notes in Computer Science*, pages 325–338. Springer Verlag.

[Dechter and Pearl, 1985] Dechter, R. and Pearl, J. (1985). Generalized best-first search strategies and the optimality af A*. *Journal of the ACM*, 32(3):505–536.

[Derisavi, 2007] Derisavi, S. (2007). A Symbolic Algorithm for Optimal Markov Chain Lumping. In *TACAS'07: Proceedings of the 13th International Conference on Tools and Algorithms for the Construction and Analysis of Systems*, volume 4424 of *Lecture Notes in Computer Science*, pages 139–154. Springer Verlag.

[Dijkstra, 1976] Dijkstra, E. W. (1976). *A Discipline of Programming*. Prentice-Hall.

[Duflot et al., 2005] Duflot, M., Fribourg, L., Hérault, T., Lassaigne, R., Magniette, F., Messika, S., Peyronnet, S., and Picaronny, C. (2005). Probabilistic Model Checking of the CSMA/CD Protocol Using PRISM and APMC. *Electronic Notes in Theoretical Computer Science*, 128(6):195–214.

[Dutertre and de Moura, 2006] Dutertre, B. and de Moura, L. M. (2006). A Fast Linear-Arithmetic Solver for DPLL(T). In *CAV'06: Proceedings of the 18th International Conference on Computer Aided Verification*, volume 4144 of *Lecture Notes in Computer Science*, pages 81–94. Springer Verlag.

[Eppstein, 1998] Eppstein, D. (1998). Finding the k Shortest Paths. *SIAM Journal on Computing*, 28(2):652–673.

[Erne et al., 1992] Erne, M., Koslowski, J., Melton, A., and Strecker, G. E. (1992). A Primer On Galois Connections. In *York Academy of Science*.

[Fecher et al., 2006] Fecher, H., Leucker, M., and Wolf, V. (2006). *on't Know* in Probabilistic Systems. In *SPIN'06: Proceedings of the 13th International SPIN Workshop on Model Checking of Software*, volume 3925 of *Lecture Notes in Computer Science*, pages 71–88. Springer Verlag.

[Ferdinand et al., 2001] Ferdinand, C., Heckmann, R., Langenbach, M., Martin, F., Schmidt, M., Theiling, H., Thesing, S., and Wilhelm, R. (2001). Reliable and Precise WCET Determination for a Real-Life Processor. In *EMSOFT'01: Proceedings of the 1st International Workshop on Embedded Software*, volume 2211 of *Lecture Notes in Computer Science*, pages 469–485. Springer Verlag.

[Flanagan and Qadeer, 2002] Flanagan, C. and Qadeer, S. (2002). Predicate abstraction for software verification. In *POPL'02: Proceedings of the 29th Annual Symposium on Principles of Programming Languages*, pages 191–202, New York, NY, USA. ACM Press.

[Fränzle et al., 2008] Fränzle, M., Hermanns, H., and Teige, T. (2008). Stochastic Satisfiability Modulo Theory: A Novel Technique for the Analysis of Probabilistic Hybrid Systems. In *HSCC'08: Proceedings of the 11th International Workshop on Hybrid Systems: Computation and Control*, volume 4981 of *Lecture Notes in Computer Science*, pages 172–186. Springer Verlag.

[Ganai and Gupta, 2007] Ganai, M. and Gupta, A. (2007). *SAT-Based Scalable Formal Verification Solutions*. Springer Verlag, Secaucus, NJ, USA.

[Ganzinger et al., 2004] Ganzinger, H., Hagen, G., Nieuwenhuis, R., Oliveras, A., and Tinelli, C. (2004). DPLL(T): Fast Decision Procedures. In *CAV'04: Proceedings of the 16th International Conference on Computer Aided Verification*, volume 3114 of *Lecture Notes in Computer Science*, pages 175–188. Springer Verlag.

[GNU, 1998] GNU (1998). Bison - the GNU general-purpose parser generator. http://www.gnu.org/software/bison/.

[Graf and Saïdi, 1997] Graf, S. and Saïdi, H. (1997). Construction of Abstract State Graphs with PVS. In *CAV'97: Proceedings of the 9th International Conference on Computer Aided Verification*, volume 1254 of *Lecture Notes in Computer Science*, pages 72–83. Springer Verlag.

[Hahn et al., 2009] Hahn, E. M., Hermanns, H., Wachter, B., and Zhang, L. (2009). INFAMY: An Infinite-State Markov Model Checker. In *CAV'09: Proceedings of the 21st International Conference on Computer Aided Verification*, volume 5643 of *Lecture Notes in Computer Science*, pages 641–647. Springer Verlag.

[Hahn et al., 2010a] Hahn, E. M., Hermanns, H., Wachter, B., and Zhang, L. (2010a). PARAM: A Model Checker for Parametric Markov Models. In *CAV'10: Proceedings of the 22nd International Conference on Computer Aided Verification*, Lecture Notes in Computer Science. Springer Verlag.

[Hahn et al., 2010b] Hahn, E. M., Hermanns, H., Wachter, B., and Zhang, L. (2010b). PASS: Abstraction Refinement for Infinite Probabilistic Models. In *TACAS'10: Proceedings of the 16th International Conference on Tools and Algorithms for the Construction and Analysis of Systems*, volume 6015 of *Lecture Notes in Computer Science*, pages 353–357. Springer Verlag.

[Han, 2009] Han, T. (2009). *Diagnosis, Synthesis and Analysis of Probabilistic Models*. PhD thesis, University of Twente, Enschede.

[Han and Katoen, 2007] Han, T. and Katoen, J.-P. (2007). Counterexamples in Probabilistic Model Checking. In *TACAS'07: Proceedings of the 13th International Conference on Tools and Algorithms for the Construction and Analysis of Systems*, volume 4424 of *Lecture Notes in Computer Science*, pages 72–86. Springer Verlag.

[Han et al., 2009] Han, T., Katoen, J.-P., and Damman, B. (2009). Counterexample Generation in Probabilistic Model Checking. *IEEE Transactions on Software Engineering*, 35(2):241–257.

[Hansson and Jonsson, 1994] Hansson, H. and Jonsson, B. (1994). A Logic for Reasoning about Time and Reliability. *Formal Aspects of Computing*, 6(5):512–535.

[Hartmanns and Hermanns, 2009] Hartmanns, A. and Hermanns, H. (2009). A Modest Approach to Checking Probabilistic Timed Automata. In *QEST'09: Proceedings of the Sixth International Conference on the Quantitative Evaluation of Systems*, pages 187–196. IEEE Computer Society.

[Helmink et al., 1993] Helmink, L., Sellink, M. P. A., and Vaandrager, F. W. (1993). Proof-Checking a Data Link Protocol. In *TYPES'93: Proceedings of the International Workshop on Types for Proofs and Programs*, volume 806 of *Lecture Notes in Computer Science*, pages 127–165. Springer Verlag.

[Henzinger et al., 2005a] Henzinger, T. A., Jhala, R., and Majumdar, R. (2005a). The BLAST Software Verification System. In *SPIN'05: Proceedings of the 12th International SPIN Workshop*, volume 3639 of *Lecture Notes in Computer Science*, pages 25–26. Springer Verlag.

[Henzinger et al., 2004] Henzinger, T. A., Jhala, R., Majumdar, R., and McMillan, K. L. (2004). Abstractions from proofs. In *POPL'04: Proceedings of the 31st Annual Symposium on Principles of Programming Languages*, pages 232–244, New York, NY, USA. ACM Press.

[Henzinger et al., 2002] Henzinger, T. A., Jhala, R., Majumdar, R., and Sutre, G. (2002). Lazy Abstraction. In *POPL'02: Proceedings of the 29th Annual Symposium on Principles of Programming Languages*, pages 58–70, New York, NY, USA. ACM Press.

[Henzinger et al., 2005b] Henzinger, T. A., Majumdar, R., and Raskin, J.-F. (2005b). A Classification of Symbolic Transition Systems. *ACM Transaction on Computational Logic*, 6(1):1–32.

[Hermanns et al., 2008] Hermanns, H., Wachter, B., and Zhang, L. (2008). Probabilistic

CEGAR. In *CAV'08: Proceedings of the 20th International Conference on Computer Aided Verification*, volume 5123 of *Lecture Notes in Computer Science*, pages 162–175. Springer Verlag.

[Hinton et al., 2006] Hinton, A., Kwiatkowska, M. Z., Norman, G., and Parker, D. (2006). PRISM: A Tool for Automatic Verification of Probabilistic Systems. In *TACAS'06: Proceedings of the 12th International Conference on Tools and Algorithms for the Construction and Analysis of Systems*, volume 3920 of *Lecture Notes in Computer Science*, pages 441–444. Springer Verlag.

[Hoare, 1978] Hoare, C. A. R. (1978). Communicating Sequential Processes. *Communications of the ACM*, 21(8):666–677.

[Kam and Ullman, 1977] Kam, J. and Ullman, J. D. (1977). Monotone Data Flow Analysis Frameworks. *Acta Informatica*, 7(3):305–318.

[Katoen et al., 2007] Katoen, J.-P., Kemna, T., Zapreev, I. S., and Jansen, D. N. (2007). Bisimulation Minimisation Mostly Speeds Up Probabilistic Model Checking. In *TACAS'07: Proceedings of the 13th International Conference on Tools and Algorithms for the Construction and Analysis of Systems*, volume 4424 of *Lecture Notes in Computer Science*, pages 87–101. Springer Verlag.

[Katoen et al., 2010] Katoen, J.-P., van de Pol, J., Stoelinga, M., and Timmer, M. (2010). A Linear Process-Algebraic Format for Probabilistic Systems with Data. In *ACSD'10: Proceedings of the 2010 10th International Conference on Application of Concurrency to System Design*, pages 213–222. IEEE Computer Society.

[Katoen et al., 2009] Katoen, J.-P., Zapreev, I. S., Hahn, E. M., Hermanns, H., and Jansen, D. N. (2009). The Ins and Outs of the Probabilistic Model Checker MRMC. In *QEST'09: Proceedings of the Sixth International Conference on the Quantitative Evaluation of Systems*, pages 167–176. IEEE Computer Society.

[Kattenbelt et al., 2008] Kattenbelt, M., Kwiatkowska, M. Z., Norman, G., and Parker, D. (2008). Game-Based Probabilistic Predicate Abstraction in PRISM. *Electronic Notes in Theoretical Computer Science*, 220(3):5–21.

[Kattenbelt et al., 2009] Kattenbelt, M., Kwiatkowska, M. Z., Norman, G., and Parker, D. (2009). Abstraction Refinement for Probabilistic Software. In *VMCAI'09: Proceedings of the 10th International Conference on Verification, Model Checking, and Abstract Interpretation*, volume 5403 of *Lecture Notes in Computer Science*, pages 182–197. Springer Verlag.

[Kemeny et al., 1966] Kemeny, J., Snell, J., and Knapp, A. (1966). *Denumerable Markov Chains*. D. Van Nostrand Company.

[Kildall, 1973] Kildall, G. A. (1973). A Unified Approach to Global Program Optimization. In *POPL'73: Proceedings of the 1st Annual Symposium on Principles of Programming Languages*, pages 194–206, New York, NY, USA. ACM Press.

[Kwiatkowska et al., 2006] Kwiatkowska, M. Z., Norman, G., and Parker, D. (2006). Game-based Abstraction for Markov Decision Processes. In *QEST'06: Proceedings of the Third International Conference on the Quantitative Evaluation of Systems*, pages

157–166. IEEE Computer Society.

[Kwiatkowska et al., 2009] Kwiatkowska, M. Z., Norman, G., and Parker, D. (2009). Stochastic Games for Verification of Probabilistic Timed Automata. In *FORMATS'09: Proceedings of the 7th International Conference on Formal Modeling and Analysis of Timed Systems*, volume 5813 of *Lecture Notes in Computer Science*, pages 212–227. Springer Verlag.

[Kwiatkowska et al., 2010] Kwiatkowska, M. Z., Norman, G., and Parker, D. (2010). PRISM web site. http://www.prismmodelchecker.org/.

[Kwiatkowska et al., 2002] Kwiatkowska, M. Z., Norman, G., and Sproston, J. (2002). Probabilistic Model Checking of the IEEE 802.11 Wireless Local Area Network Protocol. In *PAPM-PROBMIV'02: Proceedings of the Second Joint International Workshop on Process Algebra and Probabilistic Methods, Performance Modeling and Verification*, volume 2399 of *Lecture Notes in Computer Science*, pages 169–187. Springer Verlag.

[Lacan et al., 1998] Lacan, J., Monfort, J.-N., Ribal, V. Q., Deutsch, A., and Gonthier, G. (1998). The software reliability verification process: The Ariane 5 example. *DAta Systems In Aerospace*. SP-422.

[Lahiri et al., 2006] Lahiri, S. K., Nieuwenhuis, R., and Oliveras, A. (2006). SMT Techniques for Fast Predicate Abstraction. In *CAV'06: Proceedings of the 18th International Conference on Computer Aided Verification*, volume 4144 of *Lecture Notes in Computer Science*, pages 424–437. Springer Verlag.

[Littman et al., 2001] Littman, M. L., Majercik, S. M., and Pitassi, T. (2001). Stochastic Boolean Satisfiability. *Journal on Automated Reasoning*, 27(3):251–296.

[Manna and Pnueli, 1995] Manna, Z. and Pnueli, A. (1995). *Temporal Verification of Reactive Systems: Safety*. Springer Verlag, New York, NY, USA.

[McMillan, 2006] McMillan, K. L. (2006). Lazy Abstraction with Interpolants. In *CAV'06: Proceedings of the 18th International Conference on Computer Aided Verification*, volume 4144 of *Lecture Notes in Computer Science*, pages 123–136. Springer Verlag.

[Minsky, 1967] Minsky, M. L. (1967). *Computation: finite and infinite machines*. Prentice-Hall, Upper Saddle River, NJ, USA.

[Monniaux, 2001] Monniaux, D. (2001). Backwards Abstract Interpretation of Probabilistic Programs. In *ESOP'01: Proceedings of the 10th European Symposium on Programming*, volume 2028 of *Lecture Notes in Computer Science*, pages 367–382. Springer Verlag.

[Monniaux, 2003a] Monniaux, D. (2003a). Abstract Interpretation of Programs as Markov Decision Processes. In *SAS'03: Proceedings of the 10th International Symposium on Static Analysis*, volume 2694 of *Lecture Notes in Computer Science*, pages 237–254. Springer Verlag.

[Monniaux, 2003b] Monniaux, D. (2003b). Abstraction of Expectation Functions Using Gaussian Distributions. In *VMCAI'03: Proceedings of the 4th International Conference on Verification, Model Checking, and Abstract Interpretation*, volume 2575 of

Lecture Notes in Computer Science, pages 161–173. Springer Verlag.

[Monniaux, 2005] Monniaux, D. (2005). Abstract interpretation of programs as Markov decision processes. *Science of Computer Programming*, 58(1-2):179–205.

[Owicki and Lamport, 1982] Owicki, S. S. and Lamport, L. (1982). Proving Liveness Properties of Concurrent Programs. *ACM Transactions on Programming Languages and Systems*, 4(3):455–495.

[Papadimitriou and Yannakakis, 1991] Papadimitriou, C. H. and Yannakakis, M. (1991). Optimization, Approximation, and Complexity Classes. *Journal of Computer and System Sciences*, 43(3):425–440.

[Parker, 2002] Parker, D. (2002). *Implementation of Symbolic Model Checking for Probabilistic Systems*. PhD thesis, University of Birmingham.

[Pierro and Wiklicky, 2000a] Pierro, A. D. and Wiklicky, H. (2000a). Concurrent Constraint Programming: Towards Probabilistic Abstract Interpretation. In *PPDP*, pages 127–138.

[Pierro and Wiklicky, 2000b] Pierro, A. D. and Wiklicky, H. (2000b). Measuring the Precision of Abstract Interpretations. In *LOPSTR'00: Selected Papers from the 10th International Workshop on Logic Based Program Synthesis and Transformation*, volume 2042 of *Lecture Notes in Computer Science*, pages 147–164. Springer Verlag.

[Pnueli, 1977] Pnueli, A. (1977). The Temporal Logic of Programs. In *FOCS'77: Proceedings of the 18th Annual Symposium on Foundations of Computer Science*, pages 46–57. IEEE Computer Society.

[Puterman, 1994] Puterman, M. L. (1994). *Markov Decision Processes: Discrete Stochastic Dynamic Programming*. John Wiley & Sons.

[Queille and Sifakis, 1982] Queille, J.-P. and Sifakis, J. (1982). Specification and verification of concurrent systems in CESAR. In *Proceedings of the Symposium on Programming*, volume 137 of *Lecture Notes in Computer Science*, pages 337–351. Springer Verlag.

[Roscoe et al., 1997] Roscoe, A. W., Hoare, C. A. R., and Bird, R. (1997). *The Theory and Practice of Concurrency*. Prentice Hall PTR, Upper Saddle River, NJ, USA.

[Roy et al., 2008] Roy, P., Parker, D., Norman, G., and de Alfaro, L. (2008). Symbolic Magnifying Lens Abstraction in Markov Decision Processes. In *QEST'08: Proceedings of the Fifth International Conference on the Quantitative Evaluation of Systems*, pages 103–112. IEEE Computer Society.

[Schmalz et al., 2009] Schmalz, M., Varacca, D., and Völzer, H. (2009). Counterexamples in Probabilistic LTL Model Checking for Markov Chains. In *CONCUR'09: Proceedings of the 20th International Conference on Concurrency Theory*, volume 5710 of *Lecture Notes in Computer Science*, pages 587–602. Springer Verlag.

[Shoham and Grumberg, 2004] Shoham, S. and Grumberg, O. (2004). Monotonic Abstraction-Refinement for CTL. In *TACAS'04: Proceedings of the 10th International Conference on Tools and Algorithms for the Construction and Analysis of Systems*, volume 2988 of *Lecture Notes in Computer Science*, pages 546–560. Springer Verlag.

[Smith, 2008] Smith, M. J. A. (2008). Probabilistic Abstract Interpretation of Imperative Programs using Truncated Normal Distributions. *Electronic Notes in Theoretical Computer Science*, 220(3):43–59.

[Somenzi, 2009] Somenzi, F. (2009). CUDD: CU Decision Diagram Package 2.4.2. http://vlsi.colorado.edu/~fabio/CUDD/.

[Tarjan, 1972] Tarjan, R. E. (1972). Depth-First Search and Linear Graph Algorithms. *SIAM Journal on Computing*, 1(2):146–160.

[Tarski, 1955] Tarski, A. (1955). A Lattice-Theoretical Fixpoint Theorem and Its Applications. In *Pacific Journal of Mathematics 5:2:*, pages 285–309.

[Thesing et al., 2003] Thesing, S., Souyris, J., Heckmann, R., Randimbivololona, F., Langenbach, M., Wilhelm, R., and Ferdinand, C. (2003). An Abstract Interpretation-Based Timing Validation of Hard Real-Time Avionics Software. In *DSN'03: Proceedings of the 2003 International Conference on Dependable Systems and Networks*, pages 625–634. IEEE Computer Society.

[Tonetta and Sharygina, 2006] Tonetta, S. and Sharygina, N. (2006). A Uniform Framework for Predicate Abstraction Approximation. In *SVV'06: Proceedings of the International Workshop on Software Verification and Validation*, pages 61–72.

[Vardi, 1985] Vardi, M. Y. (1985). Automatic Verification of Probabilistic Concurrent Finite-State Programs. In *FOCS'85: Proceedings of the 26th Annual Symposium on Foundations of Computer Science*, pages 327–338. IEEE Computer Society.

[Wachter and Zhang, 2010] Wachter, B. and Zhang, L. (2010). Best Probabilistic Transformers. In *VMCAI'10: Proceedings of the 11th International Conference on Verification, Model Checking, and Abstract Interpretation*, volume 5944 of *Lecture Notes in Computer Science*, pages 362–379. Springer Verlag.

[Wachter et al., 2007] Wachter, B., Zhang, L., and Hermanns, H. (2007). Probabilistic Model Checking Modulo Theories. In *QEST'07: Proceedings of the 4th International Conference on the Quantitative Evaluation of Systems*, pages 129–140. IEEE Computer Society.

[Wilhelm and Maurer, 1992] Wilhelm, R. and Maurer, D. (1992). *Übersetzerbau - Theorie, Konstruktion, Generierung*. Springer Verlag.

[Wimmer et al., 2009] Wimmer, R., Braitling, B., and Becker, B. (2009). Counterexample Generation for Discrete-Time Markov Chains Using Bounded Model Checking. In *VMCAI'09: Proceedings of the 10th International Conference on Verification, Model Checking, and Abstract Interpretation*, volume 5403 of *Lecture Notes in Computer Science*, pages 366–380. Springer Verlag.

Part IV.

Annexes

Additional Proofs

This chapter contains additional detailed proofs.

Soundness of Menu-based Abstraction

This proof shows that menu-based abstraction is sound, i.e., the abstract transformers defined by it form valid abstractions of the corresponding concrete transformers:

Theorem 6.3. The proof is based on properties of the respective Galois connections and applying Definitions 6.2 and 6.1.

Part $\boxed{1}$: we need to establish equivalence of menu-based abstraction for the upper bound of maximal reachability with the corresponding best transformer. Without loss of generality, let $w^\sharp \in [0,1]^Q$, $B \in Q \setminus (F^\sharp \cup F_0^\sharp)$. By definition, we have the equality

$$(\alpha^u \circ pre_F^+ \circ \gamma)(w^\sharp)(B) = \sup_{s \in B} \max_{\pi \in Distr(s)} \sum_{s' \in S} \pi(s') \cdot w^\sharp(\overline{s'}) \ .$$

Moreover, by Definition 6.1, we have

$$\widetilde{pre}_{F^\sharp}^{u+}(w^\sharp)(B) = \max_{a \in En(B)} (\alpha^u \circ (pre[a]_F^+) \circ \gamma)(w^\sharp)(B)$$

$$= \max_{a \in En(s)} \sup_{s \in B} \sum_{s' \in S} \pi_{(s,a)}(s') \cdot w^\sharp(\overline{s'})$$

$$= \sup_{s \in B} \max_{a \in En(s)} \sum_{s' \in S} \pi_{(s,a)}(s') \cdot w^\sharp(\overline{s'})$$

which is the same as $\sup_{s \in B} \max_{\pi \in Distr(s)} \sum_{s' \in S} \pi(s') \cdot w^\sharp(\overline{s'})$. We are done.

Part $\boxed{2}$: we need to prove Inequality 6.3. Recall that function $(\gamma \circ \widetilde{pre}_{F^\sharp}^{l+})$ has type $[0,1]^Q \to [0,1]^S$. Therefore Inequality 6.3 is equivalent to the claim:

$$\forall w^\sharp \in [0,1]^Q \ \forall s \in S : \ (\gamma \circ \widetilde{pre}_{F^\sharp}^{l+})(w^\sharp)(s) \leq (pre_F^+ \circ \gamma)(w^\sharp)(s)$$

The proof has a different flavor than the previous one because we do not show equivalence to a best transformer but only validity of the abstract transformer. We first give the proof and then explain the individual steps. Let $w^\sharp \in [0,1]^Q$ and $s \in S$. Then we have:

$$(\gamma \circ \widetilde{pre}_{F^\sharp}^{l+})(w^\sharp)(s) = \gamma \circ \left(\lambda B. \max_{a \in En(B)} (\alpha^l \circ (pre[a]_F^+) \circ \gamma)(w^\sharp)(B) \right)(s) \qquad \text{(A.1)}$$

$$= \max_{a \in En(\bar{s})} (\alpha^l \circ (pre[a]_F^+) \circ \gamma)(w^\sharp)(\bar{s}) \qquad \text{(A.2)}$$

$$\leq \max_{a \in En(s)} (\alpha^l \circ (pre[a]_F^+) \circ \gamma)(w^\sharp)(\bar{s}) \qquad \text{(A.3)}$$

$$= \max_{a \in En(s)} \gamma \left((\alpha^l \circ (pre[a]_F^+) \circ \gamma)(w^\sharp) \right)(s) \qquad \text{(A.4)}$$

$$= \max_{a \in En(s)} \left((\gamma \circ \alpha^l) \circ (pre[a]_F^+) \circ \gamma)(w^\sharp) \right)(s) \qquad \text{(A.5)}$$

$$\leq \max_{a \in En(s)} \left((pre[a]_F^+) \circ \gamma)(w^\sharp) \right)(s) \qquad \text{(A.6)}$$

$$= (pre_F^+ \circ \gamma)(w^\sharp)(s) \qquad \text{(A.7)}$$

Now we explain the steps in detail. Step A.1 follows directly by definition of the transformer $\widetilde{pre}_{F^\sharp}^{l+}$. In Step A.2 we use the definition of the concretization function. Step A.3 follows because, for all $a \in En(\bar{s}) \setminus En(s)$, $0 = (\alpha^l \circ (pre[a]_F^+) \circ \gamma)(w^\sharp)(\bar{s})$, which follows directly from the definition of $pre[a]_F^+$. Steps A.4 and A.5 are simple rewrite steps. In Step A.6, we exploit that (α^l, γ) is a Galois connection, so that the function $\gamma \circ \alpha^l$ is extensive with respect to order $\geq$ and hence reductive with respect to $\leq$ as required. Finally, we only need to the definition of $pre[a]_F^+$ to arrive at the claimed result.

Part $\boxed{4}$: we need to prove Inequality 6.4. Inequality 6.4 is equivalent to the claim:

$$\forall w^\sharp \in [0,1]^Q \ \forall s \in S : \ (pre_F^- \circ \gamma)(w^\sharp)(s) \leq (\gamma \circ \widetilde{pre}_{F^\sharp}^{u-})(w^\sharp)(s) .$$

The proof method is very similar to the previous proof, however the difference is that we are now arguing about upper rather than lower bounds and about minimal rather than maximal reachability.

$$(\gamma \circ \widetilde{pre}_{F^\sharp}^{u-})(w^\sharp)(s) = \gamma \circ \left(\lambda B. \min_{a \in En(B)} (\alpha^u \circ (pre[a]_F^-) \circ \gamma)(w^\sharp)(B) \right)(s) \qquad \text{(A.8)}$$

$$= \min_{a \in En(\bar{s})} (\alpha^u \circ (pre[a]_F^-) \circ \gamma)(w^\sharp)(\bar{s}) \qquad \text{(A.9)}$$

$$\geq \min_{a \in En(s)} (\alpha^u \circ (pre[a]_F^+) \circ \gamma)(w^\sharp)(\bar{s}) \qquad \text{(A.10)}$$

$$= \min_{a \in En(s)} \gamma \left((\alpha^u \circ (pre[a]_F^+) \circ \gamma)(w^\sharp) \right)(s) \qquad \text{(A.11)}$$

$$= \min_{a \in En(s)} \left((\gamma \circ \alpha^u) \circ (pre[a]_F^+) \circ \gamma)(w^\sharp) \right)(s) \qquad \text{(A.12)}$$

$$\geq \min_{a \in En(s)} \left((pre[a]_F^+) \circ \gamma)(w^\sharp) \right)(s) \qquad \text{(A.13)}$$

$$= (pre_F^+ \circ \gamma)(w^\sharp)(s) \qquad \text{(A.14)}$$

We explain the steps in detail. Step A.8 follows directly by definition of the transformer $\widetilde{pre}_{F^\sharp}^{u-}$. In Step A.9 we use the definition of the concretization function. Step A.10

follows because, for all $a \in En(\bar{s}) \setminus En(s)$, $1 = (\alpha^u \circ (pre[a]_F^-) \circ \gamma)(w^\sharp)(\bar{s})$, which follows directly from the definition of $pre[a]_F^-$. Steps A.11 and A.12 are simple rewrite steps. In Step A.13, we exploit that (α^u, γ) is a Galois connection, so that the function $\gamma \circ \alpha^u$ is extensive with respect to order $\leq$ as required. Finally, we only need to the definition of $pre[a]_F^-$ to arrive at the claimed result.

Part ③: we need to establish equivalence of menu-based abstraction for the lower bound of minimal reachability with the corresponding best transformer. Without loss of generality, let $w^\sharp \in [0,1]^Q$, $B \in Q \setminus (F^\sharp \cup F_0^\sharp)$. By definition, we have the equality

$$(\alpha^l \circ pre_F^- \circ \gamma)(w^\sharp)(B) = \inf_{s \in B} \min_{\pi \in Distr(s)} \sum_{s' \in S} \pi(s') \cdot w^\sharp(\bar{s'}) \ .$$

Moreover, by Definition 6.2, we have

$$\widetilde{pre}_{F^\sharp}^{l-}(w^\sharp)(B) = \min_{a \in En(B)} (\alpha^l \circ (pre[a]_F^+) \circ \gamma)(w^\sharp)(B)$$

$$= \min_{a \in En(s)} \inf_{s \in B} \sum_{s' \in S} \pi_{(s,a)}(s') \cdot w^\sharp(\bar{s'})$$

$$= \inf_{s \in B} \min_{a \in En(s)} \sum_{s' \in S} \pi_{(s,a)}(s') \cdot w^\sharp(\bar{s'})$$

which is the same as $\inf_{s \in B} \min_{\pi \in Distr(s)} \sum_{s' \in S} \pi(s') \cdot w^\sharp(\bar{s'})$. We are done.

∎

B

Implementation Details

Value Iteration Algorithm for Games.

We now give the value-iteration implemented in PASS. Note that game strategies play an important role for refinement. Probabilistic CEGAR requires the induced Markov chain. For backward refinement, pivot-block selection is based on game strategies. We have assumed that optimal strategies for the lower and upper bound only differ if that is necessary to achieve the optimal value. This must be ensured in the implementation of value iteration. To this end, the algorithm first computes the probabilities and strategies for the lower bound. Then, instead of starting the computation for the upper bounds from scratch, the fixed-point iteration starts with the lower-bound values and strategies.

The value-iteration algorithm requires a criterion that decides whether two values are equal up to some specified precision $\delta > 0$. The approximate equality check is used for the termination check and to compute game strategies in a numerically robust way in presence of inexact arithmetic.

Comparing the absolute value of the difference of two values is typically not a very precise criterion because it equates all small values with each other indiscriminate of magnitude. For example, assume we set precision $\delta := 10^{-6}$ and we compare values 10^{-12} and 10^{-6}. These two values differ by six orders of magnitude, yet $|10^{-12} - 10^{-6}| < \delta$ and therefore an absolute criterion would equate them. Therefore we employ a criterion based on relative differences:

Definition B.1. *Two real values a and b are equal up to δ, denoted by $a \approx_\delta b$, if and only if, one of the following conditions is met:*

- *the numbers are the same*
- $\frac{|b-a|}{|b+a|} < \delta$.

With the relative criterion, the numbers 10^{-6} and 10^{-12} are discriminated. On the other hand, the numbers $1 + 10^{-6}$ and 1 are in the same order of magnitude and differ only at their sixth decimal place. These numbers are equal up to δ.

Both the lower and the upper bound are computed using procedure VALITER (see Algorithm 5). Its parameters control minimization and maximization for the two players. By setting $opt_1 := \max$ and $p_1^0 := -1$, we maximize for player 1. Setting $opt_1 := \min$

and $p_1^0 := 2$, we minimize player 1. Analogously, with $opt_2 := \max$ and $p_2^0 := -1$, we maximize for player 2 and minimize with $opt_2 := \min$ and $p_2^0 := 2$. Further arguments are initial values for the valuation, namely parameter v^0, and the strategies, parameters σ_1^0 and σ_2^0.

Procedure VALITER contains a while-loop. Each iteration of that loop corresponds to an application of the valuation transformer of the game to the current valuation w. In each step, the current strategy is only updated if its choice is not optimal anymore. This ensures that correct strategies are computed in presence of loops. Correctness of the computed values and strategies follows from these results [Chatterjee et al., 2006]. Our algorithm is a special case of their value-iteration algorithm for concurrent games.

To compute both lower and upper bounds, we leverage value iteration as a subroutine in procedure INTERVAL (Algorithm 6). Using VALITER, the lower bound is computed with the start valuation that assigns only 1 to the goal vertices and 0 to all other vertices. Subsequently, VALITER is used to compute the upper-bound valuation and strategies based on the lower-bound valuation w_l and strategies σ_1^u and σ_2^u. This concludes the description of the algorithm. In PASS, the precision is set to $\delta := 10^{-6}$ by default. Valuations are stored in vectors of doubles.

Observe that the abstraction procedure previously described in Section 8.1 produces a symbolic representation of stochastic games. We first convert the symbolic representation into an explicit sparse-matrix representation and then carry out value iteration on this explicit representation. As an alternative we could have used a symbolic representation based on MTBDDs for both the iteration vectors and the game, e.g, by extending the ideas of [de Alfaro et al., 2000] to games. However, Parker [Parker, 2002] showed that such representations are inferior to explicit representations if the iteration vector and the transitions of the model fit into memory.

Optimization. To improve the speed of convergence of the value-iteration algorithm, we update the player 1 vertices (line 8 of Algorithm 5) in a particular order. Following the dependencies in the evaluation order can significantly speed up value iteration [Dai and Goldsmith, 2007]. The value of a vertex depends on its successors therefore this order is determined by structure of the game. PASS performs value iteration according to a reversed depth-first order starting with the goal vertices *goal*.

Algorithm 5 Value iteration

1: **procedure** VALITER($\mathcal{G}, w^0, \sigma_1^0, \sigma_2^0, opt_1, opt_2, p_1^0, p_2^0$)
2:     $w \leftarrow w^0$ ▷ initialize valuation
3:     $\sigma_1 \leftarrow \sigma_1^0$ ▷ initialize player 1 strategy
4:     $\sigma_2 \leftarrow \sigma_2^0$ ▷ initialize player 2 strategy
5:     $done \leftarrow false$
6:     **while** $!done$ **do**
7:         $done \leftarrow true$
8:         **for all** $v_1 \in V_1$ such that $w^0(v_1) < 1$ **do**
9:             $x_{old} \leftarrow w(v_1)$ ▷ store old value of vertex v_1
10:            $x_1 \leftarrow p_1^0$ ▷ initialize current value for v_1
11:            **for all** $v_2 \in E(v_1)$ **do**
12:                $x_2 \leftarrow p_2^0$ ▷ initialize current value for v_2
13:                **for all** $v_p \in E(v_2)$ **do**
14:                    $x_p \leftarrow \sum_{v_1 \in V_1} \delta(v_p)(v_1) \cdot w(v_1)$
15:                    $x_2 \leftarrow opt_2(x_p, x_2)$ ▷ update value
16:                **end for**
17:                **if** $!(x_p \approx_\delta \sigma_2(v_2))$ **then**   ▷ update strategy
18:                    $\sigma(v_2) \leftarrow v_p$
19:                **end if**
20:                $x_1 \leftarrow opt_1(x_1, x_2)$ ▷ update value
21:            **end for**
22:            $w(v_1) \leftarrow x_1$
23:            **if** $!(x_2 \approx_\delta w(\sigma_1(v_1)))$ **then**   ▷ update strategy
24:                $\sigma_1(v_1) \leftarrow v_2$
25:            **end if**
26:            **if** $!(x_{old} \approx_\delta x_1)$ **then**   ▷ continue iteration?
27:                $done \leftarrow false$
28:            **end if**
29:         **end for**
30:     **end while**
31:     **return** (w, σ_1, σ_2)
32: **end procedure**

Algorithm 6 Computing lower and upper bounds

1: **procedure** INTERVAL($\mathcal{G}, goal$)
2:      $\sigma_1^0 \leftarrow v_2$ where $v_2 \in E(v_1)$ ▷ initialize strategy
3:      $\sigma_2^0 \leftarrow v_p$ where $v_p \in E(v_2)$ ▷ initialize strategy
4:      **if** Max for player 1 **then**   ▷ maximal reachability
5:          $opt_1 \leftarrow \max$
6:          $p_1^0 \leftarrow -1$
7:      **else**   ▷ minimal reachability
8:          $opt_1 \leftarrow \min$
9:          $p_1^0 \leftarrow 2$
10:      **end if**
11:      $(w_l, \sigma_1^l, \sigma_2^l) \leftarrow$ VALITER($\mathcal{G}, goal, \sigma_1^0, \sigma_2^0, opt_1, \min, p_1^0, 2$)   ▷ lower bound
12:      $(w_u, \sigma_1^u, \sigma_2^u) \leftarrow$ VALITER($\mathcal{G}, w^l, \sigma_1^l, \sigma_2^l, opt_1, \max, p_1^0, -1$)   ▷ upper bound
13:      **return** $(w^l, \sigma_1^l, \sigma_2^l, w^u, \sigma_1^u, \sigma_2^u)$
14: **end procedure**